P9-AFU-862

PS3571
P4
Z6
1987

128085

N. L. TERTELING LIBRARY
THE COLLEGE OF IDAHO
CALDWELL, IDAHO

PURCHASED WITH NEH
ENDOWMENT FUNDS

UPDIKE'S NOVELS: THORNS SPELL A WORD

UPDIKE'S NOVELS

THORNS SPELL A WORD

by

Jeff H. Campbell

MIDWESTERN STATE UNIVERSITY PRESS
WICHITA FALLS, TEXAS

PS 3571
P4
Z4
1987

Copyright © 1987 by Jeff H. Campbell

ISBN 0-915323-02-8

All rights reserved.

No part of this book may be reproduced in any manner whatsoever without written permission from Midwestern State University Press. Exceptions to this limitation include brief quotations in reviews and critical articles.

Requests for permission to use or copy any part of this book should be addressed to Midwestern State University Press, Midwestern State University, Wichita Falls, Texas 76308-2099.

First edition

First published in 1987 by Midwestern State University Press, Midwestern State University, 3400 Taft, Wichita Falls, Texas 76308-2099.

"A Rabbit As King Of The Ghosts" by Wallace Stevens. Copyright 1942 by Wallace Stevens and renewed 1970 by Holly Stevens. Reprinted from *The Collected Poems Of Wallace Stevens* by Wallace Stevens, by permission of Alfred A. Knopf, Inc.

Printed in The United States of America

128085

For Shelia

O body swayed to music, O brightening glance,
How can we know the dancer from the dance?
        —W. B. Yeats, "Among School Children"

N. L. TERTELING LIBRARY
THE COLLEGE OF IDAHO
CALDWELL, IDAHO

ACKNOWLEDGEMENTS

I am deeply indebted to John Updike for graciously giving me an afternoon of his time on a stormy day in August of 1976, for his help in editing the transcript of the interview, and for subsequent correspondence commenting on the novels published since the time of our interview. I am also grateful to Midwestern State University for providing the funds which made my trip to Massachusetts possible and for granting a semester's leave so that I might begin work on this volume.

This book would probably never have become a reality without the multiform aid of Shelia Campbell, who served as consultant-encourager from the inception of the project all the way through and as gadfly when sloth threatened to triumph. My thanks must also go to Jackie Davis and Donna Mansur for typing portions of the manuscript and to Elizabeth Holton for transcribing the original tape of the interview.

Portions of Chapter Four appeared, in significantly different form, in *New Mexico Humanities Review,* 1 (May 1978): 53-60, under the title "Updike's Honky Apocalypse: *Rabbit Redux,*" and in *Lamar Journal of the Humanities,* 10 (Spring 1984): 7-13, under the title "Light on Your Fur: Regeneration in Updike's *Rabbit Is Rich.*" Portions of Chapter Five were printed in the *Proceedings* of the Conference of College Teachers of English of Texas, 45 (1980): 84-92, under the title "From *Marry Me* to *Couples:* Tristan Demythologized," and in *Faculty Papers,* Midwestern State University, Second Series, 7 (1981), under the title "After

Christianity, What?: John Updike's Critique of Contemporary American Society." Permission to use material from these articles in the present context is gratefully acknowledged.

Finally, I must thank James Hoggard, editor of the Midwestern State University Press, whose belief in and commitment to the book and whose editor's eagle eye have been major factors in the final fruition here presented.

Jeff H. Campbell
Wichita Falls, Texas
July 19, 1987

THE NOVELS OF JOHN UPDIKE

The Poorhouse Fair (1959)

Rabbit, Run (1960)

The Centaur (1963)

Of the Farm (1965)

Couples (1968)

Rabbit Redux (1971)

A Month of Sundays (1975)

Marry Me (1976)

The Coup (1978)

Rabbit Is Rich (1981)

The Witches of Eastwick (1984)

Roger's Version (1986)

TABLE OF CONTENTS

CHAPTER 1

"AN EASY HUMANISM PLAGUES THE LAND":
MIDPOINT

A divided critical response greeted John Updike's first novel, *The Poorhouse Fair,* in 1959. Some critics praised Updike's dazzling prose style and his brilliant novelistic gifts while others charged him with "turning a narrow plot of ground" (Gilman 499) and "trying to make the little novel carry more weight than it is able to bear" (Hicks 58). The twenty-eight years following publication of this first novel have not altered the pattern substantially. In 1963 Norman Podhoretz confessed that he found Updike "a writer who has very little to say" (257). Howard Harper, on the other hand, affirmed in 1967 that Updike's work "has a depth, an integrity, and an ultimate concern" which reveal "a mind of impressive intelligence" (190). John Aldridge complained in 1970 of Updike's "addiction of obliqueness and stylistic preciosity" (201), but two years later Robert Detweiler was affirming that "in Updike's art one finds a direct relationship between the quality of craftsmanship and the quality of life: by doing a thing well, one creates a better self" (169). Updike's twelfth novel, *Roger's Version* (1986), continued the calling forth of contrasting evaluations. Bruce Bawer charged that Updike "establishes dramatic conflicts, but they seem, in large part, trivial and vulgar in their conception, thematically irrelevant in their development and uninspired, even halfhearted, in their resolution" (71). But David Lehman countered that the book's "power and charm lie in the terrific appeal it makes to our capacity for intellectual wonderment. It's rather thrilling to watch Updike assimilate the new vocabularies of particle physics and computer technology—and then fuse them with the ancient vocabulary of religious belief'' (64).

Despite recurring criticisms that his work is ''beautifully written, intermittently thoughtful and seriously flawed'' (Bawer 71), Updike has continued to pursue his own artistic vision, producing a steady stream of works which have earned him such awards as the National Book Award, the American Book Award, the Pulitzer Prize, and the National Critics' Circle Award. His current (1987) *oeuvre* of twelve novels, five books of poems, nine books of short stories, one play, and three collections of non-fiction pieces is a major accomplishment, and when *Esquire* magazine in the summer of 1986 asked several prominent American writers who they thought most likely to be the next American to win the Nobel prize, Updike's name was suggested more than any other. The growing body of Updike's work is eliciting more and more scholarly concern, as well. There have been nine significant book-length Updike studies, for example, since Alice and Kenneth Hamilton produced the first in 1970.[1] *Modern Fiction Studies* printed twelve serious essays on Updike in its Spring 1974 issue, and twenty-three doctoral dissertations were written on Updike between 1971 and 1984. Although there may be a few critics who still agree with Richard Rupp that Updike's work illustrates ''style in search of a center,'' most now recognize that there is a significant Updike corpus which must be reckoned with.

Critics are, in fact, discovering Updikean complexities unrecognized by the detractors. Larry Taylor, for instance, finds a complex pattern of pastoral and antipastoral concerns threading through the fiction. Furthermore, although G. F. Waller sees *Couples* as a Barthian-Calvinist parable, Joyce Markle traces the mythic underpinnings of the same novel from fertility and vegetation rituals to the story of Tristan and Iseult (125-145). David Vanderwerken interprets Updike primarily in terms of imaginative language and imagery, but Robert Regan and George Hunt probe beneath the language to find their keys to understanding in neo-Kantian epistemology and Jungian psychology, respectively. This list, brief as it is, indicates some of the philosophical, theological, psychological, and aesthetic approaches currently being taken.

I have no quarrel with the variety in Updike criticism. Updike's work is rich and complex, the product of a man of first-rate intelligence who is not afraid to use all the tools available to his linguistic skill. Multiple allusions invite diversity in critical interpretation, and many of the differing views are based on sound internal evidence drawn from the novels or stories. Therefore, most of the contrasting conclusions have their own validity. With such a plethora of approaches already available, I would hesitate to add this present study except that I believe it offers something no previous work has: an approach through the long poem *Midpoint,* a little-known Updike work in which he sets forth in his own words his outlook on life and art. I shall certainly not reject psychology, philosophy, or theology in seeking to trace Updike's growth and development as a novelist and his recurrent themes and concerns. I shall, however, begin with Updike's own statement of his position and seek to avoid superimposing upon the novels a preconceived pattern of my own. After analysis of *Midpoint,* I shall utilize the insights gained thereby to examine each of the twelve novels.

MIDPOINT

In 1968, having just passed his thirty-fifth year, the midpoint of the traditional Biblical span of three-score years and ten, John Updike undertook the writing of a long poem which would evaluate his life and set forth the framework in which he envisioned he would continue to live and write. The poem was largely ignored when it was published in 1969 and has received very little attention since, probably because, like much of Updike's poetry, it is extremely clever, and a casual reading suggests the preciosity common to much of Updike's light verse.

Despite its seemingly light, satiric tone and the slickness of its versification, however, the poem is serious, even profound, and deserves consideration as a central document in the Updike canon. In an interview first published in 1972, Updike said, "When asked about what my philosophy was I tried to write it down in *Midpoint* in handy couplets and discovered that of all my books it is the least read, and it was hardly reviewed at all. I concluded that nobody really cared what my philosophy was" *(Picked Up Pieces* 509).[2]   In August 1976, he expressed to me his pleasure that I was taking *Midpoint* seriously. The poem, he said, along with his novel *A Month of Sundays,* is "among [his] franker books." He was, he said, "trying to talk about experience as it . . . first arrives" ("Interview" 300), seeking to explain how he understands his life and his task as a writer. The serious purpose that underlies the surface cleverness of the poem is inescapable when one reads it carefully. Its five parts are artfully structured, and its philosophical and theological concerns are integral to its meaning. Although seven novels have followed *Midpoint,* Updike says that he has not altered his basic philosophical views ("Interview" 274, 302, 303). The "handy couplets" of *Midpoint,* then, offer insight into grasping the underlying intent of Updike's novels—from *The Poorhouse Fair* through *Roger's Version.*

Midpoint is divided into five cantos. Each canto is written in a distinctly different verse form, and each is preceded by a Miltonic prose argument which purports to explain the burden of the verse which follows. Canto I, "Introduction," is written in Dantesque *terza rima,* reinforcing the parallels with the most famous of the midlife poems, *The Divine Comedy.* Canto II, "The Photographs," has no words, being merely a collection of photographs of the Updike family. Canto III, "The Dance of the Solids," is made up of polished Spenserian stanzas which use allegory to explore the atomic structure of matter. Canto IV, "The Play of Memory," which uses a Whitmanesque verse form in combination with some of the pictures from Canto II, is the most personal section of the poem and includes a Shakespearean sonnet to his father. Canto V, "Conclusion," sums up the themes of the previous four parts, and in this section Updike turns to Popean couplets.

THE FIVE CANTOS

Although the verse form of *Midpoint's* Canto I is Dantesque, the opening affirmation is Thoreauvian: "of nothing but me. . . I sing, lacking another song" (3). The successful and famous writer, with his "bucket of unanswerable letters," his "wealth with its worrisome market report," the "rancid advice" from his "critical betters," and his "fretful face" peering out from *Time*'s grim cover" (10), is brought back by the "nip of night" (3) to memories of his childhood. He recalls Godlike feelings when he crushed anthills with his tricycle. But the "comma-shaped" corpses indict him with the realization that he himself could easily be "squashed on the street" if some giant "wheel from far above" should turn on him (4). Fearing that he may be only "an epiphenomenon," he then raises the crucial question "Why am I me?" (4) He finds an answer in the assertion of his own will, and sees himself as the intersection point of the cones of heaven and earth "that took their slant and spin from me alone" (7).

As he grows, however, he "half unwilling" learns "to seem a creature, to subdue [his] giant solipsism to a common scale" (7). He recognizes his participation in the common lot of humanity—"the plight of love, the fate/ of death, the need for food,/ the privileges of ignorance, the ways/ of traffic, competition, and remorse" (7). He is pleased and surprised to learn that his body has mattered—he has a wife and four children and finds himself enrolled "in the beautiful country club/ of mankind's copulating swarm" (8). He had once thought of himself as a "boneless ego" (8), the fifth point of a star, the focal point for the attentions of his parents and grandparents (9). He now advises himself to forget the hopeful burning in his ribs that is incapable of being dimmed (10-11), but concludes by rejecting that advice. He declares, instead, his "untoward faith in the eye/I pun" (11), thus insisting, as the prose argument asserted before the verse began, "on the endurance of the irreducible" (3). He has learned to "seem" a creature, to reduce his "giant solipsism," but he refuses to accept as answer to the question "Why am I me?" mere membership in the "country club/ of mankind's copulating swarm." There is something irreducible in the individual, and even though he recognizes the solipsistic nature of the affirmation, he clings doggedly to it.

Canto II, "The Photographs," is a series of pictures showing, as the prose argument explains, "a cycle of growth, mating, and birth" (12). There are pictures of Updike's parents when they were children, then as a young married couple, then as proud parents showing off baby John. Four more pages of photographs show John, alongside his parents and grandparents, in various stages of growth, and end with pictures showing him with his wife and one of his own children. The prose argument says that "the pictures speak for themselves" (12). Although this is true on an obvious level of seeing, yet another area of meaning related to the pictures calls for some interpretation since the pictures introduce and embody the pointillistic theme that is crucial to the rest of the poem. The pictures are printed in the familiar dots of newspaper engravings. The prose argument explains that these "coarse dots" "become faces" as "lost time sifts through these immutable old screens" (12). Particular faces and individuals emerge when the dots, meaningless individually, are seen from the proper distance and in the proper perspective. "Distance improves vision," the prose argument tells us (12), and we see that the dots are much more than random black spots on the page: they become screens for sifting time and experience and identity. Without the visual examples of these dots merging into significant patterns, some of the affirmations of the rest of the poem would be much less convincing.

Canto III, "The Dance of the Solids," is the only impersonal section of the poem. Sparkling Spenserian stanzas, with perfect *ababbcbccc* rhyme schemes and neat Alexandrines rounding out each self-contained stanza, present a history of the understanding of matter from Democritus through Paracelsus, Lavoisier, Hooke, and Newton on down to Fermi, Planck, and Debye. Metals, ceramics, polymers, electricity, magnetism, and atomic structure are discussed in old-fashioned allegorical style, but with current scientific understanding. The prose argument states that the point of this section is to demonstrate that "Solidity emerges intricate and giddy" (18). What also emerges is an objective, non-solipsistic affirmation of the "endurance of the irreducible," affirmed only as a personal commitment in Canto I. Utilizing the insights of modern physics, the poet shows that "Textbooks and Heaven only are Ideal;/ Solidity is an imperfect state" (20). The "Real" is "cracked and dislocated" (20), made up of "Stray Atoms," "Strange holes," "Dangling Bonds," "Unpaired electrons," and "antiparallel Domains" (20-21). In conclusion, the poet says, "How nicely microscopic forces yield,/ In Units growing visible, the World we wield!" (21).

Without speaking of soul or will or personality or the eye/I pun, the poet demonstrates that matter itself is made up of irreducible dots which present themselves. Like the engravings of the photographs, matter is a screen of innumerable points through which experience and knowledge must be sifted, and which require the proper perspective or distance to be understood as meaningful pattern. Science approaches its task inductively, accumulating the dots that are given in experience. So, too, does the individual in seeking to understand "Why am I me?"

Canto IV, "The Play of Memory," drops all suggestion of objectivity and becomes a personal recollection of and statement to those the poet has known and loved. The poetic form, Whitmanesque in its loose and flowing free verse and, in fact, including numerous direct quotations from Whitman, is combined with varying typography, arrows, dots, and some of the pictures from Canto II. The pointillism theme is fully developed as the dots of memory are sorted and sifted into various patterns. The irreducible individual nature of persons and events is recognized, but the self (the I) utilizes his vision (the eye) to gain the proper distance and perspective to see the unique pattern of his life as it emerges from the universal jumble of the points and dots of experience.

The central element of Canto IV is the sonnet to the poet's father. Its very verse form seems to assert the necessity of taking the free flow of associations and discovering some pattern inherent in them. The sonnet appears toward the end of the Canto, and it comes close to summarizing both the affirmations and the questions raised throughout the poem thus far. This sonnet, therefore, calls for quotation in its entirety:

FATHER, as old as you when I was four,
I feel the restlessness of nearing death
But lack your manic passion to endure,
Your Stoic fortitude and Christian faith.

Remember, at the blackboard, factoring?
My life at midpoint seems a string of terms
In which an error clamps the hidden spring
Of resolution cancelling confirms.
Topheavy Dutchmen sundered from the sea,
Bewitched by money, believing in riddles
Syrian vagrants propagated, we
Incline to live by what the world belittles.
God screws the lukewarm, slays the heart that faints,
And saves His deepest silence for His saints. (35-36)

The inevitability of death induces a restlessness and a sense of lack, or error. The second line of Canto I had asserted a feeling of "all wrong, all wrong—" (3). This feeling has been reiterated in Canto IV just ten lines before the sonnet. As the poet tries to sort out his experiences, he feels that somehow something is not right with his life and what he has accomplished and understood thus far. In our 1976 conversation, Updike said that he did not intend to imply a rejection of self or of specific ideas expressed. Instead, he said, "The author of middle age, the man at midpoint, has the sensation, no matter what he's saying, that something is all wrong. Things are not quite right; there's an unease pervading the poem. He sort of doubts and mocks what he's just asserted. . . . You could say original sin. I mean original sin says it's all wrong, doesn't it?" ("Interview" 299). After suggesting that his attempts are "all wrong" here in Canto IV, the poet returns to a quotation of Whitman, then inserts in italics the phrase *"try again"* (35). Immediately he launches into the sonnet, apparently as a renewed effort, a fresh attempt to understand what is "wrong."

Canto IV concludes with the affirmation of human conception—the joining of the dots of egg and sperm—as the pinnacle of the pointillism theme. The last line of Canto IV is:

most gracious   *merci* (37)

emphasizing the gratuitous nature of existence and expressing gratitude for that existence. This line of words is followed by a picture: the face of the Updike child repeated from Canto II, this time greatly enlarged so that the dots are big and the pattern of the face is difficult to discover.

The first four cantos have carefully laid the groundwork for Canto V, "Conclusion," in which the "handy couplets" seek to summarize and articulate patterns discovered in the earlier exercises. The section opens with a pair of couplets which overtly affirm the implications of the sonnet to his father and the conclusion of Canto IV:

> An easy Humanism plagues the land;
> I choose to take an otherworldly stand.
> The Archimedean point, however small,
> Will serve to lift th' entire terrestrial Ball. (38)

He rejects "easy humanism," choosing instead the "otherworldly stand" which the world belittles—presumably the "riddles" propagated by "Syrian vagrants." Further, he asserts the importance of the irreducible, insisting that, like Archimedes, he can "lift" or understand or interpret or, in a sense, create the entire world from one point. He goes on:

> Reality transcends itself within;
> Atomically, all writers must begin.
> The Truth arrives as if by telegraph:
> One dot; two dots; a silence; then a laugh.
> The rules inhere, and will not be imposed
> *Ab alto,* as most Liberals have supposed. (38)

Updike explained to me that he meant here that the writer, like the scientist, must begin inductively, being true to and careful of the small details of existence as they emerge ("Interview" 298). Whatever "rules" emerge must come from the dots of actuality, not from some abstract ideal which the individual seeks to impose upon them. The pointillistic concept is clear; the discrete elements of experience must be accepted in their irreducibility, one dot at a time. In both writing and life, one must stick to the little things, the experienced things; one trusts that the pattern and rules inhere and will eventually become clear ("Interview" 298).

The next section catalogues the poet's particular heroes, each of whom has contributed in some way to understanding the importance of the irreducible, the individual, the particular. Kierkegaard "splintered Hegel's creed," on the rock of "Existential need" (38); Barth showed how faith can save the wavering terrified soul; Henry Green demonstrated the importance of "gestures, glances, shrugs, and silly drift" (38); Disney took Goofy's successive postures and made them seem movement; Jan Vermeer salted "humble bread/ With dabs of light" (38); IBM took vast ranges of knowledge and converted them to "electric either/ors" (38).

A long view of world politics follows. Marxism and Freudianism are cited as examples of imposed theories that cannot properly interpret the entire pattern of irreducible existence. A fashionable apocalypticism is also rejected. Although "bins of textbooks" describe many holocausts, the earth continues. "Judgment Day seems nigh to every age;/ But History blinks, and turns another page" (40). The world does not go according to anyone's humanistic theory, nor is history going to end in flaming justification of any prophet of doom. Its rules inhere, and it will continue to issue its messages, Updike infers, dot by dot.

Then how does one live in such a world?

> The meanwhile, let us live as islanders
> Who pluck what fruit the lowered branch proffers.
> Each passing moment masks a tender face;
> Nothing has had to be, but is by Grace. (40)

These four lines begin a series of couplets which give directions for living. The prose argument indicates that these instructions are "intelligent hedonistic advice," and concludes by stating that the poet "appears to accept, reluctantly, his own advice" (38). Much of the advice is, in fact, intelligently hedonistic, or at least would fall under the rubric of enlightened self-interest. For example, we are told to learn the ecological lessons of nature, to take pride and pleasure in accomplishing tasks assigned to us, to accept our neighbors since they, too, are "being crowded from behind." We are told not to kill—or at least to grieve while killing if we must do it. We are told not to covet another's wife—unless we are certain that she covets us in return (40-41). Finally, we are told in couplets that are intelligently hedonistic and at the same time in harmony with the emphasis on pointillism and individuality:

> Beware false Gods: the Infallible Man,
> The flawless formula, the Five-Year Plan.
> Abjure bandwagons; be shy of machines,
> Charisma, ends that justify means,
> And oaths that bind the postulant to kill
> His own self-love and independent Will. (42)

All this "advice," however, seems trite, pat, and very much like the clichés we have thought the poet rejected in favor of his other-worldly Archimedean point. And so it is, though Updike pointed out that there are really two kinds of advice being given here. One is the ecologically sound, intelligently hedonistic advice mentioned in the prose argument. The other is the basically religious advice of "nothing has had to be"—therefore accept one's lot and be grateful for it ("Interview" 299). The first kind of advice is the kind expected of an intelligent Western man in the middle of his life, but it is the very advice that leads him to sense that something is "all wrong." He distrusts it; it makes him uneasy.

The "intelligent hedonistic advice" is followed by the

poignant question "All wrong?" and the confession that:

> Advice, however sound, depends
> Upon a meliorism Truth upends;
> A certain Sinkingness resides in things. (42)

Thus the hedonistic advice is found wanting and the balance of the poem shows that conventional humanism leads only to a "cliff of vast Indifference" (43). The second kind of advice, however, holds more promise. There is no flashing revelation, no final assurance offered, but as the poet experiences morning by Chilmark Pond, he recognizes both his participation in a complex solar galaxy and his own individuality. "I am another world," he says. He remembers his childhood with Wordsworthian pleasure, but affirms the comforts of adulthood as well. "The marsh gives way to Pond, to dunes, to Sea," he says. "Cicadas call it good, and I agree" (43).

The ten concluding couplets read:

> At midpoint, center of a Hemisphere
> Too blue for words, I've grown to love it here.
> Earth wants me, it shall have me, yet not yet;
> Some task remains, whose weight I can't forget,
> Some package anciently addressed, of praise,
> That keeps me knocking on the doors of days.
> The time is gone, when *Pope* could ladle Wit
> In couplet droplets, and decanter it.
> *Wordsworth's* sweet brooding, *Milton's* pride,
> And *Tennyson's* unease have all been tried;
> *Fin-de-siecle* sickliness became
> High-stepping Modernism, then went lame.
> Art offers now, not cunning and exile,
> But blank explosions and a hostile smile.
> Deepest in the thicket, thorns spell a word.
> Born laughing, I've believed in the Absurd,
> Which brought me this far; henceforth, if I can,
> I must impersonate a serious man. (44)

If the poet has taken his own advice, it is clearly not the

"intelligent hedonistic advice" of the earlier lines. Rather, he has taken the second kind of advice, affirming the irreducible self as the center of his own hemisphere, a self that does indeed belong to the world and will eventually go to its mother, but not until the dots or words from deep within the thicket, anciently addressed to him, have emerged into their pattern/package of praise. He cannot revive Pope or Milton or Wordsworth or Tennyson, nor can he accept a lame modernism, but he commits himself to keep "knocking on the doors of days."

UPDIKE'S COMMITMENTS

The last three lines of Canto V epitomize the ironic tone that has pervaded the entire poem. Superficially, Updike seems to say that he has been playing, posing, and toying and will from now on at least try to present a serious front. As we look back, however, we realize that the entire poem has been utterly serious, that it has presented matters of ultimate concern, that it has shown us a man wrestling with the terms of himself and his world. The cleverness, the jokes, the clowning, have been masks and disguises to provide some aesthetic distance for the frankness of personal confession. What we have seen is a man who recognizes how ludicrous it is for any individual to take himself seriously in the vastness of the universe, yet continues to do so.

The commitments Updike sets forth in this poem, therefore, provide in his own words the screens through which we may sift the complexities of his twelve novels. The insights provided by *Midpoint* will help provide the proper perspective from which the dots and laughs of the individual novels may emerge into the inherent pattern which illuminates Updike's sensibility, his fictional world, and what he has to say about life. Throughout the five cantos, Updike reveals that he is committed to the centrality of the individual, the reality of the material world, a dualistic mindset, and a life of mystery and faith.

The Centrality of the Individual

The importance of the individual is proclaimed in the opening line of the poem when the poet asserts that he will sing "Of nothing but, me, me" (3). The balance of Canto I expands this assertion as the thirty-five-year-old poet recalls his boyhood experiences. As a boy he clung to an "infinitely hard" and "luminous" point within himself (4), feeling himself to be both the "point 0" in optics where the plane "converges and passes through" to be received by the retina (6) and "the crux of radii" where the tips of the cones of heaven and earth meet and receive the determination of their "slant and spin" (7). The word "midpoint" thus has significance beyond its reference to the half-way point in the Biblical span of life. It also represents the individual who is the center of his own universe, the midpoint of the circle of his knowledge and experience. Reaffirming the midpoint imagery, Updike recalls that he thought of himself as a "boneless ego" serving "as the hub/ of a wheeling spectacle that would not pass" (8). He saw his parents as going through all their actions on his behalf and himself as "The fifth point of a star" reflecting the admiration of his parents and grandparents (9). He admits that such a claim to being the hub of the universe was a childish solipsism (7), and that he learned to subdue it as he grew. He asserts, however, in closing the Canto, that "incapable of being dimmed,/ there harbors still inside me. . ./ . . . among my ribs,/ a hopeful burning riding out the tide/ . . ." (10-11), and he concludes by reiterating his "untoward faith in the eye/I pun" (11). The eyeball is one of the smallest of the concentric circles of the universe, but it is both the center from which the subjective I looks out at its world and the center to which that world comes to be received.

Canto II continues to stress the importance of the individual, even though there are no words, only pictures. In seventeen of the twenty-one photographs, John Updike is the focus of attention. The other people pictured—his parents, grandparents, and wife—are clearly there because of their relationships to the one individual who is the center (midpoint) of the entire poem.

Canto III relates primarily to another of Updike's major commitments which will be discussed and does not deal directly with the individual, but Cantos IV and V return specifically to the subject and develop the position far beyond the childish solipsism of Canto I. Canto IV, entitled "The Play of Memory," free-flowing in both its verse form and its association of ideas, serves as a medium for the poet to remember people he has known and loved. He addresses childhood playmates, high-school sweethearts, his mother, his grandmother, his wife, and his psychiatrist, among others, without overtly distinguishing one from the other, assuming instead that the reader will sort out the distinctions. In fact, he assumes that such distinctions are secondary, since what the poet/individual feels and says is more important than the person addressed. "If my body is history," he says, "then my ego is Christ/ and no inversion is too great for me/ no fate too special" (32). A recurring thread in this complex play of memory is the awareness of sexuality as an integral part of individuality. The canto concludes with the act of conception, the joining of two discrete individuals to produce a third, and we see a picture of Updike's daughter, who, the poet has told us in Canto I, echoes his eyes and his laugh, thus projecting something of the individual onward into the future.

Canto V concludes the poem and reaffirms the centrality

of the individual with more reason and assurance than does Canto I. Although the poet's choice of the "Archimedean point" (38) recalls the intersection of cones from Canto I, the lucid, indissoluble, hard point of the will that was felt by the self-centered child is now tempered. The adult knows from Archimedes the importance of a central point on which to stand; he also knows from Heraclitus that all things flow (42), including the individual. He knows he must die, but decides to forgive himself his death "and freely flow" (42). He affirms that "We come into this World from well without" (43), thus taking the "otherworldly stand" (38), insisting that "I am another world" (43). "At midpoint, center of a Hemisphere too blue for words" (43), he is in the middle of his own life and also still the central point of his own hemisphere of meaning. Knowing that "Earth wants me, it shall have me" (44), he continues to affirm that the world of which he is the center is a good one, and he will keep "knocking on the doors of days" (44).

The mere act of writing such a poem, with its autobiographical subject matter and its self-conscious skill in versification, is in itself evidence of Updike's belief that the individual being is radically important. The poem might appear to be mere egotism without the carefully developed affirmation that the individual, whoever he or she may be, is philosophically central—that is, a part of true ego-ism where every I (ego) is pivotal. Examination of the other three major commitments of the poem will make it quite clear, however, that Updike's belief in the individual, though basic to his world-view and his work, is far from mere solipsism.

The Reality of the World

Although ideologically dedicated to the eye/I pun and the centrality of the individual, Updike seeks to avoid unchecked subjectivity from the outset of *Midpoint*. In the opening lines of Canto I, acknowledging the inevitability of death, the "nip of night" (3), he summons memories not limited to feelings of being the "crux of radii" (7). He recalls bricks, walks, grass, wood and paint, a thermometer and a broom—all solid and specific items outside himself which are parts in a "code of things" (3) testifying to a continuum: the boneless ego at one end, the wonders of Philadelphia Avenue at the other. The avenue's telephone wires, "under orders/ to find the wider world" (6) which exists beyond the child's narrow circle, join with the daily newspaper, passing automobiles, burning leaves, swirling snow, and returning spring to remind the boy that he is part of a solid material world outside himself. With growing awareness of his own physical body, the boy learns to "subdue his giant solipsism" and at least to "seem a creature" (7), even if he has not fully accepted the implications of such creatureliness.

Speaking in his mature voice, Updike fully acknowledges the outside world and its other subjective inhabitants. He addresses the reader directly (7), thus recognizing that were it not for an objective reality outside himself there would be no reason for the poem. He confesses his satisfaction in sharing with the reader the ordinary experiences of "traffic, competition, and remorse" (7). He recognizes that his physical body has mattered as he looks at his wife and children. Thus, even though the first canto concludes with the expression of his "untoward faith in the eye/I pun" (11), it also counterpoints the centrality of the individual against the ongoing material world in which the individual is simply one more factual dot among myriads of others.

Although the photographs of Canto II are clearly dominated by John Updike as individual, they also stress the fact that he is part of a cycle beyond himself: parents, grandparents, wife, and child. He may be the midpoint of the pointillistic constellation, but he is certainly neither its beginning nor its end. Furthermore, the photographs themselves are tangibly real objects, made up of numerous specific and discrete dots, presenting patterns/images to be perceived by other sets of I/eyes. The patterned dots may limn the individual, but they are products independent of his will; he did not create them, nor can he change them.

The eleven Spenserian stanzas of Canto III, "The Dance of the Solids," occupy the midpoint of *Midpoint* and, dealing as they do directly with matter itself, provide the necessary counterpoint to the emphasis on the individual prominent in the earlier and later sections of the poem. These stanzas were first published separately in the *Scientific American* in January of 1969, their insights based closely on factual materials presented in that magazine's September 1967 issue. Using allegory and personification as a writer of the seventeenth or eighteenth century might have done, Updike addresses scientists and the elements they discovered. The resulting nine-line stanzas move elegantly through the development of atomic theory from Democritus through Fermi, treating with great respect all those investigators who dealt seriously with even the tiniest dots of matter. What emerges is a testament to the scientific method which trusts the reality of its materials, allowing the bits and pieces to reveal their patterns and altering previous ideas when new dots emerge to change the pattern. There is also wonder at the complexity of matter. Man may now be able to create complex plastics and synthetics, but long ago "each primordial Bean/ Knew Cellulose by heart" (19). This canto is the most formal in the poem and the only one with no reference to the first person or I. Initially, it seems to interrupt the flow from the personal recollections of Canto I to the pictures of Canto II to the various reminiscences of Canto IV on to the more reasoned reflections and resolutions of Canto V. On close examination, however, the reader can sense the rightness of both its content and its location in the poem. It makes specific the allusions to the solidity and importance of matter offered by the first two cantos while providing a foundation for the insights in the next two cantos. By removing the I/eye from the center of the poem, Updike is able to find firmer ground for the Archimedean point of his conclusion.

The reality of connections with others outside the self is emphasized by Canto IV. The language, verse form, and thoughts expressed are idiosyncratic and speak for the importance of the I, but mother, father, wife, and others emerge as being necessary to that central ego. The fact that the poet exists in an objective literary tradition is also acknowledged by numerous quotations from Walt Whitman (significantly, of course, from "Song of Myself"). The reality and objectivity of such a literary tradition is further acknowledged, though without any overt statement, by the use of Dante's *terza rima* in the first canto, Spenser's stanza form in the third, and the heroic couplet in the fifth. By using these forms, Updike not only acknowledges himself as a part of a poetic tradition— somewhat like the line of scientific investigation from Democritus to Fermi—but he also acknowledges that such a tradition is broad enough to include a band of readers who will recognize and appreciate what he is doing. If he were only a "boneless ego," he would neither know, imitate, nor expect others to recognize such a poetic tradition.

Canto IV also deals with another major factor of objective reality—sex. Recalling a round mirror that he had cracked as a child, the poet summons his "0" symbol, which in Canto I meant the central point in the optical plane. Now he associates the 0 with the cracked mirror and concludes that "Mirrors are Vaginas" (27). In the Biblical sense, sex is a "knowing"; since, he says, "'knowing' = 'seeing'," therefore, "Penises are eyes" (28). Sex is thus associated with the centering 0, but with the addition that there is something to be known, an otherness to be experienced, which requires moving beyond self-centered egotism. The inevitable paradox emerges: the act of physical conception which confirms and continues individuality is possible only through a joining—dot of sperm must meet with dot of egg, a "twinned point" (37). "You took me in," the poet tells his wife, and it is to her that the final word—"merci"—of the canto is addressed (37).

Canto V clearly accepts the world, urging the finding of satisfaction in daily work (40). Ordinary tasks are affirmed as means of fitting into the world. The carpenter learns the secrets of wood and makes the dovetails fit. The steel-worker plunges hot metal into water and produces the proper form (41). In the concluding lines, nature-images like those in Canto I return—"Summer's touch," "cool autumnal trace," "playground dust," "Pond . . . dunes . . . Sea . . . Cicadas" (43)—all calling to mind the tangible arena in which the poet lives, even though he still asserts that he is the center of his own hemisphere.

Dualism

Updike affirms, as Emerson did, the central position of the subjective I. His insistence on the objective reality of the material world, however, stops him considerably short of Emerson's philosophical idealism which asserted that Nature is only a shadow of the soul, that matter puts itself forth through the mind of the subject (50). If Updike is going to insist on the self as the crucial midpoint of experience and at the same time insist on the solidity and reality of the world of matter, he must turn to a dualistic world-view which recognizes the interpenetration and interdependence of mind/spirit and body/matter. Such a view is exactly what *Midpoint* purveys.

31

We have already seen that Canto I combines images of the centering self—point, crux, 0, radii, hub, etc.—with images of solid reality—bricks, leaves, market reports, traffic, telephone wires, etc. The poet tells us that even as a child he "sought in middling textures part-/ icles of iridescence, scintillae in dullish surfaces . . ."(5). In the "middling textures" we find a third meaning for the word "midpoint," suggesting not only the half-way point in life's journey and the center of a hemisphere, but also a point between two extremes—a designation between idealism and materialism, between solipsism and self-abnegation, between euphoria and despair. Human life partakes of the middling quality, and the self must take hold of both horns of its dualistic dilemma in order to recognize the truth and value of both sides of its nature.

In our 1976 interview, Updike said, "I don't *mean* to be dualistic, but there is a way in which I see things as mind or spirit on the one hand and body on the other. It's more a gut way of looking at things than any sort of intellectualized position" ("Interview" 292). This spirit/body dualism is illustrated throughout *Midpoint*. Canto I, for instance describes the young boy's feeling that "The beaded curtain/ of Matter hid an understanding Eye" (5). Matter is there, to be sure, but another realm which requires a different mode of understanding is also present. Furthermore, the cones whose tips meet in the boy's consciousness are those of heaven and earth—another indication of polarity.

The photographs of Canto II also demonstrate a dualistic frame of reference. They focus on an individual, but show him dependent on others outside himself. The dots, "coarse," "calligraphic and abstract" (12), discrete spots of matter on the page, can assume meaning only by the interaction of a mind, a self from the other side of the spirit/matter duality, else there is no pattern, no meaning. The "screens" have their very real material existence apart from any ego, but without a subjective viewer there is no meaning to "sift" through the screens, and there are no faces, no vision.

Canto III centers on the reality of matter, but it reveals that even matter is "intricate and giddy" (18). Atoms, metals, ceramics, and polymers each seem to have their own personalities, just as individual human beings do. "Isotopes play pranks" and excitons "wander loose"; there are "stray atoms" and "strange holes," "Free Electrons" and hugely varied resistances (20). Matter, then, is as imperfectly understood and mysterious as spirit is. Nevertheless, "microscopic forces" (21) have yielded their secrets and their patterns, revealing a closer relationship between the poles of spirit and matter than either philosophical idealist or realist has believed.

Canto IV, with its ego-centered recollections of those persons the poet has loved, again illustrates the dualistic "gut way of looking at things." The self is central, but it is only a self as it relates outward to others. The "myriads of points" (22) or dots of experience are "out there" in objective reality, but they must be filtered through the self in order to have meaning. The sexual experience, that most intimately personal expression of the self, becomes a paradigm for this dualistic approach precisely because its success requires knowing the reality of otherness. This physical act always carries the possibilities of self-transcendence, both through the ecstatic experience of the act itself and through the procreation which it makes possible. The pair-bonding of sexual opposites is symbolic of bi-polar relationships throughout the universe.

The "heroes" cited in Canto V further reinforce the dualistic or bipolar approach. Three of the five persons cited (Jan Vermeer, Henry Green, and Walt Disney) are important to the poet for their contributions to his understanding of the artistic process. The other two (Soren Kirkegaard and Karl Barth) have provided philosophical and theological inspiration.

The Dutch painter Jan Vermeer (1632-1675), according to the poem, salted "humble bread" "as well as bricks and thread" "With dabs of light" (38). His paintings of simple and quiet domestic scenes convey what Updike has elsewhere called a sense of "graphic precision" *(Picked-Up Pieces* 36), yet the illumination achieved by the "dabs of light" gives the paintings an almost revelatory quality. As art historian William Fleming has pointed out, Vermeer's work is much more than graphic realism; Vermeer shares with the viewer his own "unique perception of the quality and texture of things" (382). Through intimate, realistic details, the painter has succeeded in combining the poles of his unique introspective vision of the world and a sense of tangible reality.

The British novelist Henry Green (1905-1973) is praised in the poem for showing how lifetimes can "sift" through seemingly insignificant "gestures," "glances," and "shrugs" (38). Green's nine novels, according to Joyce Carol Oates, are "nearly plotless comedies of manners," written in an "inimitable style" and creating "hilariously and deliberately trivial fictional worlds" (79-80). With his own idiosyncratic style Green created a distinctive and deliberately fictional world separated from ordinary reality. Yet Updike has insisted in an essay that Green gives the reader an "off-hand-and-backward-feeling of verbal and psychological accuracy" *(Picked-Up Pieces* 36). Although he pursued a deliberately eccentric personal stance, Green accomplished the unveiling of objective reality.

Walt Disney's mastery of film animation, utilizing the tricks of optical illusion to produce movement through successive still cartoon pictures, has a striking kinship with Updike's pointillistic approach. The inanimate drawings come to life through interaction with the human I/eye, illustrating the cooperation of the subject-object poles.

According to the poem, the Danish theologian Soren Kierkegaard (1813-1855) "splintered Hegel's creed/ Upon the rock of Existential need" (38). The German philosopher Hegel (1770-1831) interpreted the development of thought as a relatively smooth and objective process from a thesis to its opposite or antithesis on to a combination of the two into a synthesis. The synthesis then provided a new thesis for the process to continue indefinitely—all part of a progression toward the "Absolute Idea." According to Hegel's "creed," the real *is* the rational, and the rational *is* the real. Kierkegaard, however, found that such a rational pattern did not match human existence as he experienced it. Rather, he insisted, "subjectivity is truth," and each individual must make radical and lonely choices as he faces the stern "either/or" of life. Kierkegaard, Updike said in 1976, was crucial to him for his insistence on the importance of the individual, his speaking for the importance of existentially subjective choices in a world which often seeks to oppress or obliterate individuality ("Interview" 296).

The Swiss theologian Karl Barth (1886-1968), chief spokesman of the "neo-orthodox" movement in theology in the mid-twentieth century, is listed as a "hero" because he "told how saving Faith can flow/ From Terror's oscillating Yes and No" (38). As with Kierkegaard, there are two poles between which the self must decide. Updike wrote in 1965 that "Barth's theology, at one point in my life, seemed alone to be supporting it (my life)" (*Assorted Prose* viii). In 1976 Updike explained that what particularly attracted him to Barth was "the frank supernaturalism and the particularity of his position" ("Interview" 301). In Barth, he said, he found someone saying with "resounding definiteness and learning. . . that there was something within us that would not die, and that we live by faith alone" ("Interview" 302). Yet Barth was "very open to the world. Wonderfully alive and relaxed" ("Interview" 302). Kierkegaard and Barth, then, provide a framework for accepting the centrality of the subjective while at the same time accepting the existential reality and importance of the physical world.

As Canto V moves on to emphasize the validity of solid, worldly work, it also maintains the insistence that the "pinpoint," the "locus," (41) is in the subjective individual. The self is, indeed, in the world and a part of it, but it has come into this world from without and is, in a sense, "another world" (43). The self, then, has a dual nature and leads a dual life. As Updike summed it up in our interview:

> We are obviously very much in nature and have to be well aware of it. All of our various kinds of health depend upon some sort of recognition that we are natural beings. On the other hand, there is a radical jump between one's individual sense of me—I—and any other kind of reality. One experiences his own identity in a totally other way than he experiences the existence of all these exterior forms. ("Interview" 296)

Mystery and Faith

The foregoing bipolar dualistic stance leads Updike finally to a somewhat ambiguous affirmation. In a 1966 interview he spoke of the "yes—but" quality of his writing which recognizes the "secrecy" of reality and frequently "evades entirely pleasing anybody" *(Picked-Up Pieces* 503). Updike's particular commitment to both the centrality of the individual and the reality of the objective, material world produces a philosophy whose dualistic parts hang in uneasy suspension as he says "yes" to one side while saying "but" there is another side which must be examined as well. *Midpoint* illustrates this "yes—but" quality throughout the poem: the subjectivity is counterpointed by objective detail, but the objective detail is always qualified by the centrality of the individual ego. The ambiguity of the dualistic position highlights what is really the central question of the poem, a question raised specifically in the early lines of Canto I: "The crucial question was, *Why am I me?*" (4)

Even as a child, Updike realized that boys in China or Greece were "born as cherishing/ of their small selves" (4). As he crushed ants with his tricycle, he was made aware of the mystery that he was alive (4), and recognized that some giant "wheel from far above" could crush him just as he had crushed the ants (4). The mystery of why he should have been born in Shillington, Pennsylvania, where "Five-fingered leaves hold horsechestnuts" and "The gutter runs with golden water/ from Flickinger's ice plant" (6) is not solved by the sense of being "the crux of radii" (7). The Canto closes with a recital of the mature man's condition: fame and wealth as a writer, "a drafty house, a voluptuous spouse," four children, his face on the cover of *Time* (10). *Yes* —these things are palpable and real; *but*—he refuses to accept them as ultimate and affirms his "faith in the eye/I pun" (11). There is something "secret" about reality, a sense of mystery which cannot be explained but can only be recognized and affirmed.

Cantos II and III further illustrate the mystery. In Canto II, the photographs are "immutable . . . screens" (12). *Yes*—they are objective reality, unchangeable by individual desires or will. The dots will not move on the page. *But*—the dots are merely "coarse" and "abstract" without an individual viewer. When a person views these immutable screens, he finds that the proper "distance improves vision" (12). The individual is responsible for both the distance and the vision. Only by the mysterious partnership of mutable self and immutable screens can there be a sifting of "lost time" which allows the dots to "become faces" (12). In Canto III, matter is seen to be as mysterious as the self. "Textbooks and Heaven only are Ideal;/ Solidity is an imperfect state" (20). The real is "cracked" and "dislocated" (20). "Strange holes" and "Dangling Bonds," wavelengths absorbed and re-emitted, and "Unpaired Electrons" all suggest the "antiparallel/ Domains" and mystery of matter (20, 21). Nevertheless, the faith of the scientific method is justified, since somehow "microscopic forces yield" their patterns and help us to understand "the World we wield" (21).

The central affirmation of mystery and faith in Canto IV is the sonnet to his father, which begins with expressing restlessness brought on by awareness of nearing death—death which will obliterate the world of the central ego. In the octave of the sonnet, the poet feels that his midpoint life (both halfway through the Biblical span and center of his own universe) contains an error. His life is not working out as smoothly as the mathematical problems his teacher-father used to work on the blackboard. Mystery thus may lead to doubt and sense of lack as well as to bold affirmation. The sestet of the sonnet, however, is an affirmation of faith. It is not, now, the "untoward faith in the eye/I pun" of Canto I, but a more sober affirmation of faith "in spite of." The poet recalls his Dutch ancestors and identifies them with his father. "Believing in riddles/ Syrian vagrants propagated," he says, "we/ Incline to live by what the world belittles" (36). *Yes*—the objective world is important.. *But*—sometimes there are things beyond worldly wisdom. *Yes*—matter and spirit interpenetrate. *But*—their relationship is not always clear: sometimes "God screws the lukewarm, slays the heart that faints,/ And saves His deepest silence for His saints" (36).

The sober affirmation of mystery in the sonnet prepares the way for the opening of Canto V. Although, he says, "An easy Humanism plagues the land," the poet chooses "to take an otherworldly stand" (38). The rational credos of all sorts of philosophers are rejected in favor of the affirmation that truth arrives only one dot at a time. The dots come when and as they will. Then there may be a period of silence, or even a laugh. Human knowledge of material reality cannot fully unlock the mystery of life. In such a world one must trust "each passing moment," taking "what fruit the lowered branch proffers." One accepts the mystery of life, affirming that "Nothing has had to be, but is by Grace" (40). This line is a key affirmation of the poem. Updike said in our interview that one of his basic concerns has always been "a sense of the mystery and irreducibility of one's own identity mixed with fear of the identity being an illusion or being squelched" ("Interview" 303). This sense has been coupled with his

> philosophical obsession . . . that there is a certain gratuitousness in
> existence at all. That is, however riddles are unraveled, the one of
> why the void itself was breached remains permanently mysterious,
> and in its own way permanently hopeful-making. ("Interview"
> 299)

The mystery of the dualistic *Yes—but* is supported by what Updike calls his "sense of God the Creator, which is fairly real to me" ("Interview" 303). The mystery is not resolved; the *yes—but* is not eliminated; but the ambiguity is made acceptable by affirmation of "the permanently hopeful-making" faith in the God who originally breached the void.

The concluding stanzas of Canto V reaffirm both the mystery and faith. In Wordsworthian phrases the poet enjoys the natural scenery at Chilmark Pond. Like Wordsworth, he affirms that he has come into this world from someplace else; and, like Wordsworth, he laments the passing of childhood's simple joys but affirms the comforts of adulthood. As "marsh gives way to Pond, to dunes, to Sea" (43), he recognizes the vast cycles of nature—of which he is a part—and affirms their goodness. He still insists that he is the midpoint, "center of a Hemisphere" (43), maintaining his hold on his faith in the I. Yet he admits that earth will have him when the time comes, affirming his acceptance of the material pole of his dualism. Mysteriously, however, there is a "task" that remains, some "package, anciently addressed, of praise" (44), which will keep him living his *yes—but* life. "Deepest in the thicket," he says, "thorns spell a word" (44). Somewhere in the mystery and ambiguity of life, the dots are merging to form a pattern, a word. The "word" may be set deep in the tangled underbrush of contemporary life, but faith affirms its presence. Such faith may be what "the world belittles," and the seeker may indeed find only that "God saves his deepest silence" for him. Unlike Shelley, however, who in "Ode to the West Wind," wept, "I fall upon the thorns of life! I bleed!" (1. 54), Updike affirms that the mysterious thorny *yes—but*s of life offer a promise of meaning.

Although rich and varied, *Midpoint* offers a basically clear pattern of four inter-related commitments affirming the mystery embodied in the dualistic relation of self and world. Since Updike has admitted the frankness of the poem's attempt to set forth his philosophy, these *Midpoint* commitments will provide the prism through which we will view Updike's developing novelistic *oeuvre*.

NOTES

[1]Alice and Kenneth Hamilton, *The Elements of John Updike* (Grand Rapids: Eerdmans, 1970); Rachael C. Burchard, *John Updike: Yea Sayings* (Carbondale, Illinois: Southern Illinois U P, 1971); Larry E. Taylor, *Pastoral and Anti-Pastoral Patterns in John Updike's Fiction,* (Carbondale, Illinois: Southern Illinois U P, 1971); Robert Detweiler, *John Updike* (New York: Twayne, 1972); Joyce B. Markel, *Fighters and Lovers* (New York: New York U P, 1973); George W. Hunt, S. J., *John Updike and the Three Great Secret Things* (Grand Rapids: Eerdmans, 1980); Suzanne Henning Uphaus, *John Updike,* (New York: Ungar, 1980); Robert Detweiler, *John Updike* (Boston: Twayne, 1984); Donald J. Greiner, *The Other John Updike* (Athens, Ohio: Ohio U P, 1981); Donald J. Greiner, *John Updike's Novels* (Athens, Ohio: Ohio U P, 1984).

[2]Alice and Kenneth Hamilton, alone among Updike critics as far as I can discover, have attempted to call attention to the importance of *Midpoint*. They have written two articles ("Theme and Technique in John Updike's *Midpoint*", *Mosaic* (1970): 79-106; and "Relationships in John Updike's *Midpoint:* Personal and Aesthetic," presented as part of the program of the Updike Society at the December, 1978, meeting of the Modern Language Association in New York City) which give detailed analyses of the poem, its sources, its allusions, and its importance for understanding Updike's other work. Although the present study and those done by the Hamiltons come at their respective critical evaluations from somewhat different perspectives, the basic interpretations of Updike's philosophical position are compatible and essentially in agreement. I recommend the Hamiltons' studies to readers of this work.

WORKS CITED

Aldridge, John. *The Devil in the Fire.* New York: Harper's Magazine P, 1972.

Detweiler, Robert. *John Updike.* New York: Twayne, 1972.

Emerson, Ralph Waldo. "Nature." *Selections from Ralph Waldo Emerson,* ed. Stephen Whicher. Boston: Houghton-Miflin, 1957.

Fleming, William. *Arts and Ideas.* New York: Holt, Rinehart and Winston, 1968.

Gilman, Richard. Review of *The Poorhouse Fair. Commonweal* 69 (7 Feb. 1959): 499.

Harper, Howard. *Desperate Faith.* Chapel Hill, NC: U of North Carolina P, 1967.

Hicks, Granville. Review of *The Poorhouse Fair. Saturday Review* 17 Jan. 1959: 58.

Hunt, George W., S. J. "Updike's Omega-Shaped Shelter: Structure and Psyche in *A Month of Sundays.*" *Critique* 19 (1978): 47-60.

Markle, Joyce. *Fighers and Lovers.* New York: New York UP, 1973.

Oates, Joyce Carol. "Two Rediscoveries." *Quest/78* Nov. 1978: 79-80.

Podhoretz, Norman. "A Dissent of Updike." *Doings and Undoings.* New York: Noonday, 1964.

Regan, Robert A. "Updike's Symbol of the Center." *Modern Fiction Studies* 20 (Spring 1974) 77-96.

Rupp, Richard. "Style in Search of a Center." *Sewanee Review* 75 (Autumn 1967): 693-709.

Taylor, Larry E. *Pastoral and Anti-Pastoral Patterns in John Updike's Fiction.* Carbondale, IL: Southern Illinois UP, 1971.

Updike, John. *Assorted Prose.* Greenwich, Conn.: Fawcett, 1966.

---. "Interview Conducted by Jeff Campbell, Georgetown, MA, 9 August 1976." Published as Appendix to this volume.

---. *Midpoint and Other Poems.* New York: Knopf, 1969.
---. *Picked-Up Pieces.* New York: Knopf, 1975.
Vanderwerken, David L. "Rabbit Re-docks: Updike's Inner Space Odyssey." *College Literature* 2(1975): 73-78.
Waller, G. F. "Updike's *Couples:* a Barthian Parable." *Research Studies* 40 (March 1972): 10-21.

CHAPTER 2

"THE WOOD IS DRY":
THE POORHOUSE FAIR

In 1959, at the age of twenty-five, John Updike publish-ed his first novel, *The Poorhouse Fair*. Although the story takes place more than twenty years later, the only specific clue to the date of the events is given in a newspaper read by one of the characters. The paper mentions the up-coming celebration of the crystal anniversary of the opening of the St. Lawrence Seaway (84). The action, then, presumably takes place around 1980. The events described occur on the third Wednesday in August, as the inhabitants of the Dia-mond County Poor Home on the outskirts of the town of Andrews, New Jersey, prepare for and conduct their annual fair. The first part of the novel describes the morning's preparations. About noon, a thunderstorm arises, threaten-ing the fair and driving the old people indoors for lunch and conversation. The storm clears, however, and the fair is held as planned. Predictably, townspeople come to buy old-fashioned candy, baked goods, quilts, carved peach-stones, and other reminders of former days. The book ends with night closing down the fair's activities.

As this summary indicates, little of earth-shaking impor-tance happens in the novel. Aside from a young man of twenty-five creating a fictional group of believable old peo-ple, the chief interest of the novel is ideological. The prefect of the Poor Home is a man named Conner, a bureaucratic humanist who represents the new age of rational welfare. He stands apart from the old people, who embody the values of a by-gone era and whose chief spokesman is a ninety-four year old retired schoolteacher named Hook. The contrasts between Conner and Hook, which are highlighted in a "debate" in the book's center, provide the poles of movement and interest.

In addition to Conner and Hook, Updike creates an impressive array of lively characters. Among the old people there are the quilt making Amy Mortis with her goiter; Lucas with his perennial self-induced earache; Gregg, the rebel with a foul mouth; Elizabeth Heinemann, beautiful but blind; Tommy Fuller, who carves peach-stones; and Mrs. Lucas with her bad legs and her parakeet. In addition to the old people, the reader finds Buddy, Conner's young assistant who is attracted to his superior; Dr. Angelo, the physician who presides over the new west wing where inmates are sent to die; and Grace, his nurse, who manages to brighten the otherwise somber atmosphere. From outside the home come Ted, the young man who delivers drinks for the fair and knocks down the wall trying to back his truck through the gate; eight-year-old Mark Kegerise, who comes to the fair with his grandfather; and numerous other visitors.

STRUCTURE

One may wonder why there are so many people in a novel of only 185 pages. No single character is fully developed, and although we are fascinated by the glimpses we receive, we remain spectators and do not feel that we have genuinely come to know any of the participants. Initially, the reader might be tempted to dismiss this aspect of the book as inexperience on the part of the youthful writer. However, if one understands Updike's use of specific images to shape plot structures, one is inclined to believe that the sketchy character development is intentional.

In a television interview Updike once discussed the fact that he usually has a shape in mind as he begins a novel. In 1976 he confirmed, "It is true that with every book I do begin with some image. . . some sense of its *seizability* or some sense of its mass. I have to have that even before I begin a book ("Interview" 287).

> I . . . do see a book as having a tone before you set out and a cer-
> tain shape and texture. . . . I think that when all is said and done,
> some impetus, some direction, some tension or conflict, must be
> set up. In other words, some movement along a kind of linear
> way happens, and to some extent books do break down into this
> kind of direction or diagram. Detail is bearable only if you feel
> it's strung or bestowed on some kind of general seizable form;
> otherwise it becomes suffocating and you're lost in it. I really feel
> I can only add detail when I know where I'm going and feel the
> reader is with me. ("Interview" 287-288)

Referring to *The Poorhouse Fair,* Updike said in the television interview that the image he had in mind for this novel might be described either as a gladiola with numerous small flowers coming from a central stalk or as a skyrocket which shoots upward, spreads out into numerous spots of light, then fades away.[1] A look at the structure of the novel confirms that indeed such an image does give the "shape and texture," the "linear way" or "diagram" on which the details are "strung or bestowed" in a "general seizable form."

There are three major parts to the novel, basically following the three major divisions of the day. Part I describes the morning preparations, ended by the coming of the storm. Part II is devoted to indoor activities during the rain. Part III presents the afternoon and evening activities of the fair itself. These three parts are not ordinary narrative units, however. They are consistent neither in chronology nor point of view; instead, they are made up of forty-three individual vignettes. All are told in third-person, but from the points of view of varying characters, and sometimes the vignettes overlap one another in time. For example, while the reader is attending an incident inside the poorhouse, another event may be taking place outside which he must learn about in the next vignette.

We have in this novel, then, a series of "dabs of light"—dots emerging one by one into the reader's consciousness. Already utilizing the pointillism he later described in *Midpoint,* Updike adheres "to the testable, the verifiable, the undeniable little thing," hoping, as he has said, that "the pattern in the art will emerge" ("Interview" 298). Like the colored lights strung to illuminate the fair, the vignettes of the novel are strung, as we shall see, between the ideological poles represented by Hook and Conner—they neither build to some grand climactic insight nor fully delineate a single character, but each episode contributes its own moment of illumination in keeping with the shaping structural image.

The Poorhouse Fair is sometimes treated as the first, hesitant beginning of a young novelist and therefore not important in the Updike canon. Joyce Markle, however, finds Hook and Conner to be the archetypes of Updike's later protagonists, and she believes that, except for sexuality, *The Poorhouse Fair* presents a "surprisingly complete spectrum of Updike's thematic motifs" (2-3). Markle is quite right in pointing out the importance of this novel as a base from which later works have developed.

THE EPIGRAPH

When I asked Updike in 1976 how important he considered the epigraphs of his books to be, he replied:

> Quite important, really, and I've read very few reviews or critical articles that seem to me to take clues that the epigraphs meant to offer. I tend to discover the epigraphs at some point in the work in progress. I don't think a book as to have an epigraph—*War and Peace* doesn't have one, and so on—a book should be its own. On the other hand, I've enjoyed other people's epigraphs, and if I find a quote that seems to me to hit it, as sort of a mystical offering given to me, I use it. ("Interview" 277)

Since Updike himself considers the epigraphs significant in offering clues to the intentions of his works, I have sought in this study to utilize those clues and have chosen portions of the epigraphs as titles for its chapters, including this one. The complete epigraph for *The Poorhouse Fair*—"If they do this when the wood is green, what will happen when the wood is dry?"—is taken from the translation of the Gospel of Luke by E. V. Rieu. Updike has pointed out that his use of a Biblical epigraph was not accidental. "Certainly the book is a very consciously Christian one," he said. "I was twenty-five and very intellectually concerned. I wouldn't have been reading this modern translation of the New Testament if I weren't" ("Interview" 278). The particular verse chosen from Luke is a portion of Jesus' speech to the daughters of Jerusalem as he is being led to the cross. It is preceded by eschatological predictions of woes to come. Robert Detweiler has noted this context of the epigraph and suggested that Updike is making ironic use of the verse, since in this novel the cataclysm hasn't come and won't come because there can be no future for a humanity that surrenders itself to a bureaucratic officialdom like that of Conner (44). Such imaginative interpretation, however, exemplifies the danger of over-using critical ingenuity. When I asked Updike about the implications of the context of the verse, he responded: "I didn't know, in fact, until you said so, that the words were spoken by Jesus on the way to being crucified. . . . Throughout, I was consciously dealing with a period analogous to the early Christian period, that is, a time when the established religion was crumbling and something was trying to be born and meeting resistance. The book was written by a young man who saw the time he was living in—the Eisenhower years—as a dry period, certainly a dry period for the established church" ("Interview" 278).

The epigraph, therefore, was chosen for the specific words of the verse, not for any implications the broader context of the verse might contain. The fact that its source is Biblical, however, does indicate the author's theological concerns at this point of his life, and the sense of the present dryness projected into the future does set the tone for the work. With the tone set by the epigraph and the structural implications of the gladioloa or skyrocket image in mind, we are ready to turn to the novel's central ideological theme.

BIPOLAR DUALISM

Of the four central commitments outlined in *Midpoint,* the bipolar dualism emerges as the dominant factor in *The Poorhouse Fair.* As we examine the recurring contrasts between the worlds of individual subjectivity and objective materialism, however, we shall see that Updike maintains his commitment to both kinds of reality. The Hook-Conner polarity, developed in three stages, one in each part of the book, is the device used to articulate most fully the dualistic *yes—but* stance that would become a hallmark of Updikean fiction.

Part I

In Part I we meet Hook as he, Gregg, and Lucas chafe under Conner's labeling of each rocker on the porch of the home so that each man must sit in his particular chair. This first vignette sets forth two of Hook's key attributes: his sense of the past and his farsightedness. He knows vividly Roman history and nineteenth century American politics, the former from his grammar school education and the latter from conversations in his father's home. He can recall with clarity the scenes of his childhood near the Delaware River, and he twice repeats his conviction that "modern day workmen are not what they were" (5). Hook does not have a very high regard for or concern about the present. On the other hand, he is visually farsighted. As he looks up from the men close by him, the pain leaves his eye muscles as they lengthen to suit the horizon—and he feels positive pleasure (6). His ability to see well into the distance suggests that he can see a future beyond the actuality of the near-at-hand.

The two attributes of love for the past and farsightedness are reiterated later in the morning when Hook examines and admires one of Amy Mortis's quilts. He likes the quilt because it reminds him of his childhood and the lost arts of earlier workmen, but he also sees himself as a child wandering among the "rectilinear paths of the pattern, searching for the deeper-dyed thread. . . ." (27). He sees through the quilt to a symbolic pattern with deeper meanings.

Hook's farsightedness, however, is a mixed blessing. When Gregg brings a wounded and dying cat over the wall in an attempt to disturb the order Conner seeks to maintain, Hook is unable to find the cat because he is looking for it in the distance. The cat has actually passed near Hook's ankles, but since Hook is "blind in all directions but the forward one," he misses the cat because he is "vulnerable to approach from below" (48). Later, after Buddy, Conner's assistant, has shot the cat, Hook fails to grasp the import of what is going on because he is "incapable of receiving side impressions" (74). In Part I, then, Hook is presented as standing for a patterned past in which individual workmen crafted meaningful products. His vision, although limited in ways that make him vulnerable, allows him to see at least in one direction well beyond the limitations of his immediate environment.

Conner is introduced in the second vignette of Part I as Lucas goes to his office to inquire about the reasons for labeling the chairs. The windows in Conner's office, housed in the ornate cupola dominating the old mansion converted into the poorhouse, are equipped with venetian blinds installed by Conner. Their angular metal supports seem to conflict with the Victorian semicircles and hand-worked wood of the old house—"the stately lines [peek] above the manufactured horizontals like the upper margin of a fresco painted where now an exit has been broken through" (21). Unlike Hook, Conner has no reverence for the past. He perceives no patterns of value there, nor does he look beyond the immediate. He is "devout," but only "in the service of humanity" (14) and concentrates on the faceless administrators who will read his reports, for he believes that "beyond these blank heads [hang] the white walls of the universe, the listless, permissive mother for whom [he feels] not a shred of awe" (14).

Later in the morning, Conner, led by "proprietorial and aristocratic" emotions (41), ventures down among the old people. He feels somewhat awkward, and is told frankly by Amy Mortis that he exacts too much of his charges. "You expect us to give up the old ways, and make this place a little copy of the world outside," she says (43). Conner denies any such expectations, insisting that he is just "an agent of the National Internal Welfare Department" (43). Then he sees the wounded cat and orders Buddy to shoot it. "The thing's in pain and should be killed," he says (55). His attitude toward the cat echoes his earlier toying with the idea of "mass murder as the ultimate kindness the enlightened could perform for the others" (16).

Returning to his office, Conner reflects that he has no regrets over the cat. "He wanted things *clean*" (64). The opportunity to cleanse the world of the wounded cat had been one of his few chances to demonstrate some zealous activity, to make things happen, in his otherwise boring job as prefect of a poorhouse. He would prefer a more elevated position, one which would better utilize his abilities and his dedication to a "dynamic vision: that of Man living healthy and unafraid beneath blank skies, 'integrated,' as the accepted phrase had it, 'with his fulfilled possibilities' " (65). On another level, however, he doubts that any such dynamic individualism is possible, since he also believes that "entropia, the tendency of the universe toward eventual homogeneity," is unavoidable because, without a supernaturalism he refuses to accept, there can be "no new cause for heterogeneity" (65).

In Part I of the novel, more words have been given to describing Conner and his position than to Hook and his. Nevertheless, the sympathies of both author and reader gravitate toward Hook. He may be vulnerable, but he is made to seem much more human. As the thunder heralds the coming storm that will end both the morning's preparations and Part I of the book, there is an incident that, like the venetian blinds in the cupola, gives concrete reminder that Hook and Conner reflect not just idiosyncratic personalities but a deep-seated duality in human experience.

Ted, the young driver of the soft-drink truck, tries to back through the narrow gate of the wall surrounding the poorhouse. He succeeds, but only after scraping his truck against the wall on one side of the gate so that an eight-foot-long wedge-shaped section of the wall collapses. Most of the damage is on the inner side of the wall, because what appeared to be such a thick and substantial structure is "really two shells: . . . the old masons had filled the center with uncemented rubble, shivers [sic] of rock and smooth fieldstones that now tumbled. . . out resistlessly" (64).

The wall, a product of Hook's old-time careful craftsmen, appears well-built and solid, but it turns out to be merely two shells concealing a mass of rocks and smooth stones. In the *yes—but* world of Updike, Hook's reverence for the past may be merely misplaced nostaglia. On the other hand, the two shells that hold in the rubble suggest the two poles of the Hook-Conner dualism which are the two sides necessary to hold a pattern together. Furthermore, although the wall is seen by young Mark Kegerise as being intended to keep the old people from getting into the town, the old people see it as there to keep the changed and unwelcome new world out of their lives. The wall is broken by a truck, a mechanical agent of the modern world, suggesting that interaction between the two worlds is inescapable.

Part I closes, then, with an Updikean device that becomes common in his later novels: a verifiable objective event intrudes into and alters the lives of subjective individuals, but that event has symbolic overtones that have meaning only for minds which can sift this particular dot of experience through the proper screens to find the pattern which inheres in it. In this instance, the breaking of the wall gives objective yet symbolic reinforcement to the duality represented by Hook and Conner.

Part II

In Part II Hook is given more words and more opportunity to explain and develop his position, but weaknesses are
also exposed. At the center of the book, both physically and
ideologically, occurs the debate between Conner and Hook.
The rain has driven everyone indoors, and after lunch most
of the inmates drift into the sitting room. Conner decides to
join them, but initially they do not even notice his presence.
His attempt to ingratiate himself by lighting a fire almost
ends disastrously when he discovers that the flue is closed and
he does not know how to open it. One of the inmates comes
to his rescue, but the smoke which had escaped into the room
alerts the old people to Conner's presence. After some
jocular remarks by Amy Mortis about Lincoln and Buchanan
in heaven, Elizabeth Heinemann seriously asks Conner if he
thinks people will see in heaven. Self-righteously aware that
he is "up-to-date" whereas the others are "old-fashioned"
and "ignorant," Conner says that "vision is a function of the
eyes, and when they are gone it must follow" (97). Elizabeth
agrees with him, because she has come to believe that no one
will see in heaven, since vision separates, judges, and marks
differences. She is convinced that in heaven everyone will be
blind.

Hook suggests that heaven will probably "be something
of what each wants it to be" (104), and then Mrs. Jamiesson
and Tommy Fuller give their ideas. But Elizabeth is deter-
mined to hear Mr. Conner's full opinion. "They say you
don't believe," she says, "but I think everyone believes, in
their heart" (106). Conner feels, on the contrary, that in
their hearts no one believes—which accounts, he thinks to
himself, "for the strained, or bluff, expressions on the faces
of the few clergy he has met" (106).

Conner's response to Elizabeth's question outlines a

typical humanist utopia. Heaven is a place on earth with no disease, no oppression, and ample time for recreation. Cities will be well planned, neat, and clean. There will be no money since the state will "receive what is made and give what is needed. . . . Each man will know himself—without delusions, without muddle. . . ." There will be no pain and no waste (107). When Conner admits to Mrs. Mortis that his heaven will not come in time for her, but maybe for her children or grandchildren, she spryly says, "Well, then, to hell with it" (108).

All the old people laugh, and Conner asks Hook to explain what he finds amusing. Hook says that it is an error to believe that the absence of evil will follow from the elimination of pain (108). Conner insists that pain *is* evil, but Hook counters that there are many sorts of useful pain and that in most cases suffering is, in fact, invited by the transgressions of the sufferer. Conner believes that suffering always interferes with the fulfillment of the person, but Hook insists that it often provides the opportunity for the exercise of virtue. As Hook looks back over his own life, he finds a "marvelous fitting together of right and wrong, like the joints the old-time carpenters used to make" (110).

Conner soon moves to the question which he is sure can "drive the argument down to the core of shame that lies heavily in any believer's heart." He asks: "What makes you think God exists?" (112) Apparently unashamed, Hook responds quickly that there are two kinds of evidence: "There is what of Creation I can see, and there are the inner spokesmen" (112). Conner responds that the smoke of Hook's cigar, "twisting, expanding, fading," is "the shape of Creation." According to Conner, the whole process of life began accidentally as lightning stirred certain acids. Creation is a matter of chance. "Imagine a blind giant tossing rocks through eternity. At some point he would build a cathedral," he says (112).

Hook finds the example implausible, especially since he believes that no amount of time can generate something from nothing. Conner holds that there always was something, though relatively little. "The chief characteristic of the universe is," he says, "emptiness. There is infinitely more nothing in the universe than anything else" (113). Again Hook is not impressed. He asks: "Now why should no matter how much nothing be imposing, when my little fingernail, by being something, is of more account?" (113) Conner insists that if the universe was made, it was made by a cruel idiot, since there are no laws, and both atoms and animals simply do what they cannot help doing. "Natural history is a study of horrible things," he says (113-114). Hook admits that he does not know or understand the Creator's mind, but insists that the world which he sees is a source of consolation to him (114).

Not having shaken Hook's faith in his first kind of evidence for the existence of God, Conner moves to challenge the second. Where is the door the "inner spokesmen" can get in, he asks. All study of the human body has failed to find any evidence of a soul. Conner tells a story of a young Indian girl in whom scientists induced a vision of Christ by means of a series of electrical shocks. Hook now seems somewhat shaken, for all he can say is: "That was a cruel experiment" (115). Buddy interrupts the argument to tell bitterly the tale of his own twin brother's death from cancer, despite their prayers to God first for a cure and finally for a swift death. The doctors, according to Buddy, were kinder than God and killed his brother with drugs on his fifteenth birthday.

Hook cannot explain this suffering by his system of neat bookkeeping of virtues and transgressions, but before the debate is brought to an end by the arrival of the band engaged to play for the fair, he gets the last word. "There is no goodness without belief," he says. "There is nothing but busy-ness" (116).

Hook gets the final speech of the debate, but the results are inconclusive. For each "yes" Hook has asserted, Conner has countered with a reasonable "but." Hook has not been shaken from his affirmation of the reality of the world of spirit, but he has failed to convert or convince Conner and has been forced to fall back on a purely personal statement of faith. Edward Vargo believes that Conner lost the argument with Hook (40), but Joyce Markle thinks that Hook is defeated since he is unable to offer any convincing proof for his position (35). Actually, Conner and Hook have both given convincing arguments, and an objective judge would probably call the debate a draw. The two poles are rather equally balanced as the debate ends.

Shortly after the band arrives, the rain ceases and preparations for the delayed fair are quickly resumed. Conner is especially concerned to clean up the rubble of the shattered wall: townspeople seeing the debris would get a bad impression of the efficiency of his administration. He takes the unusual step of enlisting some of the old people (exempting Hook as too old even for light labor) to help load the stray stones into a wheelbarrow to be hauled away.

Part III

Part III opens as Conner leads the group of old people he has asked to pick up the stones from the damaged wall. He also leads the reader into another symbolic event, one that can be objectively reported but which carries in addition overtones of the "otherworldly stand" Updike affirms in *Midpoint*. Gregg deliberately tosses a stone a little too far and hits Conner on the thigh. Conner simply stoops down to pick up the stone, but this time Gregg throws another one and hits Conner on the back. As Conner straightens up, he displays both fear and "bewildered cowardice" (132). The old people see his expression, and all of them—women as well as men—start flinging small stones. Most of the stones fall short of their mark, but one hits Conner on the back of the head hard enough to stun him. Conner retreats, but only about fifteen yards, just out of range. Then he picks up a handful of the stones which have fallen around him and returns to drop them in the wheelbarrow. The old people turn and walk away from him.

The deliberately anticlimactic ending to this potentially dramatic confrontation is consistent with the rejection of apocalypticism we have seen expressed in *Midpoint*. In the poem Updike says that although violent judgment seems near to each successive age, history merely keeps on going. In *The Poorhouse Fair,* Conner is not even seriously injured, certainly not killed; and the old people suffer no wrathful retaliation from the agent of the state. Updike has said concerning the stoning incident: "I guess my experience fits *The Poorhouse Fair* that I wrote. That is, most pebbles don't brain us and most troubles are non-drastic" ("Interview" 293).

When Buddy asks him what he intends to do about the situation, Conner says he will forgive the old people. Buddy suggests that he should at least punish their leader, but Conner says, "I'm their leader" (134). At that moment, he seems close to some breakthrough of compassion as he says, "I had no idea of that much hate" (134).

The stoning incident vividly dramatizes the gulf between Conner and the old people. Although Conner technically may have "beaten" Hook in the debate in the sitting room, even he realized as it concluded that the old people "had withdrawn from him" (119). Unable to win their point with words, even the words of their most articulate spokesman, they now feel forced, in their helplessness, to futile violence to express their resentment against Conner and his scientific welfare state. This incident of conflict attests that the dualism portrayed in the novel is not just one of philosophical approaches to a discussion: there is a deeper dichotomy. Even if we do not approve of the actions of the old people, at least we understand that flinging stones at their shepherd-captor is a desperate attempt to maintain and express their own individuality.

The "stoning" also suggests parallels with the stoning of Stephen, the first Christian martyr. As we have seen, Updike felt that in writing this novel he was dealing with a period similar to the early Christian era, a time when a new religion was being born. The new religion in *The Poorhouse Fair* is that of humanism, and Updike has said that he "saw Conner as some kind of pseudo-martyr . . . really a social-humanist martyr" ("Interview" 278). When Conner says that he will forgive his assailants, we are reminded of Stephen's "Lord, do not hold this sin against them" in Acts 7:60. The fact that the parallel is largely ironic (Conner is a pseudo-martyr, not a real martyr) is clear both from the ludicrous nature of the threat of feeble old people throwing pebbles and from Conner's subsequent actions and reflections in the remaining pages of the novel.

Conner is never in any true physical danger, although he is deeply hurt by the personal rejection demonstrated. He recognizes the presence of hatred, but he fails to understand its source, and the compassion he seems to express is shown to be false. Hook had nothing to do with the stoning; he had been, in his farsighted way, "studying the clouds" (132) when the fracas started. Nevertheless, Conner believes Hook to be the ringleader, a schemer who plotted the incident to embarrass the administrator. Conner misunderstands Hook's attempts to explain what might have led Gregg to throw the first stone and ill-naturedly orders Hook to stop smoking his beloved cigars—ostensibly for Hook's own health and the safety of others in the wooden buildings.

Conner says he forgives the old people, but when he realizes that the dozen who actually threw stones were acting for all of them, that any one of the old people would have grabbed for stones if given the chance, the only explanation he can give for such action is that they resent his being better than they (156). He finds solace in imagining himself into the future—after his successful term at the poorhouse, he will go on to greater things, finally standing before a group of dignitaries to announce the discovery of the cure for cancer (157). He has been mocked by his charges, but he staunchly retains within himself "the conviction that he is the hope of the world" (158).

Conner is merely a pseudo-martyr because the only thing wounded is his pride, because he fails to understand the root cause of the enmity toward him, and because he explains things away by retreating into his own self-righteous superiority. The sympathy he earned as the old people unfairly turned on him is lost because of his pomposity and lack of compassion.

Hook, as we have seen, was initially unaware of the stoning, since he was "studying the clouds." After unsuccessfully trying to help Conner understand the incident, Hook walks around the wall of the grounds. He bears no grudge against Conner, thinking of him in terms of his schoolroom experience as "the type of dutiful good boy who had no defense but forbearance against teasing, and the knowledge that in the end he would succeed" (142). Hook thinks back over his own life, seeing it as the sort of pleasant walk he is now taking; he feels death waiting for him at the end, but he has no fear. He merely wonders what task is left waiting for him, foreshadowing Updike's observation fifteen lines from the end of *Midpoint* that "Some task remains, whose weight I can't forget."

Hook enjoys talking with Fred Kegerise at the fair—they remember old times together each year—but soon he begins thinking of going to his room, where he will read a chapter of the Gospels—"those springs of no certain bottom, which you never find dry" (175)—before going to bed. When he does get to sleep, he is awakened suddenly by difficulty in breathing and an accompanying pounding of his heart. His encounter with Conner is troubling him. He recognizes that Conner had been "grievously stricken" and that "a small word would perhaps set things right" (185). He is sure that there must be some advice he can give Conner that will serve as a bond between them and as "a testament to endure his dying" (185). As the novel ends, however, he has not found the word. He gropes for it, but it does not emerge.

In Part III the balance has shifted toward Hook and away from Conner. Although Updike has said that Hook was intended to be a tribute to his own grandfather (Serebrinck 494), Hook's final emergence as the more sympathetic character is not just a matter of personal affection or whim. While Conner remains a self-limited representative of one pole of a dualism, Hook emerges as something more. Conner's dream of human life "without muddle" suggests that he would prefer to deny the "middling textures" of the Updikean philosophy we have noted in *Midpoint*. Conner wants events fully planned, everything neat and clean. He cannot live comfortably with paradox or polarity. Hook, on the other hand, provides an illustration of the muddles of the man in the middle. He stands between and apart from both Conner's scientific humanism and the old people's inarticulate resistance to change.

Hook, therefore, is not the key spokesman of the novel merely because he is a dogmatic advocate of the "otherworldly stand" of a young author who was "very consciously Christian." To be sure, Hook is himself a conscious Christian. He finds evidence of God both in outer creation and through inner spokesmen. He drinks at the Gospel springs. Conner's hard challenges in the debate do not alter Hook's stance; he remains firm to the end. Updike, however, does not fully endorse the Christian position as expounded by Hook. He shows Hook to be "vulnerable to approach from below" (48) and as "incapable of receiving side impressions" (79). Therefore, Hook is likely to miss what is going on near at hand while his sight is fixed on things far away. Furthermore, his trust in the excellence of the past is sometimes misplaced. Although Hook does not lose the debate with Conner, neither does he win it—he cannot explain suffering and pain, and his accountant's approach to virtue is not quite satisfactory. He has the final speech in the novel, but he can only grope for the right word.

It is not so much Hook's theology that Updike endorses as his compassion. Hook seeks to understand both Gregg and Conner, for he is concerned about individuals, even those whom he does not really like and approve (like Gregg) and those who misunderstand and misuse him (like Conner). Conner may profess forgiveness, but Hook, without proclaiming his act, actually seeks reconciliation with Conner. Although Hook, spokesman for the "otherworldly stand," does not have the final answers, the balance swings in his favor because such a stand undergirds genuine individuality and concern, whereas Conner's denial of anything other than chance and reason leads to blank skies and boredom. Objective evidence of the stubborn continuation of individuality is seen in the failure of Conner's scheme to regiment the men by labeling the porch chairs. The band uses the chairs as it plays for the fair, and they remain "scrambled ever after" (150).

THE WORD IN THE THICKET

The skyrocket structure of the book prevents its degenerating into futuristic propaganda. As each vignette emerges, more light is thrown on the ambiguous polarities of existence. For a brief moment, a pattern emerges in an imaginary poorhouse. The details of that pattern, made up of minute dots of experience typical of any place or time, strike resonant chords in the reader. The light fades, however, as the skyrocket's sparks fall into darkness. We are left with a sense of mystery. Somewhere, "deepest in the thicket, thorns spell a word," Updike says in *Midpoint*. Hook, in *The Poorhouse Fair,* also believes in the reality of that "package, anciently addressed," but the skyrocket fades without revealing the mysterious word. Hook can only ask, "What was it?" 185).

In Updike's first novel, then, a dualism which recognizes the strengths of science and reason while refusing to abandon the centrality of the individual leads not to an explanation of how these two poles interact, but to an affirmation that they can and must, despite the mysterious nature of such an existence. The work also reflects Updike's perceptions of the Christian church at the time he wrote the novel. He saw institutional religion as being in a dry period, and throughout the book there is a sense of dryness in the old people's helpless nostalgia for an earlier time. On the other hand, the kind of future represented by Conner is equally sterile.

In 1968, Updike said that in this novel he was asking the question, "After Christianity, what?" (Nichols 34). His answer in *The Poorhouse Fair* is ambiguous. Certainly Conner's "easy" humanism is shown to "plague the land" with its artificiality and barrenness. On the other hand, traditional Christianity is portrayed as perhaps too dried up, too vulnerable and old-fashioned, to bring forth the necessary growth for renewed life. What will come after Christianity, then? No blueprint is given, but a strong case is presented *against* any system that fails to recognize the desires and requirements of man's individuality and spirituality.

NOTE

[1]In a 1972 interview, Updike also suggested the letter Y as a shape for this novel. See *Picked-Up Pieces* 499.

WORKS CITED

Detweiler, Robert. *John Updike.* New York: Twayne, 1972.

Markle, Joyce. *Fighters and Lovers.* New York: New York UP, 1973

Nichols, Lewis. "Talk With John Updike." *The New York Times Book Review* 7 Apr. 1968:34.

Rieu, E. V. *The Four Gospels.* London: Penguin.

Serebrinck, Judith. "New Creative Writers." *Library Journal* 134 (1 Feb. 1959): 494.

Updike, John. "Interview Conducted by Jeff Campbell, Georgetown, MA, 9 Aug. 1976." Published as Appendix to this volume.

---. *Picked-Up Pieces.* New York: Knopf, 1975.

---. *The Poorhouse Fair.* New York: Knopf, 1959.

Vargo, Edward. *Rainstorms and Fire.* Port Washington, NY: Kennikat P, 1973.

CHAPTER 3

"BETWEEN HEAVEN AND EARTH":
THE CENTAUR and *OF THE FARM*

The Centaur (1963) and *Of the Farm* (1965) provide the first of Updike's novels which call for joint consideration.[1] His third and fourth novels, they share the Olinger, Pennsylvania, setting; and in both novels the father is (or has been) a teacher in Olinger High School and is named George. In addition, the son in each house was fourteen when the family moved from Olinger to the farm at nearby Firetown; and, considered together, the two novels fill out the family picture, with the father dominating the first and the mother the second.

In Updike's short fiction, recurring characters, settings, and themes are numerous, so the interconnections in these two novels are not surprising. Updike himself has said that "there's a way in which *Of the Farm* is a sequel to *The Centaur,*" and that he likes for his work to have "some blend" ("Interview" 297). He has also said that "it becomes increasingly hard to work with things you've already established. Often it becomes necessary just to rename characters and start from scratch just to give the thing spring somehow"("Interview" 297). *Of the Farm* is evidently the product of such an effort to "start from scratch." It is only partially a sequel, for all the characters except the father have been renamed, and the protagonist, although similar in many ways to his predecessor in *The Centaur,* has certain distinctly different characteristics. Nevertheless, these two novels complement and supplement each other in ways that foreshadow Updike's "Rabbit" novels, in which he produced not only a sequel, but a sequel to the sequel.

The thematic concerns of the books provide additional connecting links. The title for this chapter—"Between Heaven and Earth"—is taken from the Barthian epigraph for *The Centaur,* but its implication of humankind caught between two worlds applies equally well to both novels. *The Centaur* emphasizes the "heaven" side of the dichotomy, and *Of the Farm* seems to stress the "earth" side. Taken together, however, the two novels do not show as much shift of emphasis as some critics have suggested. The recurrent commitments of *Midpoint* emerge clearly in each, as analyses of their structures and themes will show.

THE CENTAUR

The story in *The Centaur* revolves around the activities of George Caldwell, a science teacher at Olinger High School, and his fifteen-year-old son, Peter, a student at the school. The opening chapter describes George's attempt, on Wednesday, January 8, 1947, to lecture to an unruly class about the evolution of the world. The remaining eight chapters trace the events of Monday through Thursday of the following week. On Monday morning George and Peter drive from their farm to town, picking up a hitchhiker along the way. After school George goes to the doctor for x-rays, since abdominal pain has convinced him he may be dying of cancer. George and Peter drive to a swimming meet in Alton, after which their car breaks down, forcing them to spend the night in an Alton hotel. Tuesday morning they take a trolley back to school in Olinger while Hummel, the mechanic, takes care of the car. Tuesday afternoon George goes to the dentist, and that night both go to a basketball game. During the game a snowstorm sets in, and although the 1936 Buick has been repaired, it is unable to make it through the snow to the farm. Father and son are forced to abandon the car and walk back to Olinger, where they spend Tuesday night with the Hummels. The snow cancels Wednesday's school, but by afternoon George and Peter are able to get back home. The doctor has called to say that the x-rays are clear and that George does not have to fear cancer. Peter, however, has developed a severe cold and fever, so he stays in bed on Thursday as his father sets out for school, realizing that his fate is not to die, but to live.

This summary of seemingly trivial events may suggest that *The Centaur* is much like *The Poorhouse Fair,* the major difference being a four-day time-span. Such is not the case, however. *The Centaur* has much fuller characterization. In *The Poorhouse Fair,* although Hook and Conner are central, the shifting points of view of the forty-three vignettes do not allow for complete characterization of any of the participants in the story. In *The Centaur,* however, four of the chapters are told by Peter in first person, and two of the remaining third-person chapters are told from George's point of view. Only the central fifth chapter remains objective, detached from both George and Peter. Although the cast of characters in *The Centaur* is even larger than that of *The Poorhouse Fair,* we come to know the backgrounds, thoughts, and motivations of the central characters much more fully than in the earlier novel.

Peter's first-person chapters are told by the adult Peter, now thirty years old and a painter of abstract art who, recalling the events of this week in January fifteen years earlier, describes them to his black mistress. As he sorts through his memories, we realize that the events were not just the ordinary trials of a school teacher and his son, but crucial experiences in one boy's efforts to undertake the universal task of "finding the father." Such a perspective adds resonance and significance to the otherwise routine events described.

Even more important is the mythical overlay which Updike provides for the story. The book's title comes from Updike's identification of George Caldwell with Chiron, the noblest of the centaurs, who gave up his immortality so Prometheus might be freed from his rock. Peter is identified with Prometheus, and Mrs. Caldwell—who loves the farm—is Ceres. Hummel, the garage mechanic, is Vulcan, and his wife, Vera, the girls' physical education teacher, is Venus. Zimmerman, the principal, is Zeus.

The mythological identifications are made in various ways throughout the book. The opening chapter moves surrealistically back and forth between a two-legged high school teacher and a four-legged clattering centaur. Peter's first-person chapters (II, IV, VI, and VIII) contain mythological references such as the parallel between Peter's psoriasis and Prometheus's suffering, but except for Chapter VI, which begins "As I lay on my rock" (175), there are only oblique references to mythology. Chapter III, however, is entirely mythical, describing a group of children in a grove on Mt. Olympus. The central Chapter V is a purported obituary for Caldwell, written by one of his former students. It is the one chapter not related from either George's or Peter's point of view, and it has no mythological implications. Chapter VII, alone among the chapters in its present-tense narration, is a collection of impressionistic scenes utilizing varying points of view. Like Peter's chapters, it utilizes only metaphorical mythic references, but Chapter IX, like Chapter I, combines George the human being and Chiron the centaur, graphically re-emphasizing the parallel set up at the beginning of the novel.

The complexity and ambitiousness of intent in this novel go far beyond *The Poorhouse Fair*. This mythological complexity, however, has aroused conflicting critical opinions. John Aldridge says that the reader has no discernible reason to see any connection between the story and the myth, and that the mythology is merely an attempt to force significance on things that could not achieve importance on their own (198). David Galloway, who feels that the mythology comes very close to being a gimmick, especially criticizes Updike's addition of an index to enable the reader to identify all the mythological parallels in the story. According to Galloway, the index is among the most dramatic examples of the aesthetic self-consciousness that jeopardizes even the best of Updike's fiction (47,49). Howard Harper, on the other hand, finds that the ambiguity of the myth saves the story from sentimentality (181). Joyce Markle also affirms the validity of the mythic references, finding that they sometimes parallel the narrative and at other times satirize it, but always serve to give the "sense that the world is enriched by mystery and meaning" (69).

In order to assess the validity of Updike's wedding of myth and reality, we must understand the novel's structure and overarching themes.

STRUCTURE

In the same television interview in which he described *The Poorhouse Fair* as shaped like a skyrocket, Updike suggested that *The Centaur*'s shape was a sandwich. The fact that Chapters II, IV, VI, and VIII are told in first person does suggest a layering. Furthermore, the first-person chapters are told in the novel's dramatic present (1963), whereas the third-person chapters are set in the past (1947), reinforcing the layered effect. It seems more reasonable, however, to look upon Chapters I and IX, the two which specifically and overtly identify George with Chiron and mix mythological and real time, as the outer layers of the sandwich, the bread which holds its various ingredients together. The variety of meats, cheeses, garnishes and dressing are then held within a manageable framework. Such an approach allows for appreciation of the mythical references which flavor the whole, and it enables the acceptance of Chapter VII, in which the past becomes the present through the use of present tense.

The sandwich metaphor is helpful in providing an understanding of the use of alternating devices in the novel, and it underscores the parallel nature of the opening and closing chapters, but the epigraph suggests an even more significant way of approaching the novel's alternations and shifts. The epigraph, drawn from Karl Barth's *Dogmatics in Outline,* reads: "Heaven is the creation inconceivable to man, earth the creation conceivable to him. He himself is the creature on the boundary between heaven and earth." Updike was reading heavily in Barth's theology at the time he was writing *The Centaur,* so it is not surprising that he should find a Barthian quotation that seemed appropriate for this book. Updike came upon the quote, he says, while working on the book and "was unable to resist it because it did so tersely and definitely say that we're all on a boundary and all are centaurs" ("Interview" 279).

According to Barth, then, man is a creature who yearns for the inconceivable and is a rather uneasy combination of disparate elements. Barth had no use for any sort of mythology, insisting instead upon the objective reality of Christ, so Updike certainly did not get from Barth the idea of using the centaur—another creature representing the sandwiching together of disparate elements—to suggest the "middling" nature of man. The Barthian idea of man existing on the boundary between the conceivable and the inconceivable and the Christian concerns of the young author reading Barth did, however, suggest the integration of the myth of Chiron with the story of George Caldwell, as Updike explained in 1976.

"I think what attracted me to the Chiron thing is the notion, rather rare in Greek mythology, of the centaur sacrificing himself for somebody else," Updike said ("Interview" 293). He was quick to point out that Chiron was not a Christ-figure, since Chiron's life of pain from a continuing wound was relatively easy for him to give up to "bail somebody else out." It was, Updike said, both convenient and thrifty for Chiron to give his life for Prometheus, whereas the lives of Christ or any of the Christian martyrs were not given up out of convenience or thrift ("Interview" 293-297). Nevertheless, Chiron provided a rare example of self-sacrifice in mythology, and his unselfish deed and his double nature gave Updike the device he wanted to enrich the story of George Caldwell.

Discussing his intentions for the use of mythology in the novel, Updike said:

> The mythological references mean to show that everybody, the existence of any person, any thing, is in some way magical and highly charged, and rather strange—and gaudy. There's a gaudiness about life that means you almost have to produce an extra effect, you have to bring up fiction to the gaudiness of actuality. Something *extra* has to happen. It might be the verbal play, or these myths. From the standpoint of an adolescent boy who hasn't been anywhere else, all of these ordinary or less than ordinary people are very large and significant. That is, you live the rest of your life with the categories that you built up in these early years. . . . I'm no ancient Greek, and I'm not even a student of these stories. I still would not have written the book without the myths. They are important to me and I think give the book its proper tone of eccentricity, or surprisingness—the sense that everybody comes to us in guises. ("Interview" 293-294).

To the critics who would complain that the mythology is not fully integrated into the story, then, Updike would say that it is not meant to be. In a sense, it is only one of the ingredients in the sandwich. But he would insist that the mythology is central to the meaning and structure of *The Centaur.* The myths allude to the mysterious— "magical, highly charged, strange"—quality of each human individual who lives on the boundary between heaven and earth.

INDIVIDUAL AND WORLD

The most obvious and important thematic result of the sandwiching or layering structural device is the recurring emphasis on the interpenetration of subjective and objective spheres of experience. Peter narrates four chapters in a very personal dramatic monologue, but as he speaks in the present, he is recalling actual past events, which affected others as well as himself, filtered through the midpoint screen of his own hemisphere. Alternate chapters are narrated in third person, and one would presume them to be closer to objective reality. They are, however, layered with mythological references which suggest both the recurring universal nature of human experience and the mysterious "guises" of each individual.

Throughout the novel the contrasts or polarities are variously depicted as soul-body, man-horse, or individual-world. Nowhere is there the specific contrast between heaven and earth that is the heart of the debate in *The Poorhouse Fair.* If, however, we take "heaven" to represent the almost inconceivable world of the unique individual and "earth" to represent the readily conceivable world of scientific, rational nature, then we can better understand the boundary on which human beings live. *The Centaur,* unlike *The Poorhouse Fair,* does not concern itself with discussing an orthodox Christian heaven, but it does sandwich together the first two commitments of *Midpoint*—the central individual and the reality of the objective world. Such sandwiching illustrates Updike's bipolar dualism as it shows problems created when an individual attempts to live consistently as midpoint of his own universe.

For instance, in Chapter I, as Caldwell enters the school, he looks up "beyond the orange wall" and sees the "adamantine blue zenith" (19). The objective reality of the school building and the unyielding sky are inescapable. But as he looks, the sky "pronounces its unceasing monosyllable: I" (19). The dichotomy between self and world is stated early, and a similar dilemma arises when Venus (Vera) asks Chiron (George), "Have you ever wondered. . . if your heart belongs to the man or the horse?" (29). Where is reality? In the "unceasing monosyllable" or the "adamantine zenith," the man or the horse?

As George lectures his class at the conclusion of Chapter I, he supplies further paradoxical imagery of the boundaries at whose intersection human beings live. The volvox, he tells his class, was the first living creature to pioneer the idea of differentiated reproductive cells. By "inventing" the idea of cooperation, utilizing certain cells for specific functions for the good of the whole, the volvox introduced to our planet something like what we mean by life. But as George points out, the volvox also virtually "invented" death. Specialization of cells and the cooperation thereby necessitated brings a kind of sacrificial death for the good of the whole. Previously there were only cells "sitting around forever in a blue-green scum" (42). Now there is cooperative life, but there is also certain death. Individualization, then, brings a new sort of life, apparently superior to that of the "blue-green scum," but separation from the mass also implies death.

In Chapter II Peter illustrates the individual-world interpenetration as he describes his ambition to paint like Vermeer, the Dutch painter whose unique personal style of realism made him one of Updike's *Midpoint* heroes. Riding to school on Monday morning, Peter imagines himself painting like the Dutch master and achieving the fame and wealth Vermeer himself never knew. He is not sure just what his own work will look like, but that does not bother him; he makes "its featureless radiance. . . the center of everything" (78). His self-centered and self-satisfied adolescent world is shaken by the interpenetration of the outer world, however, as George picks up a dirty hitchhiker, and Peter confesses: "That my existence at one extremity should be tangent to Vermeer and at the other to the hitchhiker seemed an unendurable strain" (83).

In Chapters IV and VI, Peter provides three more examples of interpenetration of spheres of experience. Peter follows George to the doctor's office on Monday afternoon and enters in time to hear the conclusion of the doctor's conversation with George. Dr. Appleton (Apollo) tells George: "You have never come to terms with your own body" (128). Instead, he continues, "You believe in the soul. You believe your body is like a horse you get up on and ride for a while and then get off" (129). Once more the flesh has entered in, reminding both George and Peter that the "unceasing monosyllable" and the central "featureless radiance" exist on the boundary of a different world.

At the end of Chapter IV, as Peter prepares to go to bed in the hotel room in Alton on Monday night, he actually experiences for the first time the substantive interpenetration of worlds he has only been told of before or at best known peripherally. He thinks of the city of Alton, and his inner world expands: "My sense of myself amplified until, lover, loved, seer and seen, I compounded in several accented expansions of my ego, the city, and the future, and during these seconds truly clove to the center of the sphere, and out-muscled time and tide" (165-166). Clearly, Peter is affirming the centrality of his own personality; he is the midpoint of his own hemisphere. The moment, however, does not last. The world is not impressed—"the city shuffled and winked beyond the window unmoved, transparent to my penetration, and her dismissal dwindled me terribly"(166).

But the ego is not shattered. Peter feels "like a dry seed lost in the folds of the earth," but as the sheets warm around him he enlarges "to human size" and then begins to feel enormous, including in himself all galaxies and all time. Then he returns to the "plane of everyday" and becomes "aware of details" (166). The world challenges and repulses the overarching ego, but the individual does not remain mere-ly a dry seed, but insists on its "human" size amid the world of myriad details.

In Chapter VIII George and Peter each give one more ex-ample of the self-world interaction. They are at home after the snow storm, and they know that the x-ray report showed no cancer. The mother suggests that George might quit teaching and do something that would get him close to nature. George responds: "I hate Nature. It reminds me of death" (291). George apparently still believes in the soul, as Dr. Appleby has said. Nature to him is the death that threatens his own unique individuality. Peter, sick with a cold, watches his father leave through the snow to go to school, and comments that George's "posture made no con-cession to the pull underfoot; upright he waded out through our yard and past the mailbox. . ." (293). As he watches, Peter says: "I knew what this scene was—a patch of Penn-sylvania in 1947—and yet I did not know. . . . I burned to paint it, just like that, in its puzzle of glory; it came upon me that I must go to Nature disarmed of perspective and stretch myself like a large transparent canvas upon her in the hope that, my submission being perfect, the imprint of a beautiful and useful truth would be taken'' (293). Peter both knows and does not know what the scene is. Objectively, it is just a patch of Pennsylvania snow. But it is also a "puzzle of glory," which must be interpreted by a self fully aware of its uniqueness but also ready to participate in the mysterious interaction of self and world.

THE WORD

The first three commitments of *Midpoint* (the centrality of the self, the reality of the world, and the resulting dualism) are illustrated in *The Centaur* through both structure and theme. The realities of both individual and world are layered together to embody a dualistic approach to life. Both sides are presented faithfully, with careful attention to each dot/detail. Neither side is allowed to dominate, but as the novel sifts events and personalities and shifts time and point of view, the search for an affirmative, if ambiguous, word emerges, as it did in *The Poorhouse Fair*.

In the opening chapter, George's story of the evolution of the world is told with no reference to any supernatural force. The mystery of how the void was breached remains unsolved; the universe George describes is much like Conner's in *The Poorhouse Fair*. Conner assumed that there was always something, and George describes life as originating from the freezing of various gases (39). After the volvox invented both cooperation and death, "the flint-chipping, fire-kindling, death-foreseeing, . . . tragic animal" —man—merged (46) rather quickly (in terms of evolutionary time). There is nothing here that a scientific rationalist could not accept, but this version of the story does not satisfy

George himself. "His very blood loathed the story he had told" (46). George (and Updike) is not willing to accept a purely rational, naturalistic word concerning the origin of man and matter.

In Chapter III, the only chapter given an entirely mythological setting, Chiron, the centaur, is instructing a group of Olympian children. As they conclude their opening hymn to Zeus asking for a sign, a black eagle flies across the sun. A word has been given: the eagle of Zeus ascending. Chiron must puzzle, however, for although the eagle is on the children's right, which is a propitious sign, the eagle is on his left. What is the word, then? Is it a comforting answer or a threat? Even in the world of mythology, ambiguity prevails. Furthermore, Chiron's daughter foresees a time when Zeus will be "taken by men as a poor toy" and "branded a criminal" (98). Even gods who give signs, then, do not always last.

In Chapter IV, as Peter and George settle down in the Alton hotel on Monday night, there is a moment between them when it seems that something significant may be spoken. Peter says, "There was a word—I did not know it but believed he did—that waited between us to be pro-nounced" (164). Peter feels that his father has the necessary word, but he is disappointed. George says only, "I guess you can go to sleep" (164). The next morning, as father and son arrive at school, there is a little whirlwind that springs up before them and leads them along. Peter almost expects the whirlwind to have the needed word. Unlike Job's whirlwind, however, Peter's merely "dance[s] from one margin of grass to another and sigh[s] its senseless word" (170). Peter feels the need of a word, but he cannot find it. He wants to stop before the whirlwind, but George keeps on striding, ignoring the whirlwind and Peter's need.

In Chapter VI Peter reverses the situation and seeks to give a word to his father. At the end of the day on Tuesday, after sitting in his father's class, Peter tells George, "I have something to tell you" (189). "I have hope," he says. George says he never had any hope, and that Peter must have gotten it from his mother. Peter insists that he got it from George, and when George asks if Peter really has hope, Peter replies, "with a little lie. . . 'Yes' " (190). Not hearing the affirmative word *from* his father, Peter attempts to offer a needed word *to* his father, but he must lie a little, and the word is not convincing.

In Chapter VIII the thirty-year-old Peter is still seeking the word he wants. He admits that his father puzzled him—he never really knew his "upper half," but was more familiar with his legs. He knows, however, that he is inescapably his father's son, and he likens the stains on the ceiling of his artist's studio to an "all-wrong discoverer's map." He grows frightened thinking of "the earnestly bloated canvases I conscientiously cover with great streaks straining to say what even I am beginning to suspect is the unsayable thing" (270). He is very aware that his own present life is somehow "all wrong" (as was Updike in *Midpoint*), and he finds his aesthetic-artistic approach to finding the right word ultimately unsatisfactory.

Before the chapter is over, however, Peter has recalled going home through the snow with his father on that Wednesday evening in 1947. As Peter walks in his father's footsteps in the heavy snow, they see a bright star. Peter asks George its name, and George identifies it as Venus. Peter asks if one can steer by it, and George replies he doesn't know. Peter says that he can never find the North Star because he always expects it to be larger than it is. George replies, "I don't know why the hell they made it so small" (285). Since 1947 Peter has indeed attempted to steer by

Venus, brighter and easier to find than the North Star, but less dependable. Even at age thirty, Peter has not found the way to continue to walk in his father's footsteps toward the small North Star, but George, in the final chapter, does find the elusive word.

In Chapter IX George merges once again with Chiron, giving him a timelessness and dignity that lift him beyond a specific snowy evening in Pennsylvania in 1947. The whiteness of the landscape suggests both the barrenness of the earth and the barrenness of a purely material explanation of life. Bare sticks protrude from the snow, and George/Chiron sees them as "calligraphic"—beautiful, elegant handwriting. As he "search[es] their scribble for a word," however, he finds none (295). The elegant calligraphy is as blank as the snow. He reflects, however: "Yet even in the dead of winter the sere twigs prepare their small dull buds. In the pit of the year a king was born. Not a leaf falls but leaves an amber root, a dainty hoof, a fleck of baggage to be unpacked in future time. Such flecks give the black thatch of twigs a ruddy underglow" (295-296).

Although the prose says "the Centaur" had these thoughts, it is clearly George Caldwell thinking, both because of the Christian references to a king being born in the pit of winter and because he goes on to recall an experience with his minister-father outside a saloon. As a boy, George was repelled by the "cruelty and blasphemy" of the "poisonous laughter" which emerged, but his father said, "All joy belongs to the Lord" (296). As a boy Caldwell realized that "wherever in the filth and confusion and misery, a soul felt joy, there the Lord came and claimed it as his own"; "all the rest, all that was not joy, fell away" (296). As a man, he is glad now that he will continue to live, that he can sustain his family and his students "for yet a space more." He has "discovered that in giving his life to others he has entered a total freedom," and he affirms, "Only goodness lives, but it does live" (296-297).

Chiron accepted death, but Caldwell realizes that he must accept life. For him there will be no change, no momentous journey (298). The abyss he must face is the daily one of Zimmerman, his students, and his lessons in Room 204. And as he comes to this realization, he finds the word that Peter has not yet located: "His will, a perfect diamond under the pressure of absolute fear, uttered the final word. *Now*" (298-299).

The epilogue of the novel explains that Zeus took pity on the centaur and set him among the stars after his death as the constellation Sagittarius. Caldwell had pointed out in his lecture on evolution in Chapter I that Sagittarius is in the center of our Milky Way galaxy (37). Updike says in the epilogue that very few people look respectfully to the heavens any more and even fewer bother to learn the names of the stars (299). Although George Caldwell did not die and is not placed in the stars, the word he found is still at the center of human existence, though most persons, like Peter, do not look up to find it. In the freedom of living for others in the now, George found the mysterious word that bridges self and world.

As Updike did in *Midpoint,* George finds that death is inevitable—"Earth shall have me." But, as Updike adds in *Midpoint,* "yet not yet." George learns to abandon his preoccupation with death to live now, recognizing that nothing has had to be. Like *The Poorhouse Fair, The Centaur* concludes by affirming the mystery and centrality of the individual. Hook is unable to find a word in the former novel; in *The Centaur,* although he apparently has not succeeded in passing it on to his son, George Caldwell finds the word which enables him to go on living.

OF THE FARM

Of the Farm describes an August weekend in the life of thirty-five-year-old Joey Robinson. Since no date is specified, one assumes the events take place in or near 1965, the year of the book's publication. On Friday evening, Joey, an advertising executive, drives from New York with his new second wife, Peggy, and her son, Richard, to his mother's farm near Firetown, Pennsylvania. Joey's father has been dead a year, and this visit will serve a dual purpose: Joey will mow the field his mother has become too old to mow, and the mother will get to know her new daughter-in-law. Joey does mow the field, and the two women do get to know each other, though not without some tense moments. Joey's mother is afraid that Joey wants to sell the farm to encroaching real estate developers, but he promises not to do so unless it becomes absolutely necessary. On Sunday afternoon, Mrs. Robinson has a mild heart attack on the way home from attending church with Joey, but she recovers enough so that Joey, Peggy, and Richard leave for New York as planned late that same afternoon.

Echoes from *The Centaur* abound, making clear why Updike says *Of the Farm* is in a sense a sequel. The road to the Robinson farm (to which the Robinsons moved when Joey was fourteen, just as the Caldwells moved when Peter was fourteen) is exactly like the road to the farm in *The Centaur;* even the neighbors have the same name: Schoelkopf. The family name is different, but the father, although dead a year in this novel, was named George and was a high school teacher. George Robinson, like George Caldwell, never liked the farm and moved to it only to please his wife. Mrs. Robinson, like Mrs. Caldwell, wears her father's old wool sweater around the house. As Grandfather Kramer in *The Centaur* always bade everyone "Pleasant dreams" before retiring, so, Joey and Mrs. Robinson call to mind, did Grandfather

Hostetter in *Of the Farm*. Numerous other such shared details could be cited, but these few are sufficient to indicate that in many ways *Of the Farm* is like a return visit to some of the scenes and people of *The Centaur*.

Despite the similarities, including the fact that Joey is thirty-five in this novel, whereas Peter would have been thirty-three in 1965, there are differences. Joey is an advertising executive, not an artist, and Joey is the twice-married father of three children, not the paramour of a black mistress. *Of the Farm* has no complex impressionistic shifts of time or point of view, since the entire story is told by Joey in a first-person narration, and there is no mythological overlay. In fact, the actions and conversations in the book might be explained by references to Freudian psychology—as Peggy herself implies, suggesting that Mrs. Robinson had emasculated her husband and is trying to do the same to Joey.

Although the structure and technique are much simpler and more naturalistic than those in *The Centaur,* the interpenetration of the subjective and objective spheres that motivated the earlier novel is strikingly evident here as well.

A FARM NOBODY FARMS

As the book opens, Richard asks Joey, "What's the point of a farm nobody farms?" (4). Unable to answer, Joey suggests that he ought to ask Mrs. Robinson. Richard finds his chance the next day, and presses Mrs. Robinson to tell him what use there is to her farm. Richard mentions having seen a bird sanctuary, and Mrs. Robinson takes her cue and says, "We can call this a *people* sanctuary. . . . A place . . . where people can come, and be refugees like me, for an hour or two, and let their corners rub off, and try to be round again'' (71).

Mrs. Robinson is half joking, of course, but her more seriously expressed feelings about the farm elsewhere in the book confirm that she does indeed see the farm as a place where refugees from the city, like Joey and Peggy, might find sanctuary. She has developed her own mythology, quite different from the sky-oriented Olympian mythology layered into *The Centaur.* Hers is an earth-centered nature worship. Just before she proposes her farm as a people sanctuary, she has said that she believes only in what she can see or touch. Richard is surprised, because Joey had told him that Mrs. Robinson believed in God. Mrs. Robinson replies that she sees and touches God all the time (70). "If I couldn't see and touch Him here on the farm, if I lived in New York City, I don't know if I'd believe or not," she goes on (70). As Caldwell believed in the soul, she believes in tangible nature.

Yet she has not surrendered the centering privilege of her own ego. She looks at nature in an idiosyncratic way. Joey sees that she has made a mythology of her own life, "like a mathematician who, having decreed certain severely limited assumptions, performs feats of warping and circumvention and paradoxical linkage that an outside observer, unrestricted to the plane of their logic, would find irksomely arbitrary" (31). Mrs. Robinson, Joey says, "surreptitiously read into the animate world . . . a richness of motive that could hardly be there—though, like believers everywhere, she had a way of making her environment supply corroboration" (23). So, although *Of the Farm* centers more on earth than on heaven, it, like *The Centaur,* emphasizes the dualism of self and world.

The farm, then, supplies Mrs. Robinson with the source of her own personal mythology and belief, but what is its significance to Joey? He is, after all, the narrator of the story, its protagonist and central consciousness. The first word of the novel's title suggests possibilities that are developed in the book's structure and themes. The first and most obvious meaning of "of" is "about." Thus this story may be simply "about" the farm. While it is true that the story is set *on* the farm, it would not be adequate to say that it is *about* the farm. Rather, it is about Joey, his mother, and his wife, who are gathered at the farm on a particular weekend. "Of" can also mean origin or derivation, and in this sense the story is about Joey's origins, about a man who is "of" the farm, who has left it, and who must return there to come to terms with himself. "Of" may also indicate belonging or possession. Does Joey belong to the farm? Or does it belong to him? Or are both statements true? Such intersections of meaning suggest an approach to the book's theme and structure.

INTERSECTIONS

Updike has identified the shape he had in mind in writing *Of the Farm* as an X (*Picked-Up Pieces* 499). Divergent forces intersect during this brief weekend but, after a momentary convergence, continue to move further apart. These forces may be variously labeled, but essentially represent the two basic polarities embodied in Mrs. Robinson and Joey. The polar factors may be diagrammed as follows:

Mrs. Robinson—Joey
mother—son
farm—city
female—male
age—youth
past—present

There is no resolution of the dualism; the two representatives meet and then continue their own ways. The

Sartrean epigraph Updike chose affirms that "Man is a being in whom existence precedes essence" and that when one accepts this fact, then one "can only want the freedom of others." Thus neither Joey nor Mrs. Robinson can—or should—expect the other to adopt his/her viewpoint. Nevertheless, in the meeting, the crossing or intersection, there is mutual understanding. As Updike has said, "In a way the mother and Joey forgive each other and there's some kind of mutual blessing bestowed at the end" ("Interview" 280). Each has granted the other his or her freedom, has voluntarily surrendered any false claims on the other. In granting freedom to the other, each has found new freedom for him/herself, similar to the freedom Caldwell found in living for others. Examples of some of the intersections in the novel will illustrate how, despite the continuing divergences, the book is, as Updike has said, "in a way, about community" ("Interview" 280).

Joey, normally the representative of the urban present, finds himself ironically changing places with his mother as they drive to town on Saturday afternoon for groceries. He is shocked to find that the familiar road he had traveled so often with his father has been "abolished," replaced by a smooth new highway (84). Mrs. Robinson is "exhilarated" by the new road, but Joey feels "like a visitor from the dead," remembering the acres where the new shopping center is located as a city dump (84-85). He is afraid that he will "be left with nothing but this present, this grim echo of his mother and . . . this acreage of brightly shoddy goods, this sordid plenty" (85).

Saturday night, as Joey goes to the cellar for firewood, he realizes he "had forgotten the cellar" (115). He had forgotten his subterranean roots, but the cellar reminds him of his father, who had stacked the fragrant logs standing ready for the fire. He also remembers the day he and his father had poured the cement floor for the cellar, and notices with surprise that "the floor we had made that day was smooth and level and innocent of seepage; it was as if the day itself were preserved, an underground pond, a lake of treasure in a vault" (115). The past is a part of him, even though he had momentarily forgotten it.

Joey is irritated by all the pictures of himself his mother has around the house and would like to get rid of them. Mrs. Robinson, however, says, "Don't you touch them. Those pictures are my son. Those pictures are the only son I have" (119). At this point she is still seeking to keep her son alive in the saga of her own mythology, and the pictured son of the past is more important to her than the live thirty-five-year-old son of the present.

The climax of the weekend occurs after dinner on Saturday night. Joey tells Richard a bed-time story about a frog that felt like a king inside his castle in his body. His eyes were turrets, his tongue like a crossbow, his mouth like a drawgate, but he wondered about "the dungeon of his guts, where he had never been" (130). He had been told there was a great treasure there, so one day in fall he started "down a circular staircase out of his head" and went down and down until he disappeared (130). Richard comments that the story sounds like Dr. Seuss, but Joey says he intended it to be like Dante (130). When Richard asks, "He died?" Joey explains that he was merely hibernating and that he woke up in the spring, went back up the circular stairs, and opened his eyes to the blue sky (131). The story is simple and childish enough, but Joey, like Dante as he followed Virgil through the Inferno (and like Updike in *Midpoint*), is thirty-five years old as he returns to the farm of his origins and goes down into its cellar. The frog's emergence from the "dungeon of his guts" metaphorically suggests a similar emergence for Joey.

As Joey comes down the stairs from Richard's room, he is conscious of the "faint familiar tint of vapor" which he thinks nostalgically must be emerging from the "stones, plaster, wood, and history of the house" (132). He realizes, however, that the "presence" he feels is not the past but is "rising from a damp towel tossed onto the landing, . . . the hoarse scent of Peggy's wet hair" (132). He is brought "up" from any nostalgic resting in the cellar of his past by a reminder of the now. He is not a little boy whose mother can lean over his bed or whose father can drive him to school on familiar roads. He is a grown man with a very real wife to whom he must respond in the present. Like Caldwell, he finds that the word he seeks is "now."

Peggy and Mrs. Robinson are arguing about the roles of Joey and his father and the farm. Peggy believes that Mrs. Robinson has undervalued Joey's father and actually destroyed him by bringing him to the farm, which was, in fact "her giant lover" (134). Joey dismisses her opinion because it painfully fails "to harmonize with the simple, inexpressible way things had been" (134-135). On the other hand, he finds his mother's "fabulous counter system" equally untrue. Then he reflects:

> Perhaps they were both right. All misconceptions are themselves data which have the minimal truth of existing in at least one mind. Truth, my work had taught me, is not something static, a mountain top that statements approximate like successive assaults of frostbitten climbers. Rather, truth is constantly being formed from the solidification of illusions. (135)

Joey is coming to see that he can grant both his wife and his mother the freedom of their own truths.

As his mother sleeps after her heart attack on Sunday, Joey looks at her and sees, for the first time, not a mythological figure, but merely an old woman. "In sleep my mother had slipped from my recognition and blame and had entered, unconsciously, a far territory, the arctic of the old"

(167). And as his mother becomes merely an old woman instead of one whom the son must please or blame, he comes to a new vision of the farm. He thinks of the nurture his mother has expended on the various growing things, and imagines himself filling the same role: "my heart expanded to the limits, the far corners and boundary-stones, of the farm; soon it would be fall, the trees transparent, the sky clean, the stars pressing at night, asters everywhere, the first frost" (168). He has a "momentary vision of the farm, the farm as mine, in the fall, the warmth of its leaves and the retreat of its fields and the kind of infinity of its twigs" (170).

But this vision is only momentary. He understands the farm now in a way he has not before, but he is unable to see both Peggy and the farm at the same time, and soon it is clear where his life must be: "New York, . . . the living memento of my childish dream of escape, called to me, urged me away, into the car. . . ." (174). His life must be in the now, not in the past. He is truly *of* the farm, but his future is not *on* the farm.

As Joey recognized Mrs. Robinson as an old woman and freed both her and the farm of the burden of blame for his own life, Mrs. Robinson, awaking from her sleep after her attack, accepts Joey and Peggy and frees them to live in the present. She tells them how happy the weekend has made her, and urges them to return to New York. She compliments Joey on the "man-sized" job he did in mowing the field, and tells Peggy, "He's a good boy" (173). She also asks Peggy to have a picture made to hang in the farmhouse—a final gesture of acceptance of Peggy as a member of the family. Granting Joey the freedom to sell the farm, she requests, "When you sell my farm, don't sell it cheap. Get a good price." Joey, however, responds: "*Your* farm? . . . . I've always thought of it as our farm" (127).

The divergence of the intersecting forces is not absolute.

There is a mutual blessing bestowed, and although the son will go back to the city to live in the present, he goes with new insight. Joey finds what Peter Caldwell did not find. Peter at thirty is still looking at a map that is all wrong, and he has almost decided that there is no word that can be meaningfully expressed. Joey, like George Caldwell, accepts the present and his responsibility for others. Despite whatever regrets he may have about his first wife and his children, he accepts Peggy as his wife *now,* and by the end of the book he is even thinking of Richard as his son rather than stepson.

Joey qualifies his statement to his mother about the farm being "theirs" by explaining to the reader: "We were striking terms, and circumspection was needed. I must answer in our old language, our only language, allusive and teasing, that with conspiratorial tack declared nothing and left the past apparently unrevised" (174). Despite the ambiguity suggested by Joey's acknowledging of his "conspiratorial tack," however, he has responded out of mature compassion for his mother. He has given her the freedom to have what she wants.

RELATIONSHIPS

The Centaur is concerned primarily with the centering self; *Of the Farm* emphasizes the impinging world of community interaction. Both illustrate the Updikean dualism, and both portray characters seeking a word. Both deal with the necessity for the acceptance of death and of the now. Caldwell is clearly presented as a hero—almost a saint. Updike has said, "George Caldwell I do see as exceptional in his altruism. . . . He'd be my candidate for sainthood—if I had one" ("Interview" 289). Joey, on the other hand, is neither heroic nor saintly, but he does succeed where Peter Caldwell fails.

In comparing these two novels to *The Poorhouse Fair,* one notes many relationships. First, there are the autobiographical overtones. Hook in *The Poorhouse Fair* was intended as a tribute to Updike's grandfather; George Caldwell in *The Centaur* is modeled in many ways on Updike's father; and Mrs. Robinson in *Of the Farm* has many characteristics of Updike's own mother. In addition, George Caldwell stands opposed to Zimmerman in *The Centaur* as Hook opposes Conner in *The Poorhouse Fair;* and despite its heavy dose of Greek mythology, *The Centaur* seems to be just as consciously Christian in outlook as *The Poorhouse Fair,* whereas *Of the Farm* is much less overtly Christian.

The language and structure of *The Centaur* are quite different from the dry, calibrated prose of *The Poorhouse Fair.* *Of the Farm* has some of the limited focus of *The Poorhouse Fair,* but its structure and language are quite different. Sexuality, so vital to Updike as a paradigm of duality and mystery, is more important in the latter two novels than in the first, but even in these it remains peripheral rather than central. In Updike's other novels, however, as we shall see, sexuality assumes a much more prominent thematic role.

NOTE

[1]Although *Rabbit, Run* was published in 1960, its sequels, *Rabbit Redux* and *Rabbit Is Rich* were not published until 1971 and 1981, respectively. Since these books are so integrally related, serious analysis demands that they be considered together. I have, therefore, chosen to delay consideration of *Rabbit, Run* until Chapter IV rather than forcing the two later books into a spot before the two novels of the early sixties.

WORKS CITED

Aldridge, John. *The Devil in the Fire*. New York: Harper's Magazine P, 1972.

Galloway, David. *The Absurd Hero in American Fiction*. Austin: U of Texas P, 1970.

Markle, Joyce. *Fighters and Lovers*. New York: New York UP, 1973.

Updike, John. *The Centaur*. New York: Knopf, 1973.

---. "Interview Conducted by Jeff Campbell, Georgetown, MA, 9 Aug. 1976." Published as Appendix to this volume.

---. *Of the Farm*. New York: Knopf, 1965.

---. *Picked-Up Pieces*. New York: Knopf, 1975.

CHAPTER 4

"IT TOOK ME QUITE A WHILE TO FIND YOU, BUT NOW I'VE GOT YOU": *RABBIT, RUN, RABBIT REDUX,* and *RABBIT IS RICH*

John Updike's second novel, *Rabbit, Run* (1960), is radically different from his first, *The Poorhouse Fair* (1959). In the earlier novel, the young author audaciously experimented by imagining himself into the minds of a group of old people in a future welfare state. *Rabbit, Run* is also boldly experimental, but in a quite different way. It turns from a fictional future which the author can control and manipulate with relative ease to the immediate present, with its myriad of details which the author must render accurately if he would make his story believable. It turns from the narrow, almost hermetically sealed world of the poorhouse to a broad cross section of American urban life. It turns from a dry, calibrated prose style to the impressionistic, cinematic immediacy of present tense narration. And it turns from a purely imagined world to draw heavily on the author's own personal experiences. The Brewer/Mt. Judge setting is modeled closely after the Shillington, Pennsylvania, area where Updike grew up, and the intimate details of daily life have the authentic ring of experienced reality. Updike had already discovered the rich possibilities in mining his own background for short stories, especially the "Olinger Stories," which center around a boy growing up in the mythical town of Olinger, Pennsylvania. He was to continue mining the personal vein in his novels, staying with the Pennsylvania background for *The Centaur* and *Of the Farm* and then moving to the suburbs of Boston and New York in *Couples, Marry Me,* and *The Witches of Eastwick*. He thus moved from recreating scenes of his childhood and youth to reflecting the life of upper-middle-class suburbia, which he himself was living in the 1960s, 1970s, and 1980s. *Rabbit, Run,* however, marks the initial exploration in novel form of what has become Updike's characteristic use of immediate personal experience as the matrix for his fictional world.

The second novels of young authors are often disappointing, somehow failing to deliver the achievement that a promising first novel suggested, but in Updike's case his second novel has become his most widely known and praised work. In fact, Updike has confessed that the novel's reputation as his "best" and "the tendency of strangers to mutter 'Run, rabbit, run,' as [he] walk[s] past have led [him] to harbor something of a grudge against the book," although he loved it as he was writing it. ("Special Message—*Rabbit, Run*" 849). Updike did not originally intend to continue the story of Harry Angstrom beyond the scope of *Rabbit, Run,* but "a little over ten years later, as the interminable sixties were drawing to their end, the idea that Harry . . . was still out there and running suddenly excited [him]," and he returned to Rabbit, now a "paunchy Middle American" whose "reluctant education," Updike said, offered "the parable that nobody else, in those shrill years, was offering" ("Special Message—*Rabbit Redux*" 858). With the publication of *Rabbit Redux* in 1971, Updike was committed to the continuing saga and promised that there would be a third Rabbit book—*Rural Rabbit*—in 1981, and even a fourth—*Rabbit Is Rich*—in 1991 ("Bech Meets Me" 13). 1981 brought *Rabbit Is Rich* instead of *Rural Rabbit,* but three of the promised four novels in the saga of Updike's "angst-ridden Everyman" ("Special Message—*Rabbit, Run*" 850) are now completed.

Rabbit, Run, Rabbit Redux, and *Rabbit Is Rich,* both singly and as a trio, are given more frequent critical discussion than any other of Updike's novels, often with the assessed judgment that they represent his best and most mature work. Charles Samuels, for instance, avers that only in Rabbit has Updike succeeded in presenting a hero whose value is neither exaggerated nor unconvincing (37). Joseph Waldmeir finds *Rabbit, Run* to be Updike's "best, most profound novel" (27), and Wayne Faulk thinks *Rabbit Redux* is Updike's only novel with a vision tough enough to withstand truth (61). Peter Prescott insists that *Rabbit Is Rich* shows "an assurance, a complexity of response, even a kind of serenity" that make the book "one of his very best yet" (89), and Roger Sale finds it "the first book in which Updike has fulfilled the fabulous promise offered. . . twenty years ago" (34).

Although not all critics join in praising these novels—Anthony Burgess complains that it is a "democratic heresy" to pour such richness of language on characters and situations so trivial (557); Eugene Lyons insists that *Rabbit Redux* is jarring and offensive to both mind and taste, an example of "breath-taking ineptitude" (44); and James Wolcott refers to the three novels as "a moribund saga" (20)—Updike has created in Harry Angstrom a hero who has taken his place in the American imagination alongside such other quixotic questers as Jay Gatsby, Quentin Compson, Holden Caulfield, Jay Yossarian, and Augie March. The three Rabbit novels also provide touchstones of thirty years of Updike's career.

Rabbit, Run, published eight years before *Midpoint,* clearly foreshadows the poem's concerns and commitments. *Rabbit Redux,* following the poem by three years, coherently develops the *Midpoint* philosophical stance, and *Rabbit Is Rich* a decade later demonstrates that Updike has not abandoned the approach to art and life outlined in the poem.

Taken together, these three novels provide further evidence of the usefulness of *Midpoint* as a prism through which to view both continuity and change in Updike's developing *oeuvre*.

RABBIT, RUN

Through the striking use of present tense narration, Updike brings the reader immediately into the stream of events in the life of Harry "Rabbit" Angstrom as he heads home from work on the Friday before Palm Sunday in March, 1959, the next to the last year of the Eisenhower era. Updike has pointed out that the present tense, "a piece of technical daring in 1959, though commonplace now," was chosen "to emphasize how thoroughly the zigzagging hero lived in the present" ("Special Message—*Rabbit, Run*" 850). The original subtitle of the book was "A Movie," and Updike has explained that "the present tense was in part meant to be an equivalent of the cinematic mode of narration" *(Picked-Up Pieces* 496).[1] Updike has also said that *Rabbit, Run* was "originally to be one of two novellas bound into a single volume; with its companion, *The Centaur,* it would illustrate the polarity between running and plodding, between the rabbit and the horse, between the life of instinctual gratification and dutiful self-sacrifice" ("Special Message—*Rabbit, Run*" 849-850). Both Harry Angstrom and George Caldwell, however, expanded under their creator's hand to demand full novels of their own. Reading the completed version of *Rabbit, Run,* one finds it difficult to imagine how these rapidly unreeling scenes, filled with exact and minute details spliced together so that one not only sees and hears, but also tastes, smells, and feels the experiences centering around Rabbit for three months, could possibly have been truncated into a novella.

Twenty-six-year-old Rabbit, who had been an outstanding basketball star in high school, now demonstrates a gadget called "Magipeeler" in dime stores. He married Janice Springer six months before their son, Nelson, was born three years ago. Janice is now pregnant again, and Rabbit finds her in their apartment half drunk, intently watching the Mousketeers on television. She has been shopping with her mother, and has left Nelson with Rabbit's mother and the car at her mother's. As Rabbit sets out to retrieve both the car and the child, he is struck with the mediocrity of his life and impulsively decides simply to run away from it all. He heads south in the car, planning only as far as reaching the Gulf of Mexico by morning. He gets lost on an intricacy of rural roads, however, and heads back to Brewer. He does not return to Janice; instead, he seeks out his old high school coach, Tothero, who lets him sleep through the day in his room at the Sunshine Athletic Club.

That night Tothero introduces Rabbit to a prostitute named Ruth, and Rabbit spends the night with her. The next day, Palm Sunday, Rabbit returns to his apartment to leave Janice the car and pick up some clothes for himself. He is spotted by Jack Eccles, the minister of the Episcopalian church the Springers belong to, who tells him of the concern he has caused everybody but does not try to force Rabbit to return to Janice. Instead, he gets him to promise to play golf the following Tuesday.

Eccles arranges for Rabbit to work as a gardener for a wealthy widow while Rabbit continues to live with Ruth and to play golf with Eccles. By Memorial Day, Ruth knows she's pregnant, but she has not yet told Rabbit when a few days later Eccles notifies him that Janice has entered the hospital to deliver her baby. Rabbit immediately leaves Ruth and goes to Janice. He finds himself accepted back, and things go rather smoothly until the Sunday after Janice brings the baby home from the hospital. Rabbit goes to Eccles' church and afterwards walks home with Eccles' wife, Lucy, finding himself sexually stimulated by her. He returns to Janice filled with desire, but Janice rejects his advances because it is too soon after the baby's birth.

In frustration, Rabbit runs once more. When he does not come home the next morning, Janice spends the morning drinking, then accidentally drowns the baby while attempting to bathe it. This tragedy brings Rabbit home again, and it seems as if shared sorrow may bind him and Janice together for good. At the funeral Rabbit feels for a moment the reality of "humans knitting together" (290). He hears and believes Eccles' words of comfort and feels that he has broken free into a patch of light. When he turns and sees Janice's grief-stricken face, however, the light is blocked, and he blurts out, "Don't look at *me. She's* the one" (293). As the shock and horror register on the faces around him, Rabbit turns and runs a third time. He runs over the mountain back to Ruth, who tells him she is pregnant and that he is "Mr. Death." He leaves Ruth with the intention of buying some food to bring back, but "guilt and responsibility slide together like two substantial shadows inside his chest" (305), and in a "kind of sweet panic" (307), for the fourth and final time he runs.

Edward Vargo finds a sharp division of opinion about the character of Rabbit. He suggests that readers see Rabbit as either a completely insensitive, irresponsible cad or as a saint and the only man of integrity in the novel (51). The plot summary shows that Rabbit does indeed act impulsively on his own momentary feelings, with no consideration for others; judged by his actions alone, he appears in a strongly negative light. Understanding the possibility of saintliness and integrity, however, requires looking beneath the mere events of the action into the minds and motives of the characters. An analysis of the structure of the novel and a consideration of the relationship of its epigraph to that structure will help explain why critics such as David Galloway, Robert Detweiler, Joyce Markle, Dean Doner, Alice and Kenneth Hamilton, and others see more to Rabbit than an insignificant human speck (an angstrom is a unit of measure indicating one/ten billionth of a meter) and find in him a representative of the universal *angst* of modern man.

ZIGZAG STRUCTURE: SELF VERSUS WORLD

In the same television interview in which Updike identified the "shape" of *The Poorhouse Fair* as a skyrocket or gladiola and that of *The Centaur* as a   sandwich, he stated that *Rabbit, Run* was shaped like a Z. In 1976 he explained that the Z suggested the "zigzaggy shape" of the book, which, he said, "settles on no fixed point" ("Interview" 279). The book, he said, was "a deliberate attempt to present both the escapist, have-it-my-way will to live versus the social restraints" ("Interview" 295).   In terms of the *Midpoint* commitments, the result is a dramatization of the self-world polarity. Rabbit Angstrom clearly thinks of himself as the midpoint of his own I-centered universe and refuses to use his eye to look beyond himself and recognize that his individual world is also one of the dots which relate to other individuals in a larger pattern of objective social reality.   George Caldwell in *The Centaur* was finally able to affirm and maintain his individuality while at the same time recognizing his place in a larger pattern. He overcame the "giant solipsism" of the childish assertions in early *Midpoint* by accepting the mysterious interpenetration of the two poles of self and world. Rabbit, however, remains a solipsist and fails in this book to achieve integration of the two worlds. That is the principal reason for the book's lacking the final unity of *The Centaur,* why it finally "settles on no fixed point." Rabbit illustrates the plight of the individual who refuses to relinquish his affirmation of the centrality of his own ego and is unable to succeed at fulfilling his potential because the objective world of social involvement continually exposes his shallow solipsism.

The novel's three major sections clearly show the zigzag structure created by self and world pulling at each other. In Part I, Rabbit thoughtlessly and impulsively runs, but finds himself quickly brought back into the social involvements he sought to escape. In Part II, he is back at home with Janice, apparently once more a responsible husband and father with a job. But when his own desires and impulses are thwarted, he flees again. In Part III, the tragedy of the baby's death has brought Rabbit back into the net of responsibility, but his thoughtless outburst of self-justification breaks the web and he is off running alone once more. The solipsistic immaturity of Rabbit's attempts to affirm himself as the sole midpoint of his own I-centered universe is shown by the fact none of his flights lead to an escape from the world around him, and clusters of zigzag reversals in each of the three sections of the novel further demonstrate the ineffectual nature of solipsism.

In Part I, the first confrontation of self-world poles comes when Rabbit is dressing to go out with Tothero to meet Ruth. He easily sheds any remorse over having left Janice and the familiar walls of their apartment. The "reflexes" of social responsibility, being "shallowly scratched," are quickly spent, and he feels the flooding of "deeper instincts" of "freedom like oxygen everywhere around him." So perfect is his feeling of freedom that "the clutter of the world" has been "vaporized." When he finishes dressing, he adjusts the knot of his tie "as if the little lines of this juncture of the Windsor knot, the collar of Tothero's shirt, and the base of his own throat were the arms of a star that will, when he is finished, extend outward to the rim of the universe" (49-50). Like the child in *Midpoint,* Rabbit feels himself the center of a star which includes the whole universe. This "zig" toward solipsistic, escapist freedom is, however, immediately countered by the "zag" of the voices of social restraint, not so easily shed as Rabbit had thought. "Clots of concern"—memories of his home, his wife, his job—return to mar his euphoria (50), and after describing to Ruth and Tothero the feeling he often got on the basketball floor that he *knew* he could do anything (65), he is reminded of his marriage and "a big bubble, the enormity of it, crowds his heart" (68).

The next zigzag occurs as he leaves Ruth's apartment after their first night together to return to leave the car for Janice and pick up some clothes. He "feels clean, narrow, hollow," self-sufficient and free. The car "smells secure," "a sheath for the knife of himself" (96). But quickly "his mood of poise crumbles as he descends into the familiar houses of Mt. Judge" (96). He finds that he is afraid of seeing Janice, and even "the bare possibility makes him so faint that when he gets out of the car the bright sun almost knocks him down" (97). "All the things inside his skull, the gray matter of his brain, the bones of his ears" (97), and the sights which present themselves to his eyes force him to recognize that there is an objective, patterned world in which his actions have consequences.

Finally in Part I, Rabbit confesses to Eccles that he had had no particular plan, that he was just suddenly struck with how easy it was simply to walk out, to get away from the mediocrity he felt was destroying him (103-104). He refuses to be bothered by Eccles' suggestion that he is not mature, for, he says, as far as he can make out, being mature is "the same thing as being dead" (106). He doesn't know or care what Janice may be feeling. "All I know is what's inside *me*," he says (106). He leaves Eccles with the confident feeling that when one lives for himself "the world just can't touch you" (107). But before this Palm Sunday is over, that world does indeed touch him. As he and Ruth stand atop Mt. Judge, Rabbit looks down on the city and recognizes that "his day has been bothered by God." "It seems plain" to him "that if there is this floor there is a ceiling, that the true space in which we live is upward space" (112-113). He strains to see if he can detect the soul of a dying man springing upward from the apparently illusory city that lies at his feet. But "silence blasts him. Chains of cars creep without a noise; a dot comes out of a door" (113). The city is not illusory, but recalcitrantly real. It is an example of the objective world and its patterned dots which deny his airy upward feeling and pull him downward. He wonders: "What is he doing here, standing on air? Why isn't he home?" (113). Frightened, he asks Ruth to put her arm around him. Clasping her makes him feel better, makes the city seem somehow a shelter of love and security. But he presses this warmth and security too far, asking Ruth in the voice of a spoiled child, "Were you really a whore?" The love, security, and warmth are suddenly gone; Ruth hardens, twists away, and asks Rabbit, "Are you really a rat?" (113). Part I concludes with this cluster of images which juxtapose Rabbit's naive assumption of the importance and centrality of his own ego with recurrent rebuffs from the world in which he is merely another dot, not the midpoint.

Part II presents more zigzag reversals as the central ego seeks to assert itself against the claims of the objective world. Ruth and Rabbit run into Ronnie Harrison, one of Rabbit's old high school teammates, at a night club. Rabbit is revolted by Harrison's pot belly and his crude talk about sex, and is especially angered by the knowledge that Harrison has in the past been sexually intimate with Ruth. He realizes that although he has been thinking that somehow he is special and different, in fact to Ruth there may be no difference between himself and Harrison. Forcing Ruth to admit that she had performed fellatio for Harrison, he insists that she do the same for him, claiming that it will prove that she is his. Rabbit's sleep after this experience is interrupted by Eccles' call to tell him that Janice is in the hospital delivering their baby. As

Rabbit prepares to leave for the hospital, he regrets what he had made Ruth do. He admits he doesn't even know why he did it, "except it felt right at the time" (191). He had wanted to stop her, but he didn't until it was too late, and instantly the floating, high pride that he had felt was plunged into shame (191). At the hospital the feeling of remorse and guilt continues. "He is certain that as a consequence of his sin Janice or the baby will die. His sin a conglomerate of flight, cruelty, obscenity, and conceit . . ." (196). "His life seems a sequence of grotesque poses assumed to no purpose, a magic dance empty of belief" (198). But such feelings cannot last long because for Rabbit "everything seems unreal that is outside of his own sensations" (197). Soon he is feeling joy (198), and the next day he tells Eccles' wife, Lucy: "Last night driving home I got this feeling of a straight road ahead of me; before that it was like I was in the bushes and it didn't matter which way I went" (209). For awhile he is almost forced to the realization that he is like other men; for awhile he feels the weight of the consequences of his actions; but now he is quickly back to trusting his own sensations, sure that the straight road ahead is there just for him.

As he waits for Janice to come home from the hospital, however, Rabbit feels cramped and afraid. When he tries to sleep, he is "like an unsteered boat," and "he keeps scraping against the same rocks: his mother's ugly behavior, his father's gaze of desertion, Ruth's silence the last time he saw her, his mother's not saying a word. . . ." "Though he's lying there alone he feels crowded, all these people troubling about him not so much their faces or words as their mute dense presences, pushing in the dark like crags under water and under everything like a faint high hum" (230-231). When Janice comes home from the hospital, however, all this changes. He finds that "thick, sweet love burdens his chest" (233) and "considers himself happy, lucky, blessed, forgiven . . ." (234). Such emotions motivate him to want to give thanks by attending worship at Eccles' church. The church experience is unsatisfying, however, because Rabbit "has no taste for the dark, tangled, visceral aspect of Christianity, the *going through* quality of it, the passage *into* death and suffering that redeems and inverts things, like an umbrella blowing inside out. He lacks the mindful will to walk the straight line of a paradox. His eyes turn toward the light however it glances into his retina" (237). He still sees everything only as it relates to his own central ego. He walks Lucy Eccles home after church and is sexually stimulated by what he interprets her to mean by inviting him in for coffee. Whether he is right or wrong about Lucy Eccles' intentions, he returns to Janice filled with sexual desire. When Janice refuses him because she must wait six weeks after the baby's birth and asks, "Why can't you imagine how I *feel*?" he responds, "I can but I don't want to, it's not the thing, the thing is how *I* feel. And I feel like getting out" (248). So for the second time Rabbit follows his own impulses, thinking predominantly of his own desires, and runs aways. This second running leads directly to Janice's drunkenness the next day and her fateful attempt to bathe the baby. The I-centered ego which responds only to the light that glances into its solipsistic retina has this time collided with the world of social responsibility in a way that results in genuine tragedy.

Part III opens with indications that Rabbit may be surrendering his solipsistic egoism. Recognizing that what kept him from going home and thus preventing the baby's death was his feeling that "somewhere there was something better for him than listening to babies cry and cheating people in used car lots" (270), he tries to kill this feeling, and when he gets to the Springers' home "he feels he will never resist anything again" (271). He even tells Janice that it wasn't her fault, but his, and "they cling together in a common darkness; he feels the walls between them dissolve in a flood of black" (277). Then he has a dream in which he sees a pale, transparent disk eclipse a bright, dense disk, with the resulting awareness that he has witnessed the explanation of death: "lovely life eclipsed by lovely death" (282). The experience causes him, in the dream, to feel that he must go forth and found a new religion, but upon awaking he realizes it was only a dream, and "that he has nothing to tell the world" (282). As he walks over to the apartment with Janice and Nelson to get clothes for the funeral, he is struck by the strangeness of the familiar surroundings and faces

> the riddle, Why does anyone live here? Why was he set down here, why is this town, a dull suburb of a third-rate city, for him the center and index of a universe that contains immense prairies, mountains, deserts, forests, coastlines, cities, seas? This childish mystery—the mystery of 'any place,' prelude to the ultimate, 'Why am I me?'—starts panic in his heart. (282-283)

He seems on the verge of affirming the mysterious interpenetration of objective and subjective worlds outlined in *Midpoint*. At the funeral, he "feels these humans knit together" (290), and the reader almost believes that Harry may be close to finding that mindful will to walk the straight line of paradox which relates self to world. But such discovery is not to be, at least not for another twenty years.

In the final, crucial zigzag, his "heart turns again, a wider turn in a thinning medium to which the outer world bears a decreasing relevance" (290). Harry has settled once more on himself as the only midpoint. He feels freedom and forgiveness; he has cast all his burdens on the Lord and feels a new strength. As he moves from the undertaker's tent into the sunshine, "it is as if he has been crawling in a cave and now at last beyond the dark recession of crowding rocks he has seen a patch of light" (293). But that light is the selfish, egocentric specialness he has always lived for. When he turns, he finds that "Janice's face, dumb with grief, blocks the light" (293). Unable to accept anything that blocks the light of his newly regained sense of strength and freedom, he blurts out the fateful words: "Don't look at *me*. . . .*I* didn't kill her. . . . *She's* the one" (293). Recognizing that even his own mother is horrified at what he has said, he is blinded by a sense of injustice as he turns and runs for the third time. He runs to Ruth, who offers a final condemnatory judgment when she asks him:

> "Why don't you look outside your own pretty skin once in a while? . . . . I see you very clear all of a sudden. You're Mr. Death himself. You're not a rat, you don't stink, you're not enough to stink. . . . Maybe once you could play basketball but you can't do *anything* now. What the hell do you think the world is?"

All Rabbit can say is: "I don't know. I don't know any of these answers. All I know is what feels right. You feel right to me. Sometimes Janice used to. Sometimes nothing does." But Ruth responds, "Who cares? That's the thing. Who cares *what* you feel?" (330-333).

Despite her harsh words, Ruth says that if he will face up to the situation, make a choice, and divorce Janice, she will marry him. If he won't work it out, however, both she and his unborn child will be dead to him. Rabbit has hardly listened to Ruth: "it is too complicated and, compared to the vision of a sandwich, unreal" (304). He is still convinced that "if he can just once more bury himself in her. . .that . . . he'll come up with his nerves all combed" (304). He goes down the stairs, ostensibly to buy something to eat to bring back, but "as he goes . . . worries come as quick as the sound of his footsteps. Janice, money, Eccles' phone call, the look on his mother's face all clatter together in sharp dark waves; guilt and responsibility slide together like two substantial shadows inside his chest" (305). The objective world of social restraints keeps challenging the midpoint ego. "He decides to walk around the block, to clear his mind and pick a path," but he begins to reflect:

> Funny, how what makes you move is so simple and the field you
> must move in so crowded. . . . Goodness lies inside, there is
> nothing outside, those things he was trying to balance have no
> weight. He feels his inside as very real suddenly, a pure blank
> space in the middle of a dense net. I don't know, he kept telling
> Ruth; he doesn't know, what to do, where to go, what will hap-
> pen, the thought that he doesn't know seems to make him in-
> finitely small and impossible to capture. . . . It's like when they
> heard you were great and put two men on you and no matter
> which way you turned you bumped into one of them and the only
> thing to do was pass. So you passed and the ball belonged to
> others and your hands were empty and the men on you looked
> foolish because in effect there was nobody there. (306)

In the final zigzag of the book, Rabbit refuses to give
weight to all the outside things he has been called on to
balance. The only reality he finds is himself. This final reaf-
firmation of the inside-self as true midpoint of his universe
restores his happiness, and

> the steps and window sills seem to twitch and shift in the corner of
> his eye, alive. This illusion trips him. His hands lift of their own
> and he feels the wind on his ears even before, his heels hitting
> heavily on the pavement at first but with an effortless gathering
> out of a kind of sweet panic growing lighter and quicker and
> quieter, he runs. Ah: runs. Runs. (306-307)

The solipsistic illusion of his own central vision as that which
gives life to the world about him stirs him to light, quick,
quiet action, but since that action is based also on rejecting
the pole of objective reality and responsibility, the action can
be nothing more than escapist flight.

The zigzag structure of the book, then, leads, as Updike
said, "to no fixed point." The conflicting claims of the
self/world polarity are presented dot by dot as they emerge,
but there is no resolution. Rabbit has apparently learned
nothing; he is still affirming the centrality of his own ego, and

the only course of action he can discern is the negative one of running away. If analysis were limited to this structural aspect of the book, one would be led to conclude that Rabbit is, indeed, extremely insensitive and irresponsible, that his young creator was struggling with an ego/world conflict which he was unable to resolve, and that Rabbit is simply a negative figure who shows the author's limits, at least at that time.

With Updike, however, the response is "yes—but." Rabbit *is* irresponsible, ultimately unsuccessful—but. He also has a certain inner integrity. There is a sense in which the others in the book are all false, as Rabbit concludes at the funeral. Rabbit alone seems to have the yearning, the awareness that there is "something out there that wants me to find it," that there is a realm of meaning beyond Magipeelers, Mousketeers, and used cars. That other side of Rabbit is indicated by the Pascalian epigraph Updike chose for this book, and examining the book in light of that epigraph will show why some critics see a kind of saintliness in Rabbit and will help explain both the possibility of and the need for a sequel to this particular segment of Rabbit's story.

"THE MOTIONS OF GRACE, THE HARDNESS OF THE HEART: EXTERNAL CIRCUMSTANCES"

The epigraph for *Rabbit, Run* is Pascal's Penseé 507: "The motions of Grace, the hardness of the heart: external circumstances." Updike has said that he first read Pascal when he was in his twenties and found himself strongly "attracted to his particular line of Christian thought" ("Interview" 279). Although he had read some in St. Thomas Aquinas, he said that he found the Augustine-Pascal-Kierkegaard approach to Christianity to speak more directly to his plight than the more rational, Scholastic Thomistic approach. ("Interview" 279). The impact of the Christian existentialism of Pascal and Kierkegaard on him helps explain why Updike's protagonist experiences the *angst* and absurdity common to characters created by Sartre and Camus but resists the heroic defiance of the transcendent voiced by Sartre's Orestes or Camus's Sisyphus. Pascal and Kierkegaard—and Updike and Rabbit—assume the reality of a transcendent realm with its motions of grace. Rabbit's *angst* comes from his inability to find a way to bridge the gap between his unique individual ego with its yearning for that transcendent realm and the world of external circumstances that continually confronts him. He refuses to accept the affirmation of nothingness, of mere existence without a prior essense, that is central to the Sartrean version of existentialism.

Updike has said that this particular quotation from Pascal struck him as appropriate for the novel both because "its darting, fragmentary, zigzaggy form fits the book" ("Interview" 279) and because the three things Pascal mentions seem to him to describe Rabbit's life. The "external circumstances" in this case are

> the pregnancy and family responsibilities and financial necessities. The motions of grace represent that within . . . which seeks the good, . . .the . . . nonmaterial, non-external side. . . . Clearly Rabbit shows hardness of heart, and there's a way in which the hardness of heart and the motions of grace are intertwined. . . . And I think there seems to be an extent to which hardness of heart is tied in with being alive at all. ("Interview" 278-279)

It is the numerous manifestations of the nonmaterial, non-external side of Rabbit which seeks the good, which responds in some inchoate way to the motions of grace, that prevents the reader or critic from dismissing Rabbit as merely a self-centered reprehensible egotist.

On his initial flight, Rabbit has an experience that indicates his inability to accept the "easy humanism" that seems to govern the lives of those around him. He stops at a filling station and asks for a map. The farmer-attendant asks, "Son, where do you want to go?" (26). Rabbit confesses that he doesn't exactly know. The man tells him, "The only way to get somewhere, you know, is to figure out where you're going before you go there." Rabbit, however, responds: "I don't think so" (28). He believes that there is something more to life than rational decisions based on objectively presented external circumstances. Later he does pick up a map, but he sees it as a "net, all those red lines and blue lines and stars, a net he is somewhere caught in." He feels that the filling station attendant with his reference to maps and plans has been mocking him, mocking "the furtive wordless hopes that at moments made the ground firm" for him (36). He thinks: "Decide where you want to go and then go: it missed the whole point and yet there is always the chance that, little as it is, it is everything" (36). Harry is not ready to accept that little as everything, however. He feels that if he had simply trusted his instincts he would already be in South Carolina. Instinct alone is not enough, though, for when he turns onto a highway following his instincts, he turns north, not south, and soon finds himself back in Brewer.

Harry, unlike Conner in *The Poorhouse Fair,* does not believe that man can map out the perfect life. Like Hook, he senses some sort of providence beyond that will give the final meaning. Also like Hook, however, Harry is unable to see clearly that which is close at hand. Hook could not see the dying cat at his feet and was unaware when the old people started throwing stones at Conner. Harry, looking for something more than Magipeelers and Mousketeers, is unable to recognize and deal with the inescapable, external circumstances whose recurrent zigzags entangle him in a net of social involvement.

Harry's first night with Ruth gives evidence of his "non-material, non-external" side. Ruth would like to treat him as just another customer, but he cannot be content with "just her heavy body. . . . He wants whole women, light as feathers" (73). Rabbit is "unconscious of their skins, it is her heart he wants to grind into his own, to comfort her completely" (75). "It is not her crotch he wants, not the machine; but her, her" (78). Ruth taunts him, saying, "You all think you're such lovers," but Rabbit assures her, "I am. I am a lover" (76). Unconsciously Rabbit seeks in sex and love the mysterious interpenetration of separate worlds suggested in *Midpoint*. Ruth finds the view from her window "dismal," but Rabbit focuses not on the gray, somber church that presents itself, but on its rose window. The lights are burning behind the window so that to Rabbit "this circle of red and purple and gold seems in the city night a hole punched in reality to show the abstract brilliance beneath"(80). Ruth is disgusted by Sunday mornings because she once had a man with her who woke her up at eight o'clock because he had to go teach Sunday School. Ruth insists she doesn't believe in anything, but Rabbit affirms that he does believe in God. He winces as he makes the confession, and "wonders if he's lying. If he is, he is hung in the middle of nowhere, and the thought hollows him, makes his heart tremble" (89). Inarticulately raising the basic *Midpoint* question of why the void was breached at all, Rabbit asks Ruth, "Well now if God doesn't exist, why does anything?" (90). Rabbit has neither the clear vision nor the mindful strength of will to pursue his question to resolution, but his affirmation of an unseen world, his ability to catch glimpses of the brilliance burning underneath mundane reality, leads Ruth to confess the most important reason she likes him: "Cause you haven't given up. Cause in your stupid way you're still fighting" (91).

Rabbit's first night with Ruth, then, provides the second instance in Part I of what separates Rabbit from the rest of the characters in the novel. Even Ruth, who finally makes the harshest condemnation of his immaturity, recognizes Rabbit as having both the ability to love in a way that goes beyond the techniques of sex and the tenacity to continue to fight for the possibility of an unseen world when others have given up. The potential for loving and fighting gives Rabbit stature and keeps him open to the motions of grace. He is the first Updike protagonist to demonstrate these two qualities that Joyce Markle finds so characteristic of Updike's major characters that she titles her study of his work *Fighters and Lovers,* and it is these two qualities that lift Rabbit beyond negative significance and thereby justify a continuation of his story beyond the irresponsible flight which ends the novel.

Even the minister, Jack Eccles, whom some critics have interpreted to be the central example in the novel of the motions of grace seeking the lost sinner, Rabbit, turns out to be really only the representative of a humanistic ecclesiasticism, lacking Rabbit's sense of transcendent possibilities. On the way to the golf course, Rabbit tells Eccles that he feels "that somewhere behind all this. . . there's something that wants me to find it" (127). Eccles, straying for a moment from his carefully cultivated Rogerian non-directive counseling technique, replies, "Of course, all vagrants think they're on a quest. At least at first" (127). Rabbit is indeed uncertain of his quest; he frequently confesses he has no plan, no answers. But he is more than a vagrant, and he soon realizes that behind Eccles' pressing him to identify exactly what this "it" is that wants him to find it is a real desire to be told. Rabbit realizes that "underneath all this I-know-more-about-it-than-you heresies-of-the-early-Church business [Eccles] wants to be told about it, wants to be told that it is there, that he's not lying to all those people every Sunday" (133). Rabbit is irresponsible and inarticulate, but he is closer to the truth than Eccles, who cannot love in a meaningful way and who has quit fighting and accepted a role in an institution whose central assertions he does not really believe.

As we have seen, after the death of the baby, Rabbit seeks to kill the feeling inside him that there is an opening somewhere, that there is something better that he must try to find (270). He also feels that he will never resist anything again (271)—the loving and the fighting seem all gone out of him. The fact that he turns once more to his own inner reality at the funeral, however, proves that he has not succeeded in killing that feeling, that he does still have resistance within him. When he runs away, it is true that he is merely running toward some unidentified light. He still has no taste for the "dark, tangled, visceral aspect of Christianity, the *going through* quality of it. . . ." He still "lacks the mindful will to walk the straight line of a paradox" and so he is left empty when, as he runs from Ruth for the final time, he looks up again to the church window to find it "unlit, a dark circle in a stone facade" (306). He has not succeeded in "going through"; he has not learned to combine his "I" and his "eye"; but the very fact that he runs proves that he has *not* killed the feeling inside that there is an opening somewhere, shows that he is still resisting the external circumstances which seek to deny the reality of his individuality—and enables Updike to continue his story. Ten years later Rabbit is forced to learn a great deal about the interpenetration of the poles of self and world.

RABBIT REDUX

In *Rabbit Redux* the juxtaposition of self and world that characterized *Rabbit, Run* is continued, but the external circumstances which intrude on Harry Angstrom (almost nobody calls him Rabbit anymore) in 1969 are of a scale significantly different from those he confronted in 1959. Political and philosophical apathy typified the next-to-last year of the Eisenhower era, but the first of the Nixon years is characterized by the Vietnam war, its counter-culture opponents, black militancy, and the conquering of outer space through man's first successful flight to the moon. In both novels there is the immediacy of present tense narration, and the verisimilitude is heightened by the inclusion of a wealth of detail from actual events of three months of a particular year, but in *Rabbit Redux* those details are not just items such as popular songs that come over the radio or the words of Jimmy, the head Mousketeer. This story opens on the very day of the moon launch, and the first chapter closes with the televised report of man's first steps on lunar soil. The Vietnam war and race riots in the cities are subjects for heated debates among the characters, and Harry's home is invaded by a runaway hippie and a radical black militant. The issues of family and financial responsibility he refused to balance against the inward reality of his own insistent ego in 1959 are still present, but the deliberate expansion of the "external circumstances" to national, international, and even cosmic levels suggests that the solipsistic escapism he pursued ten years earlier, whatever tenuous elements of heroism it possessed then, is impossible now.

Unlike, *Rabbit, Run,* whose three major divisions are indicated not by chapter titles or even numbers but only by the starting of new sections on fresh pages, *Rabbit Redux* has four numbered and titled chapters, each with its own epigraph. The epigraphs are drawn alternately from the recorded conversations of Russian cosmonauts and American astronauts, and are intended, according to Updike, "to remind the reader that these domestic events are occurring simultaneously with this unparalleled adventure into space" ("Interview" 282).

Chapter I, entitled "Pop/Mom/Moon," opens on a Wednesday in mid-July as Harry and his father leave their work as linotype operators at Verity Press in Brewer, where Harry has been working with his father for the past ten years. They stop in a bar to share a drink before Harry takes the bus to the suburban home in Penn Villas that he and Janice bought three years earlier. As the television shows the astronauts blasting off for their flight to the moon, Harry's father reports on the state of Mrs. Angstrom's continuing struggle with Parkinson's Disease and tells Harry that his mother is bothered by gossip she has heard about Janice. Janice is now working at her father's automobile agency; unlike Harry, who has settled into a routine anonymity so that "his prime is soft, somehow pale and sour" (4), Janice has found new energy and purpose; she is no longer the "dumb" girl Rabbit condescended to ten years ago. The gossip is accurate: Janice is having an affair with Charlie Stavros, a salesman at her father's lot. Harry has no suspicions, largely because he has lost interest in sex. After the baby's death he had refused to let Janice have another child because "it had all seemed like a pit to him then, her womb and the grave, sex and death" (27).

When Rabbit confronts Janice with the gossip his mother has heard, she admits her affair with Stavros and is prepared to tell Stavros that she will not see him again, but Harry suggests that she go on seeing him if she wants to and then heads off to a baseball game with Nelson and Mr. Springer. When he returns, he finds a note from Janice saying that she has left to have a few days to think things out— she was shocked by his suggestion that she continue having a lover, and she wonders now if she ever meant anything to him at all. Harry assures Nelson that she will be back, and on Sunday they both go to the elder Angstroms' home to celebrate Harry's mother's birthday while the television shows the moon landing.

Chapter II, entitled "Jill," opens on a Saturday in August, after Janice has been gone approximately two weeks. Rabbit is conned by one of the men he works with into visiting a black bar. A young white girl, a freaked-out runaway suburban hippie named Jill, has attached herself to the group at the bar, and they need to get rid of her in order to avoid suspicion of the law. Rabbit meets the girl and Skeeter, a pusher who is also a black militant; and almost before he realizes it, he has taken Jill home with him. Nelson is surprised but delighted to find Jill there when he comes home the next morning, and after about three weeks things have settled into a more or less comfortable routine, even though Jill is in many ways Harry's opposite. He finds the books she reads—yoga, psychiatry, and zen—"spooky." "The light of common day, the sights and streets that have been the food of Rabbit's life, seem to strike her as poisonous and too powerful" (158). Rabbit finds himself "entranced" by the kinds of things Jill talks about. He thinks, "Never too late for education. With Janice and Old Man Springer you could never have this kind of conversation" (160).

Chapter III, "Skeeter," is dominated by the young black militant Harry met in the bar the same night he met Jill. Skeeter has been arrested for possession of marijuana, but jumps bail and comes to Rabbit's home for asylum in early September. Soon he has maneuvered the whole group into reading black history, Rabbit into smoking marijuana, and Jill back into using hard drugs. He dominates the scene with his rhetoric of violence and his claims of Messiahship in a new age of anarchy and chaos, and the promised apocalypse of the new dark Christ does indeed take place. While Rabbit and his son are away for the evening, the house burns and Jill dies a fiery death within it. It is possible that Skeeter himself set the fire, but it is more likely that the neighbors, who had tried to warn Rabbit about allowing blacks and drugs into the neighborhood, have set the fire to teach him a lesson. Either way, Skeeter has been the instigator of a fiery violence, destroying Jill and whatever semblance was left of Rabbit's former life.

Chapter IV opens three days after the fire as Rabbit gets the news that he is losing his job at Verity Press because new and cheaper methods of printing are replacing the linotype process. The chapter takes its title, however, from Rabbit's sister, Mim, who returns from Las Vegas both to see her sick mother and to offer what help she can to get Rabbit put back together. Rabbit and Nelson are living with the elder Angstroms, and Rabbit seems perfectly happy to regress into a childhood role with no job and no responsibilities. Mim tries to sting him into some decisive action; although her attempts with Rabbit have no apparent effect, she does trigger a change in Janice. Mim meets with Stavros, finds out that he has a bad heart and is really eager to be free of the responsibility Janice has brought into his life, and subsequently sleeps with Stavros three times. Janice reacts violently to Charlie's involvement with Mim, jealously questions him about it, and forces him to make love to her. Charlie has a heart attack, and Janice, unable to find the right pills for him, covers him with her body and by sheer force of love and will drives death away. She recognizes that "this love that has blown through her has been a miracle. . . . Spirits are insatiable but bodies get enough. She has had enough, he has had enough; more might be too much. She might begin to kill. . . . The lone thing worthy of . . . this love. . . is to leave" (388). Janice calls Rabbit and suggests that they meet. She picks him up in their old Falcon, and after driving by the burned-out house, they stop at a motel. As they get into bed together, Rabbit "feels they are . . . adjusting in space, slowly twirling in some gorgeous ink that filters through his eyelids as red. In a space of silence. . . he feels them drift along sideways deeper into being married" (405). Rabbit confesses to Janice that he feels guilty about everything, but she tells him, "Relax. Not everything is your fault" (406). As he and Janice lie in bed together, "the space they are in, the motel room long and secret as a burrow, becomes all interior space" (406). In the final paragraph of the book, Rabbit feels himself microcosmic, and instead of feeling sexual stimulation in Janice's body, he runs his hand over "the familiar dip of her waist, ribs to hip bone, where no bones are, soft as flight, fat's inward curve, slack, his babies from her belly. He finds this inward curve and slips along it, sleeps. He. She. Sleeps. O.K.?" (407).

Rabbit's role in all of these events is essentially passive. He has apparently abandoned the urgency of maintaining and defining his inward self. He works at a routine job; he accepts the fact that Janice has a lover and makes no move to reclaim her; he allows himself to be manipulated into taking Jill into his home; he lets Skeeter come in and dominate him; he regresses to irresponsibility when he loses Jill, his home, and his job; he waits for Janice to take the initiative for their reunion. He seems to have succeeded in his resolution in *Rabbit, Run* to kill his sense of something better wanting him to find it, to have followed through on his feeling that he would never resist anything again. Yes—but. The inward self is not totally gone. The self that felt guilty inside and ran from the funeral and from Ruth is still there, and now it is the objective world of social involvement that continually intrudes and challenges that self to live. The world will not let the self retreat into itself and escape. External circumstances themselves become examples of the motions of grace. "There is a way," Updike has said:

> in which the television set invades the guy's life. That is, these are sort of headline figures who come upon him, and I think it was true of a lot of us in the late sixties that all the things we preferred not to think about became unavoidable. So in a way he is the middle class man whose living room becomes the scene of atrocities and teach-ins and all those things. ("Interview" 286)

In this novel, then, the inward self is jarringly forced into acceptance of the reality of the objective world and its larger patterns, and instead of a zigzag structure which settles on no fixed point, there is a much more complex structure which illustrates the mysterious interpenetration of the poles of self and world.

MÖBIUS STRIP AS STRUCTURAL METAPHOR

In the same television interview in which he described the "shapes" of *The Poorhouse Fair, The Centaur,* and *Rabbit, Run,* Updike mentioned that he felt the traditional form of the novel might well be worn out and that novelists should seek to shape novels in new ways. He suggested that perhaps a star or even a Möbius strip might provide interesting possibilities. In our 1976 interview, Updike said that he was not conscious of having any specific shape in mind as he worked on *Rabbit Redux* ("Interview 285). He said that he had written the book rather rapidly, and had "forgotten the composition" except that he was "trying to let out [his] own anxieties and doubts, puzzlement over the issues that are raised" ("Interview" 286). Nevertheless, when I reminded him of his suggestion of the Möbius strip as a promising shape for a novel and suggested some of the ways *Rabbit Redux* reflected the qualities of a Möbius strip, he responded positively. Therefore, because the Möbius strip works in so many ways as a metaphor to help explain the complex and subtle movements in the novel, I have chosen to approach it from this perspective, even though Updike did not consciously shape the book with this goal in mind.

The Möbius strip, a one-sided band of paper, was first described by the German mathematician and astronomer

Augustus Ferdinand Möbius (1790-1868) in an article published posthumously. The Möbius strip is made from an ordinary strip of paper which is given a half twist and then glued together at the ends to make a closed ring. If one traces around the band with a pencil, he discovers that, unlike an ordinary paper ring, this one has not two sides, but only one. The pencil line will return upon itself, leaving no blank side. The strip has further peculiarities, as well. If one draws a line down the middle of the strip and then cuts along that line, the strip does not become two strips; instead, it becomes one strip, twice the size of the former, but now with two sides, not one. If, on the other hand, one cuts the Möbius strip one third of the way in from the edge, he will find that the scissors make two complete trips around the strip, but only one continuous cut. The end result of the cutting leaves two intertwined strips: one is a large two-sided hoop, and the other is a new Möbius strip of the same diameter as the original.

This twisted world of one-sided surfaces, in which paper strips refuse to be cut in half or surprisingly become two separate but interlocked strips with different properties, was discovered by a mathematician—a scientist who might well have been mentioned in Canto III of *Midpoint*. Although his accomplishments hardly match the significance of those of Planck, Fermi, and Debye, Möbius, like them, proved that solid matter is often "intricate and giddy" *(Midpoint* 18). In the Möbius strip we see further illustration of "dangling bonds" and "antiparallel domains" which contribute to the mystery and complexity of the objective world and find a metaphor for the interlocking relation of that world to the world of the individual ego.

The three basic characteristics of the Möbius strip which shed light on the structure of *Rabbit Redux* are as follows. First, when the strip of paper is given a half-twist and its ends fastened together, a one-sided surface is produced. There is no "other" side. Second, when the strip is cut down the middle, one two-sided strip results. Third, when the strip is cut beginning one-third of the way in from the edge, two interlocking strips are produced—one one-sided and the other two-sided. Let us examine each of these characteristics in turn as they relate to the novel.

One Side—Twisted

The original one-sided twisted strip may be taken to represent the world of the central ego, midpoint of its own universe. We have seen that throughout *Rabbit, Run* Harry Angstrom takes a consistently solipsistic view of the world, either ignoring or defying the claims of social responsibility. He lives only inside his own skin, doing those things that feel right to him at the time. Although in *Rabbit Redux* Harry has become considerably more passive, he still shows little comprehension of the meaning of things outside himself. How *he feels* seems to be the only yardstick by which he measures his actions. Janice tells Stavros, for instance, that she thinks Harry probably came back to her and Nelson "for the old-fashioned reasons," that he now wants "to live an old-fashioned life, but nobody does that any more and he feels it. He put his life into rules he feels melting away now" (53). Harry's early middle age is "soft, somehow pale and sour" (4) because he *feels* that he's missing something since he gave up pursuing the thing out there that wanted him to find it. Janice recognizes that something in Harry has changed when she tells him: "There've been a lot of days . . . when I was sorry you came back. . . . You were a beautiful brainless guy and I've had to watch that guy die day by day" (74). Harry has given his ego a half-twist by trying to live the life of a responsible citizen according to the old rules, but he still is living a one-sided life. He has not truly acknowledged the reality of the objective, "out-there" world, because he still judges everything by his own feelings. He tells his mother at the end of Chapter I, "I don't feel anything yet" (100). He makes this comment just after having watched Neil Armstrong take the first human step on the moon; Janice's leaving him has introduced a radical new era into his life just as the moon landing has introduced a new era for man's explorations, but neither means anything to Harry because *he* doesn't *feel* it.

Further evidence that Harry has continued to see the world from his one-sided midpoint is found in Chapter IV. Harry and Nelson have moved in with the elder Angstroms, and Nelson and Mr. Angstrom are arguing about the Vietnam war. Harry is amused at the passion of their argument, because he "feels none." Now that he is home again, he "feels protected," saved from worrying about the world outside (349). When Mim comes home and seeks to help Harry, he denies any responsibility for all that has happened, insisting that he did only "what felt right" (358), and that what other people make of it is their problem. Mim, however, tells him that he is "just big Mr. Muddle" (369). In words that strongly echo the judgment of Ruth at the end of *Rabbit, Run,* she says, "Everybody else has a life they try to fence in with some rules. You just do what you feel like and then when it blows up or runs down you sit there and pout" (370). When Rabbit counters that he went to work every day for ten years, she responds, "You felt like it. It was the easiest thing to do" (370).

Thus, although a new decade has brought some significant twists to the life of Harry Angstrom, his existence is still one-sided. Despite the twists and turns, the self is basically the same as it has always been. Although in Harry's case the examples of this persistency of the self indicate a continued solipsistic egoism, there is nonetheless a positive side: the integrity of his individual ego persists through the changes of external circumstances. In spite of Harry's life being turned inside out by the events of these three months of 1969, there is a continuity through his internal consciousness that supports the reality of self and sets up a possibility that self may intentionally and decisively interact with the larger world outside.

Two-sided Reality

The two-sided band produced when a Möbius strip is cut down the middle can be taken to represent the objective, two-sided outer world, in which there is not only "me" but also "them," in which there are objective natural laws that dictate certain inevitable consequences, in which inner reality is counterbalanced by a palpably real outer world of things, persons, and events. The fact that the original strip does not become two but remains one suggests that Harry cannot be cut off from the outer world. He cannot successfully ignore it or run away from it or withdraw from it. There is a unity to the two poles of reality, even though the two sides of the strip indicate the dualism necessitated by recognizing the two poles.

Certainly the events of the novel force Harry into acknowledging the existence of a world beyond himself. Outer space is there, challenging the technological and scientific knowledge of mankind. The successful moon shot serves as forceful reminder of the cosmic universe of matter and law in which man lives. Harry doesn't like the newscaster's comparing the voyage of the astronauts to that of Columbus, because he sees it as the exact opposite: "Columbus flew blind and hit something, these guys see exactly where they're aiming and it's a big round nothing" (22). Columbus followed his own instincts and feelings and discovered a marvelous new world. This is the way Harry would like his life to be. The astronauts, however, represent the point of view expressed in *Rabbit, Run* by the old filling station attendant: they have carefully looked at the map of reality, planned where they wanted to go, and they have reached their destination. Although Harry still prefers the instinctual, ego-centered approach, he acknowledges the relationship between his own world and that of cosmic outer space when he tells Nelson that it is time to leave Mom's birthday party with these words: "We better rendezvous with our spacecraft" (99).

Significant as the moon shot is in bringing Harry to the realization that he lives in a world governed by cosmic laws, other events closer to home have greater personal impact on him. His argument with Charlie Stavros about America's involvement in Vietnam forces him to recognize a world of international involvements about which many people have "feelings" quite different from his own, and the racial violence in York, Pennsylvania, confronts him with flaws in the America he has so strongly defended. But it is the entry into his life and home of Jill and Skeeter that most dramatically brings Harry in contact with an "other" side of reality.

Jill introduces him to a type of thinking totally foreign to his previous experience. With her he begins to venture out on a side of life suggested by the epigraph for Chapter II: "It's different but it's very pretty out here." The words are Neil Armstrong's but they reflect Harry's own reaction to Jill. He is fascinated, for instance, by her description of matter as "the mirror of the spirit. . . . Inside it are these tiny *other* mirrors tilted this way and that and throwing the light back the wrong way. Because to the big face looking in, these little mirrors are just dark spots, where He can't see Himself" (159). Even so, Harry has difficulty accepting all that Jill says. He tells her that she's always had things too easy, has had things handed to her, doesn't know about fear. "Fear," he says. "That's what makes us poor bastards run. You

don't know what fear is, do you, poor baby? That's why
you're so dead." Jill responds in true flower-child fashion:
"People've run on fear long enough. Let's try love for a
change." Unimpressed, Harry sticks to the party line that he
has felt is right: "Then you better find yourself another
universe" (170).

It is Skeeter who finally forces Harry all the way out onto another side beyond his own ego. Skeeter initiates
readings from and discussions of black history, gets Harry to
smoke marijuana, and finally proclaims: "I am the Christ of
the Dark Age. Or if not me, then someone exactly like me,
whom later ages will suppose to have been me. Do you
believe?" As "Rabbit drags on his own joint, and feels his
world expand to admit new truths as a woman spreads her
legs, as a flower unfolds, as the stars flee one another," he
responds, "I do believe" (243).

Despite this confession of faith, Rabbit's world has not
expanded and changed quite so much as the thinks at the moment. We have already seen that after the fire, Jill's death,
and Skeeter's departure, Rabbit is still very much the same
self he was before. He cannot be substantively cut apart from
his original personhood, but he has at least experienced a
cosmos—things, nations, and persons—of which he himself is
not the midpoint.

Interlocking Bands

The one-sidedness of the Möbius strip coupled with its
paradoxical two-sidedness when cut in half suggests the
bipolar dualism of self and world affirmed in *Midpoint*.
The final characteristic of the strip—the interlocking bands,
one one-sided and the other two-sided—suggests the paradox
ical and ultimately mysterious interpenetration of these two

realms of reality. On the one hand, there is the twisted, one-sided band representing the continuity of the central ego. It has been partially molded by Pop, Mom, Janice, and Nelson, and it cannot be separated from its origins no matter how sharply the scissors of external circumstances may cut. The self that knew the validity of inner reality does not renounce commitment to its own feelings. Yet that twisted, one-sided, solipsistic world is now interlocked with, inseparably bound to, the reality of the outer world. Rabbit's recognition of the truth of that interlocking nature of these worlds justifies the title of the novel. Literally, *redux* means "led back"; figuratively, it means "cured." By venturing forth into new worlds, Rabbit learns something, is "led back" to a more viable position, and is "cured" of the solipsism of *Rabbit, Run.*

Rabbit tells Mim in Chapter IV that he "has learned some things" (358). Updike agrees. He says that Rabbit shows the peculiarly American quality of openness in his willingness to "entertain these outlanders in his house" and affirms, "I do think he's learned something" ("Interview" 285). For example, in Chapter IV Rabbit asks his mother, "Where do you think I went wrong?" In the halting speech caused by Parkinson's Disease, Mom responds, "Who says. You did?" Rabbit points out that he has no house, no job, no wife, that his kid hates him, and his sister says he's ridiculous. His mother sees his confession as a sign he's growing up. When Rabbit tells her that Mim has said he never learned any rules, she says, "You haven't had to." Rabbit exclaims that if this were "any decent kind of world, you wouldn't need all these rules" (373).

Even though he still wishes for a world in which what he feels inside himself is all that matters, his very admission that he has gone wrong somewhere supports his mother's observation that he may be growing up, that he may at last find himself learning some rules. He is beginning to acknowledge the verity that time and environment do not exist for him alone; that admission marks a giant step toward potential maturity. As Rabbit looks out of his mother's bedroom window, he thinks how these familiar sights had once "excited him with the magic of his own existence. These mundane surfaces had given witness to his life; this chalice had held his blood; here the universe had centered, each downtwirling maple seed of more account than galaxies" (373). He realizes now that Jackson Road is an ordinary street anywhere. "Millions of such American streets hold millions of lives, and let them sift through, neither notice nor mourn. . ." (373). Rabbit realizes that no more can this site seem to him the center of a universe. If the maple trees remain, they cannot hold back his mother's moment of death. If the trees are cut down, her long years of looking at them will not save them. "Time," he thinks, "is our element, not a mistaken invader. How stupid, it has taken him thirty-six years to begin to believe that" (374).

Shortly after Mim leaves to return west, Rabbit, sleeping in his childhood bed, feels Jill's presence. When he turns his head to kiss her, she is gone, but her presence has wakened him and "through this rip in her death a thousand details are loosed" (380). He does not want to remember those details: "He had retreated into deadness and did not wish her to call him out. He was not ready, he had been hurt. Let black Jesus have her, he had been converted to hardness of heart" (380). But he does remember. His heart is no longer quite so hard. He wakes and cries; "grief rises in him out of a parched stomach, a sore throat, singed eyes; remembering her daughterly blind grass-green looking to him for more than shelter he blinds himself, leaves stains on the linen that need not be wiped, they will be invisible in the morning" (381). Symbolically he blinds himself through his tears so that he may really see; the stains will be invisible in the morning, but they will remain in his heart. He has learned to accept a depth of genuine grief that cannot be escaped by a retreat into deadness and that will not allow true hardness of heart.

Rabbit's learning to perceive and accept an environment of complex reality beyond himself and to feel grief for the fate of others is demonstrated by his confession to Janice in the concluding paragraphs of the book. "I feel so guilty," he says. When she asks about what, he replies, "About everything." Although she tells him, "Relax. Not everything is your fault," he says, "I can't accept that" (406). Such a confession of guilt would not be surprising or particularly revelatory coming from almost any of the other characters, but Rabbit throughout two books has steadfastly refused to accept any guilt or responsibility for anything that has happened. His confession then stands in direct contrast to his "Don't look at me . . . . *I* didn't do it" just before he runs from the funeral at the end of *Rabbit, Run,* and indicates that Rabbit has been led back to a place where he may start a life in which claims of the outside world may interact with the imperatives of his inner reality.

The need for recognizing the interlocking of the realms of subjective ego and objective world is reinforced by Rabbit's continuing quest for inner meaning being set against the exploration of outer space. According to Updike:

> Rabbit's adventures in this book are a kind of launching free of the very terrestrial world of Pop and Mom and Janice to a kind of no man'a land. In some way I felt the little ranch house to be a space capsule spinning in a kind of way, and the reunion with Janice—even their bodily jockeyings were meant to be a kind of jockeying in space, like these linkups. . . the whole thing, the whole fantasy of the book—and the book is a touch fantastic—is related to the true fantasy of our space invasion. ("Interview" 282).

The epigraphs, recorded words of astronauts and cosmonauts, were chosen to reinforce the sense of cosmic and personal interlocking. Updike found that the space men's words indicated that after all they were

> very much just men. . . . Even though they're way out there. The things they said were so mundane. . . . I especially love Armstrong saying that it's kind of different out here but pretty. This seemed to me much more a natural remark than the first words he had prepared—much less stilted. ("Interview" 282)

Neil Armstrong and Vladimir Shatalov, though one is American and the other Russian, have the same needs, feelings, and problems that Harry Angstrom does. Shatalov's words following the successful link-up in space become the epigraph for Chapter I: "It took me quite a while to find you, but now I've got you." These words express not only a cosmonaut's feelings about his space mission, but also Rabbit's feelings about Pop, Mom, Janice, and Nelson—and himself and his ongoing quest—and thus offer the appropriate title for this chapter.

The final paragraph of the book predictably utilizes the imagery of space flight and at the same time applies it to the sense of inner reality: "He lets her breasts go, radiant debris. The space they are in, the motel room long and secret as a burrow, becomes all interior space" (406). Rabbit's hand finds the familiar curve of Janice's waist, "fat's inward curve. . . . He finds this inward curve and slips along it, sleeps" (406). As the cosmonauts found the right outward curve and slipped into the linkage of the two space ships, Rabbit finds the inward curve and slips into a peaceful sleep next to his wife.

The two-sided external world still exists in this linkage, for there is "He" and there is "She"—two discrete selves, of opposite sexes. But they are at this moment united in sleep.

The final word of the novel is a question: "O.K.?" and it recalls the words of astronaut Armstrong used as epigraph for this last chapter. After following Buzz Aldrin's instructions for leaving the space craft to step onto the lunar surface, Armstrong said: "O.K., Houston, I'm on the porch." Everything about the moonshot was perfect. Outer space has been successfully conquered by man and his machines. Can inner space be similarly conquered and succesfully related to that outer world? Updike offers no clear answer, and has insisted that "the question that ends the book is not meant to have an easy answer" ("Special Message—*Rabbit Redux*," 859). But Rabbit and Janice, in their small personal world, do seem to be, like Neil Armstrong, O.K. and on the porch. Since one of the meanings of *redux* is "cured," Updike seems at least to suggest that the steps Rabbit takes off that porch will be in the right direction.

The zigzag structure of *Rabbit, Run* gave full recognition to the conflicting claims of central ego and wider world, but it did not enable Rabbit to resolve his conflict. In *Rabbit Redux* Harry—and the reader—is led to accept the fact that reality, like the Möbius strip, is both one-sided and two-sided. The one-sided world in which the ego is its own midpoint is inevitably and inextricably intertwined with the two-sided objective phenomenal world. Rabbit's recognition of that doubleness of reality has led him back and opened the way for another sequel in which Updike shows even more conclusively that Rabbit has "learned something" ("Interview" 285).

RABBIT IS RICH

Rabbit Is Rich (1981), which won for Updike both the Pulitzer Prize and the National Book Award, is set in the summer and fall of 1979 and the first few days of the new decade of 1980. These were the last months of the Carter administration, times of long lines at gasoline pumps, high inflation rates, and the stalemate over the hostages in Iran. Harry Angstrom has been the manager of the Toyota agency in Brewer since his father-in-law, Fred Springer, died in 1974, leaving half the business to his wife and the other half to Janice and Harry. Harry and Janice have been living in the Springer house since their own house burned in 1969. Their son Nelson has been studying at Kent State University but, as the book opens, is in Colorado for the summer.

"Running out of gas," Rabbit thinks as he stands in the showroom of Springer Motors watching the sparse traffic on the last Saturday in June (1). James Wolcott finds this opening phrase of the book the key to its dominant imagery and theme. He finds the novel "dramatically static," its basic message being that "everything is running down." "The force of entropy," he says, "bends all the action to a futile droop" (20, 22). Wolcott has correctly pinpointed one of Updike's important themes. Recurrent images reinforce the notion that Rabbit is running out of gas as he nears the end of his fourth decade and that America is running out of gas as she enters her third century.

Rabbit notes, for instance, that producing gas pump shrouds has become a new industry (20). Everywhere he looks in Brewer, "once the fourth largest city in Pennsylvania but now slipped to seventh, structures seem to speak of expended energy" (32). There are "great shapely stacks that have not issued smoke for half a century" and "scrolling cast-iron light stanchions not lit since World War II" (32). On a personal level, Rabbit finds that his desires and wants have shriveled. "Freedom, that he always thought was outward motion, turns out to be this inward dwindling" (97). When discussing the decline of American industry with his son, Nelson, Harry insists that "We used to be the best," but Nelson only responds, "So I'm told" (20). Harry feels that "his own life has closed in to a size his soul had not yet [quite] shrunk to fit" (285). Thinking of his father, Nelson observes that Rabbit once "had this crazy dim faith about himself left over from basketball or growing up as everybody's pet or whatever," but now "that spark is gone, leaving a big dead man on Nelson's chest" (314). When a friend asks Harry if he has seen *Jaws II,* he responds in a way that allows Updike to turn the entropy imagery into a clever barb aimed at himself: "D'you ever get the feeling that everything these days is sequels? . . . Like people are running out of ideas" (403).

These images, merely a sampling of many which could be cited, indicate that the running-out-of-gas imagery figures importantly, especially in the first three of the book's five sections. Wolcott, however, has seen only one side of Updike's usual "yes—but" technique. In September of 1981, as a companion piece to the *New York Times Book Review*'s review of *Rabbit Is Rich,* Updike imagined himself being interviewed by his own fictional creation, Henry Bech, writer-hero of two Updike short story collections. In this "interview," Updike says he has recently been re-reading Herman Melville. "A wonderful man he was," he says, "refusing all his life to call the puzzle solved." And he quotes a Melville poem: "Yea and Nay—/ Each hath his say;/ But God He keeps the middle way" (875). Updike has also always kept the middle way, adroitly resisting since *Midpoint* "the flawless formula, the Five-Year Plan," or any bandwagon *(Midpoint* 42).

Rabbit, Run was "a deliberate attempt to present both the escapist, have-it-my-way will to live versus the social restraints" ("Interview" 295). *Rabbit Redux* showed Harry venturing out into new worlds yet still inextricably rooted in the same self, and ended with a question rather than an answer. *Rabbit Is Rich* also follows the *Midpoint* pattern of dualism and polarity. Updike presents a sociological analysis of the pervading presence of entropy in Rabbit's personal life and that of his culture in such loving and intimate detail that a shock of recognition forces us to say, "Yes, he's right; things are running down; time is running out." But there is another side to be examined. In the "interview" with Bech, Updike confessed that the aim of his fiction was

> bringing the corners forward, or throwing light into them. . . . Singing the hitherto unsung. That's applied Christianity for that matter. I distrust books involving spectacular people, or spectacular events. Let *People* and *The National Enquirer* pander to our taste for the extraordinary; let literature concern itself, as the Gospels do, with the inner lives of hidden men. The collective consciousness that once found itself in the noble must now rest content with the typical. . . . I don't want to write gushers. I want to write books that are hard and curvy like keys, and that unlock the traffic jam in everybody's head. Something like $E = mc^2$, only in words, one after the other. (873-874)

Clearly Updike did not intend *Rabbit Is Rich* to be "swollen with forlorn rue" (Wolcott 20), but to be an attempt to find an equation to unlock the unquestioning acceptance of degeneration and decay which the Second Law of Thermodynamics seems to predict. As we have seen, the central section of *Midpoint* is a brilliant analysis of some of the insights into reality offered by modern physics. One of those insights that fascinated Updike in *Midpoint* was Max Planck's $E = h\nu$ equation, a formulation which defines the relationship of energy and frequency. The equation does not deny that light is made up of particles as Newton's experiments indicated, but asserts that light also must be understood as waves. Although the many implications of wave theory and wave mechanics were clear enough to Updike to allow him to versify his understanding in Spenserian stanzas published in *Scientific American* as well as at the midpoint of *Midpoint,* I cannot claim such expertise. Physicists Ernest C. Pollard and Douglas C. Huston suggest, however, that the "sensational" successes of the applications of wave theory are "almost mystical" (313). And these "almost mystical" successes offer Updike a way of saying "yes" to entropy while adding his customary "but," examining another side of the puzzle. Physics says, "Yes, light is made up of particles," and then adds, "but it also consists of waves." Quantum theory affirms that absorption of energy is continuous, but counters that emission proceeds discontinuously in quanta of energy which depend on the frequency of the oscillation of electrons. Just so, Updike sees a regenerative force which contradicts and counteracts entropy.

"LIGHT ON YOUR FUR"

A look at the epigraphs Updike has chosen for *Rabbit Is Rich* gives the first clue to the "yes—but" equation the book offers. The first and most easily interpreted of these epigraphs is from Sinclair Lewis's *Babbitt*: "At night he lights up a good cigar, and climbs into the little old 'bus, and maybe cusses the carburetor, and shoots out home. He mows the lawn, or sneaks in some practice putting, and then he's ready for dinner." This quotation suggests the shallow, crass, and empty materialism of American middle-class success satirized by Lewis. Babbittry has become synonymous with Mencken's scathing term "booboisie," and it takes the shift of only one consonant to turn Rabbit into Babbitt. The implication is that whatever dreams and hopes made Rabbit run in his earlier years, whatever motives gave his story some semblance of a significant quest, he has now succumbed to the entropy of middle age and middle America.

Yes—but. The other epigraph is three lines from Wallace Stevens's poem "A Rabbit as King of the Ghosts": "The difficulty to think at the end of the day,/ When the shapeless shadow covers the sun/ And nothing is left except light on your fur. . ." At first these lines seem to support the running-on-empty suggestions of the Babbitt epigraph. If Rabbit is a king of ghosts, his kingdom is made up of those who are dead and gone, who have no power in the modern materialistic world. Furthermore, if it is difficult "to think," if a "shape-less shadow covers the sun," and "nothing is left," surely there is not much to do except to mourn the loss of vitality and hope. Yes—but. Just as the Babbitt epigraph suggests the whole context of Lewis's novel, this epigraph must be seen in light of Stevens's complete poem:

> The difficulty to think at the end of day,
> When the shapeless shadow covers the sun
> And nothing is left except light on your fur—
>
> There was the cat slopping its milk all day,
> Fat cat, red tongue, green mind, white milk
> And August the most peaceful month.
>
> To be, in the grass, in the peacefullest time,
> Without monument of cat,
> The cat forgotten in the moon;
>
> And to feel the light is a rabbit-light,
> In which everything is meant for you
> And nothing need be explained;
>
> Then there is nothing to think of. It comes of itself;
> And east rushes west and west rushes down,
> No matter. The grass is full
>
> And full of yourself. The trees around you are for you,
> The whole of the wideness of night is for you,
> A self that touches all edges.
>
> You become a self that fills the four corners of night.
> The red cat hides away in the fur-light
> And there you are humped high, humped up,
>
> You are humped higher and higher, black as stone—
> You sit with your head like a carving in space
> And the little green cat is a bug in the grass.

As Robert Pack has pointed out, in Stevens's work, "reality, based on the most rigid discipline of accurate perception, is changed by the imagination into a fuller reality" (69-70). In this poem the rabbit represents the power of the imagination. The light of the sun, representing objective perception, is gone, but there is still "light on your fur," "a rabbit-light," the moonlight, the power of imagination. The cat, the rabbit's natural and fearful enemy, shrinks from a "monument of cat" to become "a bug in the grass." The rabbit becomes the center of his world just as all men are, when thinking of themselves, the centers (midpoints) of their own universes. Through a quantum jump, the imagination emits new energy on a different frequency that transforms the insignificant rabbit into a self that "touches all edges." "King of the Ghosts" now seems to suggest not an impotent realm of the dead but a realm in which spirit may transcend objectively perceivable reality. By the light of tomorrow's sun the cat will still be "slopping its milk," but reality is more complex than the "fat cat, red tongue, green mind," and "white milk" imply.

So despite the darkness and emptiness promised by the continuing expending of energy, there is a counter force represented by the "light on your fur," an interrelationship of the poles of individual self and objective world that offers regeneration in spite of a continuing energy shortage. Counterpointing the rational and sociologically precise entropy imagery of growing darkness, there is a contrasting pattern emphasizing the pervasive and prevailing importance of a life force that emits regenerative power that must be seen by a different light, the "rabbit-light" on one's fur, the light of mystery and faith. These images, present rather sparingly in the first sections of the book, become more and more important until they dominate the metaphorical texture of the final section, which is "a hard and curvy key" to "unlock the traffic jam" ("Updike on Updike" 874) of the downward lock-step of entropy.

Although Rabbit opens the book by raising the possibility that the "world is running out of gas" (3), he also offers the first challenge to accepting such an outcome as inevitable. "They won't catch him," he thinks, because his Toyotas get excellent gas mileage and give lower service costs (3). When a young farm boy comes in to look at cars, bringing with him a girl of about nineteen, Rabbit wonders if the girl could possibly be his daughter, the result of his liaison with Ruth Leonard twenty years ago during the time he tried to run away from Janice. The girl looks enough like Ruth and himself for him to imagine her to be the child that Ruth was carrying when he left her to return to Janice. Excited by the possibility, Rabbit finds it "wonderful to think" of "a secret message carried by genes all that way through all these comings and goings all these years, the bloody tunnel of growing and living, of staying alive" (34). Though the world may be running out of gas, Rabbit has not given in. His cars will buck the trend, and the secret messages carried by genes will continue the life process.

Echoing the *Midpoint* assertion that "The Judgment Day seems nigh to every age;/ But History blinks, and turns another page," Rabbit reflects that although "the world keeps ending. . . new people too dumb to know it keep showing up as if the fun's just started" (88). He may echo fashionable ideas of decay and loss of energy, but fundamentally he affirms the continuation of human vitality. And when Nelson returns home from Colorado, he brings with him a young woman named Melanie, who says, "I believe the things we're running out of we can learn to do without. . . . as long as there are growing things, there's still a world with endless possibilities" (97-98).

In Part II Rabbit pursues the chance that the young farm girl might be his daughter far enough to locate the rural home near Galilee where Ruth (now a widow) lives. He does not have the courage to actually face Ruth, but as he watches her house from near the road, he crowds against a tree and is struck with "the miracle of it: how things grow, always remembering to be themselves" (113). Later he comments, "What a threadbare thing we make of life! Yet what a marvellous thing the mind is, they can't make a machine like it, . . . and the body can do a thousand things there isn't a factory in the world can duplicate the motion" (139). And he thinks, "Funny about feelings, they seem to come and go in a flash yet outlast metal" (163).

These scattered images of a "rabbit-light" prepare the way for the first really significant image suggesting a counter-force to entropy. Nelson has come home from Colorado because his girl, Teresa (Pru), is pregnant, and he must get a job and prepare to accept responsibility for her. The other young woman, Melanie, had come just to look out for Pru's interest and be sure that Nelson did not run away as his father once did. She works as a waitress all summer, but leaves to return to Kent State at summer's end. But on the Sunday before Labor Day, Pru arrives, and Rabbit finds out that he is to become a grandfather. The news of this impending new life immediately makes Harry feel that all the souvenirs of the dead and the signs of dying life around him now "bristle with new point, with fresh mission" (184). From this point on, the regenerative counter-images become more frequent and more significant.

In Part III a cluster of images suggests that entropy is not the reigning force. Rabbit finds himself scanning the "new up-close photos of Jupiter, expecting to spot a clue all those scientists have missed: God might have a few words to say yet" (271). He complains to Charlie Stavros, his Senior

Sales Representative with whom Janice had her affair ten years earlier, that he wishes he had some of Charlie's freedom, but Charlie tells him, "You've got freedom you don't even use" (272). The next day Rabbit finds that the disco music on the car stereo sets "that hopeful center inside his ribs to jingling" (274), and he laughs at his Rotarian Babbittlike friends. "The thing about these Rotarians," Rabbit thinks:

> if you knew them as kids you can't stop seeing the kid in them, dressed up in fat and baldness and money like a cardboard tuxedo in a play for high-school assembly. How can you respect the world when you see it's being run by a bunch of kids turned old? That's the joke Rabbit always enjoys at Rotary. (275)

It is Part V, the concluding section of the novel, however, in which the regenerative images are dominant. His granddaughter has been born, and Rabbit and Janice have just moved into a house of their own after having lived with Janice's mother for twelve years. It is January, the beginning of a new year and the new decade of the eighties. Furthermore, it is Super Sunday, the day of the Super Bowl football game. Rabbit feels that the emptiness of his furniture-less new house is a "species of new possibility" (431) which excites and pleases him. In this new house one has to step down into the den. Harry thinks that in this room he "might begin to read books, instead of just magazines and newspapers, begin to learn about history, say." The "small difference in plane hints to him of many reforms and consolidations now possible in his life, like new shoots on a tree cropped back" (453). Although he is aware that he has no habits to cushion him in this new house, his life seeming to stretch emptily on all sides, and "that moving in any direction he's bound to take a fall" (456), he nevertheless feels that on this Super Sunday he is "king of the castle" (446). He feels that "maybe God is in the universe the way salt is in the ocean, giving it taste" (462). He also notes that even at this dead point of winter the days have already "begun lengthening against the grain," and that "the planets keep their courses no matter what we do" (463).

But it is the new granddaughter whose presence in the last paragraph of the book provides a concluding moment which manages to include the inescapable truth of the Second Law of Thermodynamics while challenging it with a quantum jump of new energy:

> Teresa comes softly down the one step into his den and deposits into his lap what he has been waiting for. Oblong, cocooned little visitor, the baby shows her profile blindly in the shuddering flashes of color jerking from the Sony, the tiny stitchless seam of the closed eyelid aslant, lips bubbled forward beneath the whorled nose as if in delicate disdain, she knows she's good. . . . Through all this she has pushed to be here, in his lap, his hands, a real presence hardly weighing anything but still alive. Fortune's hostage, heart's desire, a granddaughter. His. Another nail in his coffin. His. (467)

Rabbit's daughter-in-law steps down into the new plane which suggests reforms, consolidations, and new shoots and gives him what he has been waiting for—a sign that as the days lengthen against the grain, so does life; human individuality, uniqueness, keep coming. A visitor, not unlike Wordsworth's child trailing clouds of glory, the baby brings a new spirit into a world using up its energy prodigally, a world which is illuminated by shuddering flashes from Japanese rather than American technology. The stitchless seam of her eyelids, the bubbling of her lips, and her whorled nose defy and transcend all technologies, whether American or Japanese. Although she weighs little and has no force or energy to be measured in material terms, she knows she's good, has somehow pushed to be here—a real presence. These two words recall Martin Luther's insistence that when Jesus said "This is my body," he meant what he said. Although Luther could not believe the Catholic doctrine of transubstantiation which asserts that the elements of the Eucharist are literally changed into the body and blood of Christ, neither would he accept the Calvinist-Reformed position that the sacrament is merely a memorial. He offered instead his own doctrine of consubstantiation, insisting on Christ's "real presence," a presence which does not change the actual substance of the bread and wine, but adds to those material elements, is there along with them.

I think it is not stretching interpretation too far to stress the Lutheran implications here because Updike confessed to me in 1976 that "Christianity is the only world-frame I've been exposed to that I can actually look through," and that his Lutheran upbringing molded him in important ways. "In the county I was from," he said:

> the Lutheran and Reformed churches existed on the same block, but they were distinctly different churches. The Calvinist church just gives off a different vibe. I do think that in some way the personalities and fundamental emphases of the two great founders show through still. Lutheranism is comparatively world-accepting; it's a little closer to Catholicism than Calvinism. I don't feel much affinity with the New England Puritan ethos insofar as it still persists. No, I would call myself a Lutheran by upbringing, and my work contains some of the ambiguities of the Lutheran position, which would have a certain radical otherworldly emphasis and yet an odd retention of a . . . rather rich ambivalence toward the world. ("Interview" 291)

The final passage of *Rabbit Is Rich* echoes this Lutheran paradox of "a certain radical otherworldly emphasis" while maintaining its "rather rich ambivalence toward the world." The new baby is what Rabbit has been waiting for. As Updike said in his "interview" with Henry Bech, "Ever since his baby girl drowned in *Rabbit, Run,* Harry has been looking for a daughter. It's the theme that has been pressing forward, without my willing it or understanding it exactly, through these novels" (871). So this new baby is the daughter he has wanted, his heart's desire, a hostage to fortune—and she is his; she can belong to no one else in quite the same way.

Her presence does not change the outward reality of the empty house where he is bound to take a fall, nor does she reverse the aging process—she is another nail in his coffin, another sign of his moving closer to his own eventual death. Rabbit is running down. All things run down. But there is still the rabbit-light on one's fur that affirms the real presence of an audacious, unique human personality looking out from its own midpoint. Or as Updike told me more succinctly: "Entropy may triumph in the eventual heat-death of the universe, but not in human lives" ("Response").

WHAT RABBIT HAS LEARNED

Rabbit himself would certainly not be likely to understand and interpret the meaning of his experiences in terms of equations involving wave theory, quantum jumps, and uniquely human forces countervailing the heat-death of the universe. As Roger Sale has suggested, Rabbit "can never be described as large-minded." That, however, has not prevented "Updike from imagining him largely" (32), and Updike himself has said that "authors. . . create characters to dramatize issues and tensions" ("Response"), not to speak their own philosophies directly. Furthermore, Updike does see Rabbit as characterized by a "great willingness to learn." "He, like me," Updike says, "has been taught a lot not only by individual instructors, but by the times" (qtd. in Kakutani 15). And in 1976, Updike told me that he felt that Rabbit had learned something through the first two installments of his saga, and that he "would like to write a sequel showing that he did learn something" ("Interview" 285). What, then, has Rabbit learned in *Rabbit Is Rich*? How does the middle-aged Harry compare to his earlier manifestations?

He still thinks of himself as the "star and spearpoint" (4), no longer on the basketball court, but in the Toyota agency. He is the "front man" for the twenty-four employees of the agency, and he even has his old basketball clippings framed and on display to reinforce his sense of stardom. However, he "avoids mirrors, when he used to love them," for he weighs 210 pounds, has a forty-two inch waist and "a chaos of wattles and slack cords. . . beneath his chin" (6). More significantly, he finds his inner life less rich than in previous decades: he "dodges among more blanks than there used to be, patches of burnt-out gray cells where there used to be lust and keen dreaming and wide-eyed dread" (13). Although intensity may have diminished, his inner life maintains some of the same longings and fears he has always had. As he drives home with Janice from a party at the home of Webb Murkett, one of his prosperous and fashionable new friends, "he feels a scared swift love for something that has no name" (71). He is not sure whether it is love for Janice, his own life, or the world, but as he sees the spire of the Lutheran church where he went to Sunday School, he remembers the stern old preacher Fritz Kruppenbach, "who pounded in the lesson that life has no terrors for those with faith, but for those without faith there can be no salvation and no peace. *No* peace" (71). He is still the same Rabbit who ran in zigzags but could not escape the net of social involvement, the same Rabbit who was open enough to venture out on the other side of reality with Jill and Skeeter, but he is much more at peace now and considers himself happy for the first time in his life. "He sees his life as just beginning, on clear ground at last, now that he has a margin of resources, and the stifled terror that always made him restless has dulled down" (97).

He has outgrown the giant solipsism that was the chief source of his hardness of heart in *Rabbit, Run* and which kept him basically passive in *Rabbit Redux*. He now comes to realize that the "houses and porches and trees . . . in Mt. Judge fed the illusions of . . . little boys that their souls were central and dramatic and invisibly cherished" (136). Like the poet in *Midpoint,* he comes to recognize the reality of a world beyond his own ego and surrenders the illusion that he alone is central. He "feels love for each phenomenon and . . . seeks to bring himself into harmony with the intertwining simplicities that uphold him, that were woven into him at birth" (138). He recognizes that there were circumstances that were given him, not chosen by him, at birth, and he tries to reconcile himself with the givenness of external reality. Furthermore, he acknowledges that "at about the age of forty he came out of that adolescent who-am-I vanity trip" (377).

Rabbit is still a runner, but now his is not a zigzag effort to escape the nets of responsibility. In fact, he now runs purposefully, "as a way of getting his body back from those sodden years he never thought about it, just ate and did what he wanted" (224). As he runs, he thinks. He remembers Janice asking him "why is his heart so hard toward Nelson" (226), and we are reminded of the hardness of heart suggested in the epigraph of *Rabbit, Run.* He runs along the gutter "where the water from the ice plant used to run" (226), and we are reminded that the poet in *Midpoint* cited the "golden water from Flickinger's ice plant" (6) as one of the wonders of Philadelphia Avenue that first made him aware of the objective existence of a world of phenomena outside himself. Rabbit, however, is reminded of the "edge of green slime" that rimmed the water, and thinks: "life tries to get a grip anywhere, on earth that is, not on the moon" (226).

Rabbit remembers falling into that ice-plant water as a child and having to run home to change out of his wet knickers. "He hated being late for school," he remembers, also recalling that he has had a life-long fear of being late drummed into him by his mother. Now he realizes that "he no longer ever feels he is late for somewhere, a strange sort of peace at his time of life like a thrown ball at the top of its arc for a second still" (227). The release from fear and the sense of a sort of peace are among the most important differences between the young Rabbit and the middle-aged one. The second of stillness at the top of the arc of a thrown ball also provides the best metaphor to represent the structural principle of the book. As we noted in Chapter II, Updike has said that he usually begins a book with some image of a visual shape in mind, "some sense of its 'seizability'." But he said in 1976, "I think I'm maybe running out of shapes!" and that he doubted that he had a specific shape in mind for *Rabbit Redux* ("Interview" 284). Although a definite shape such as the Z that dictated *Rabbit, Run* or the Y that characterized *The Poorhouse Fair* or the X of *Of the Farm* is missing from *Rabbit Is Rich,* the image of the thrown ball pausing momentarily at the top of its arc does provide a visual metaphor for the novel's structure. The book is not static as James Wolcott avers (22), nor is it characterized by "a willful circularity" as Michiko Kakutani suggests (14). There is definite movement and growth, as our continuing discussion of what Rabbit has learned will show, but there is also a sense of momentary rest in the book and in Rabbit's life. Middle age is a plateau between the anxieties and upward struggles of youth and young manhood and the inevitable decline of old age. The arc is there, just as the hill of life was there in the early drawings of the poet in *Midpoint* (10), and the inexorable movement will continue. But at this particular period in his life, Rabbit feels at rest.

This sense of peace, however, does not mean that Rabbit has lost all of his sense of life as a quest. As he continues his run, he thinks, "Middle age is a wonderful country, all the things you thought would never happen are happening." He also reflects that "if a meaning of life was to show up you'd think it would have by now" (231), but then adds, "At moments it seems it has, there are just no words for it, it is not something you dig for but sits on the top of the table like an unopened dewy beer can" (231). Harry seems closer now to the poet who wrote in *Midpoint:* "let us live as islanders/ Who pluck what fruit the lowered branch proffers./ Each passing moment masks a tender face;/ Nothing has had to be, but is by Grace" (40). Like Updike himself, who said in 1976 that he had, with the help of Karl Barth, conquered "this sort of existential terror" and now "as a middle-aged person" found himself "somehow . . . permanently reassured. . . and able to open to the world again" ("Interview" 302), Rabbit is more relaxed and open to the world beyond his own ego; but he also has not lost all sense of "something out there" that wants him to find it. Harry reflects:

> When [he] was little God used to spread in the dark above his bed . . . and then when the bed became strange and the girl in the next aisle grew armpit hair He entered into the blood and muscle and nerve as an odd command and now He had withdrawn, giving Harry the respect due from one well-off gentleman to another, but for a calling-card left in the pit of the stomach, a bit of lead true as a plumb bob pulling Harry down toward all those leaden dead in the hollow earth below. (231).

This recognition and acceptance of the pull toward death is one of the most significant things that Harry has learned. "Each day he is a little less afraid to die" (47), and he feels that the dead have left room for him. As he runs, "he is treading on them all, they are resilient, they are cheering him on, . . . he is a membrane removed from the hosts below, their filaments caress his ankles, he loves the earth. . . ." (141-142). He identifies more specifically with the dead as he looks in a mirror and gazes into his own eyes:

> Oh but blue still the spaces in his eyes, encircling the little black dot through which the world flows, a blue with white and gray mixed in from the frost of his ancestors, those beefy blonds in horned helmets pounding to a pulp with clubs the hairy mammoth and the slant-eyed Finns amid snows so pure and widespread their whiteness would have made eyes less pale hurt. Eyes and hair and

skin, the dead live in us though their brains are black and their eyesockets of bone empty. (303).

Harry is newly aware of his place in the continuity of life. Earlier he had noticed "his own father talking in his own brain sometimes" (46), and although he cannot really understand or reach out meaningfully to Nelson, he does recognize himself in his son. "You're too much me," he tells him (208). He recognizes his part in creating difficulties for Nelson as he was growing up, and when Janice seeks to reassure him by saying "We did what we could. . . . We're not God," Harry acknowledges, "Nobody is" (312). Although he scares himself with this statement, he has made a real step in acknowledging the limitations of his own ego and his place in a chain of humanity.

Although his solipsism is greatly chastened, he has not lost his faith in the centrality of the individual. When thinking of his blue-eyed ancestors, he had noted that the eye is "the little black dot through which the world flows," echoing the *Midpoint* affirmation of the eye/I pun, acknowledging each individual's eye as the midpoint of his/her own hemisphere. And when he and Janice join the Murketts and the Harrisons (Ronnie Harrison is the old high school teammate whose relationship with Ruth Rabbit had so resented twenty years earlier, but now they are regular golf partners at the Flying Eagle Club) for a mid-January Caribbean vacation and the wives decide to swap husbands, we find Harry reaffirming both his belief in himself and his dedication to the importance of sex as an expression of individuality. Thelma Harrison suggests that the husband-swapping reflects "simple female curiosity . . . about the penises, what they look like" (408). Harry says, "They're ugly as hell. Most of the pricks I've seen are." But Janice responds, "And yet he loves his own." Harry protests, "I don't love it. . . . I'm stuck with it." But Cindy Murkett quietly says, "It's you" (408-409). In *Midpoint* Updike had affirmed that sex was a "knowing" and that "knowing" = "seeing," and concluded, therefore, that penises are eyes (28). That Harry's penis is closely associated with both his eye and his "I" is demonstrated by the results of his night with Thelma Harrison.

Harry has been lusting after Cindy Murkett all through the early parts of the novel, and he is deeply disappointed that it is Thelma who takes him to her bed rather than Cindy. But he finds in Thelma more than he expected. Thelma confesses that she has been attracted to him for years. Since she is in the middle of her period, she suggests that she and Harry engage in anal intercourse. Harry finds the sensation "a void, a pure black box, a casket of perfect nothingness. He is in that void" as he experiences orgasm (417). He tells Thelma that he feels embarrassed, but she says she feels full of him and explains what it is about him that has "turned her on":

> The way you never sit down anywhere without making sure there's a way out. . . . Your good humor. You *believe* in people so—. . . Janice, you're so proud of her it's pathetic. It's not as if she can *do* anything. . . . You're so grateful to be anywhere, you think that tacky club and had hideous house of Cindy's are heaven. You're so glad to be alive. . . . It kills me. I love you *so much* for it. And your hands. I've always loved your hands. . . . And now your prick, with its little bonnet. . . . (418)

Harry can't quit thinking of the "void, inside her. . . that nothingness seen by his single eye" (418-419). The old sense of "something that wanted him to find it" is revived by the physical proof of love Thelma has offered him, and

> he trusts himself to her as if speaking in prayer, talks to her about himself as he has talked to none other: about Nelson and the grudge he bears the kid and the grudge the boy bears him, and about his daughter, the daughter he thinks he has, grown and ignorant of him. . . . [and about] his sense of miracle at being himself, himself instead of somebody else, and his old inkling,

now fading in the energy crunch, that there was something that wanted him to find it, that he was here on earth on a kind of assignment. (419)

Harry has confirmed and reaffirmed his own individuality by coming to know Thelma through the eye/I of his penis, affirming his unique selfhood through experiencing the otherness and oppositeness of Thelma, also a unique self. The paradox of finding self through union with another becomes a paradigm in Updike's work (much more fully developed in *A Month of Sundays,* his seventh novel) of the interpenetration and interdependence of mind/spirit and body/matter. Harry's experience with Thelma reminds him of his former belief that he has "some kind of assignment here on earth," but it does not jar him loose from the firm commitments he has made to the social nets that hold life together. As he thinks back on his night with Thelma, "it seems in texture no different from [a] dream. Only Janice is real" (427). Janice is real because of all they have been through together. "What more can you ask of a wife in a way than that she stick around and see with you what happens next?" Rabbit asks (460). Rabbit once ran when Janice's "fear contaminated him," "but in these middle years, it is so clear to him that he will never run that he can laugh at her, his stubborn prize" (455).

Thelma not only reminds Harry of his former feelings of some special mission. She also tells him directly that he should confront Ruth to find out if the girl he saw in the Toyota showroom is really his daughter. He follows the advice although when he had first located Ruth's house out beyond Galilee he had bolted and run when the dog began barking. As he pulls into the driveway this time, he thinks, "This is crazy. Run." But this time he finds the courage to stay and knocks on the door. "As with dying," he thinks, "there is a moment that must be pushed through, a slice of time more transparent than plate glass; it is in front of him and he takes the step" (437). "Pushing through" has never been one of Harry's strong points. In *Rabbit, Run* Rabbit failed to respond to the sermon the Sunday he went to Eccles' church because "he had no taste for the . . . *going through*" quality of Christianity, "the passage *into* death and suffering . . ." (237). Now he recognizes the importance of pushing through, and does it. Ruth denies that the girl is his daughter, insisting that her two sons and a daughter are all children of her husband, Mr. Byer. But Rabbit has pushed through to face the moment. He apologizes to Ruth for having "left [her] in such a mess way back then." No longer so condemnatory as when she told him twenty years ago to "look outside of your own pretty skin once in a while" and called him "Mr. Death" *(Rabbit, Run,* 330), Ruth now says, "Well, . . . I guess we make our own messes" (449). Rabbit recognizes that "once he escaped by telling her, *I'll be right back,* but now there is not even that to say. Both know, what people should never know, that they will not meet again" (449-450). He has finally pushed through his fantasy about Ruth and his daughter to face, accept, and shape reality.

So Rabbit has learned a great deal in the ten years since Updike asked if he and Janice were O.K. He has outgrown the crippling solipsism of his earlier years by coming to terms with the objective world of phenomena and social responsibilities in which he lives. He has come to love the world which he has been given and to feel peaceful and at ease in it. And, most significantly, he has learned to accept death without surrendering the miracle of his own selfhood and the mystery of sex and has found the strength to "go through" moments that require commitments and decision. Although he cannot articulate equations involving quantum jumps of energy or philosophical nuances distinguishing between the heat-death of the universe and the power of the human imagination and therefore is not qualified to speak directly for his creator, he does serve, as Updike has said an author's characters should, "to dramatize issues and tensions" ("Response"). Like the poet at the conclusion of *Midpoint,* Harry knows that earth wants him and shall have him, "yet not yet" (44). For Harry, too, "Some task remains.../ Some package, anciently addressed, . . ./ That keeps [him] knocking on the doors of days" (44). So he tells his son, Nelson, "Maybe I haven't done everything right in my life. I know I haven't. But I haven't committed the greatest sin. I haven't laid down and died" (381). In a new life in a new house stimulated by a new granddaughter, Harry will keep looking in the thicket for the thorns that spell a word. Like his creator, the *Midpoint* poet, Harry has "believed in the Absurd." And he, again like the poet, has at last learned to "impersonate a serious man" *(Midpoint* 44).

Updike has thus unfolded the saga of his middle-American Everyman through three decades. As Michiko Kakutani has suggested, these three books form "something of an epic" (15), tracing the evolution not only of Harry Angstrom but also of America. Updike sees Harry's "tolerant curiosity and reluctant education" as typical American qualities, and has pointed out that both Harry and America have "suffered, marveled, listened, and endured" ("Special Message—*Rabbit Redux* 858). In 1976 Updike told me that he had "committed [him]self to writing four books about this man" ("Interview" 285), and in his "interview" with Bech in 1981 he reaffirmed his intention to "rendezvous with [his] ex-basketball player and fellow pilgrim one more time" (975). We may, therefore, look forward to hearing more about Harry Angstrom and the America in which he lives as Rabbit moves beyond the peaceful plateau of a rich middle-age and moves toward his own sixth decade and the ninth decade of the twentieth century.

NOTE

[1]Warner Brothers actually made a movie version of *Rabbit, Run,* but it was not successful either artistically or financially. Updike commented in 1977:

> *Rabbit, Run* was to be subtitled "A Movie." The cinematic art knows no tense but the present. I even had an introduction, discarded, leading the reader down the aisle to his seat. The opening scene, of boys playing basketball around a telephone pole, was meant to be the background for the title and credits, but when a real movie was made of the novel, the scene was not used in this way. Warner Brothers' *Rabbit, Run* lost them two million dollars and made vivid to me certain differences between word and image. The film medium, superb mirror of the visible furniture of our lives, cannot show the shadow of moral ambiguity. Without this impalpable novelistic substance, this unspoken but constant discussion between reader and author, the actions make insufficient sense. Watching the movie, I felt I had put the actors in a glass box, which I wanted to smash, to let them out; James Caan, the hero, later echoed this claustral hallucination by saying, in an interview, of the movie, *"Rabbit, Run* wasn't released; it escaped." *(Hugging the Shore* 850)

WORKS CITED

Burgess, Anthony. "Language, Myth, and Mr. Updike." *Commonweal* 83 (11 Feb. 1972): 557-559.

Falke, Wayne. *"Rabbit Redux:* Time/Order/God." *Modern Fiction Studies* 20 (Spring 1974): 59-75.

Kakutani, Michiko. "Turning Sex and Guilt Into an American Epic." Review of *Rabbit Is Rich. Saturday Review* Oct. 1981: 14-15; 20-22.

Lyons, Eugene. "John Updike: The Beginning and the End." *Critique* 14 (1972): 44-59.

Markle, Joyce. *Fighters and Lovers.* New York: New York UP, 1973.

Pack, Robert. *Wallace Stevens.* New Brunswick, NJ: Rutgers UP, 1958.

Pollard, Ernest C. and Douglas C. Huston. *Physics.* New York: Oxford UP, 1969.

Prescott, Peter S. "Rabbit Rides Again." Review of *Rabbit Is Rich* by John Updike. *Newsweek* 28 Sep. 1981: 89-90.

Sale, Roger. "Rabbit Returns." Review of *Rabbit Is Rich* by John Updike. *New York Times Book Review* 27 Sep. 1981: 1; 32-34.

Samuels, Charles. *John Updike.* Minneapolis: U Minnesota P, 1969.

Stevens, Wallace. "A Rabbit as King of the Ghosts." In *The Palm at the End of the Mind.* New York: Vintage, 1972. 150-151.

Updike, John. "Interview Conducted by Jeff Campbell, Georgetown, MA, 9 Aug. 1976." Published as Appendix to this volume.

---. *Midpoint and Other Poems.* New York: Knopf, 1969.

---. *Picked-Up Pieces.* New York: Knopf, 1975.

---. *Rabbit Is Rich.* New York: Knopf, 1981.

---. *Rabbit Redux.* New York: Knopf, 1971.

---. *Rabbit, Run.* New York: Knopf, 1960.

---. "Special Message to Purchasers of Franklin Library Limited Edition, in 1981, of *Rabbit Redux*." Rpt. *Hugging the Shore*. New York: Knopf, 1983. 858-859.

---. "Special Message to Purchasers of Franklin Library Limited Edition, in 1977, of *Rabbit, Run*." Rpt. *Hugging the Shore*. New York: Knopf, 1983. 849-851.

---. "Updike on Updike." An "interview" conducted by Henry Bech on the occasion of the publication of *Rabbit Redux*. *New York Times Book Review* 27 Sep. 1981: 1; 34-35. Rpt. *Hugging the Shore*. New York: Knopf, 1983. 870-875.

Vargo, Edward P. *Rainstorms and Fire: Ritual in the Novels of John Updike*. Port Washington NY: Kennikat P, 1973.

Waldmeir, Joseph. "It's the Going That's Important, Not the Getting There: Rabbit's Questing Non-quest." *Modern Fiction Studies* 20 (Spring 1974): 13-28.

Wolcott, James. "Running On Empty." Review of *Rabbit Is Rich* by John Updike. *Esquire* Oct. 1981, 20-23.

CHAPTER 5

"WE LOVE THE FLESH":
MARRY ME, COUPLES, and
THE WITCHES OF EASTWICK

Although *Marry Me* (1976), *Couples* (1966), and *The Witches of Eastwick* (1984) are not as closely related as either *The Centaur* and *Of the Farm* or the three Rabbit novels, they do call for joint consideration. Each of the three is set in a small New England town; each is a carefully rendered sociological study of American culture of the 1960s; and, as Updike himself has pointed out, "all [three] deal with marriage, in progressive states of deterioration, . . . and people in deteriorating states of innocence, in small-town Edens" ("Response"). Furthermore, each novel, as we shall see, asks the same question posed by Updike's first novel, *The Poorhouse Fair:* "After Christianity, what?" There is implied judgment on American culture in the settings chosen for these novels and the specific names given the towns described. The three novels take us from Greenwood, Connecticut, with its Edenic allusions, to Tarbox, Massachusetts, suggestive of one of Dante's bolgias in *The Inferno,* to Eastwick, Rhode Island—the colony to which Anne Hutchinson fled after being banished from Massachusetts, but where now a coven of witches and their Satanic consort are an accepted part of community life. As these novels show, the 60s began with the idealistic if shallow dreams of the children of the Age of Aquarius, moved on through a disillusioning identification of eros with thanatos, and ended with the welcoming the devil himself.

MARRY ME

Even a casual reading of *Marry Me* and *Couples* suggests that they be considered together. In *Marry Me* the men of Greenwood, Connecticut, commute to New York, while in *Couples* the men of Tarbox, Massachusetts, commute to Boston, but their lives are much the same. The ostensible subject of both novels is the adulterous sex lives of young couples in their thirties; and both protagonists, Jerry Conant of *Marry Me* and Piet Hanema of *Couples,* believe in God, fear death, and seek release in sex. The action of *Marry Me* occupies the year from the spring of 1962 to the spring of 1963, while the events of *Couples* fill the months from the spring of 1963 to the spring of 1964, almost as if one story picks up where the other leaves off. And although the adulterous affairs of *Marry Me* are limited to two, *Couples* outlines the complex involvements of ten couples, again almost as if one book were preparing the way for the other.

The eight-year gap between the publication dates of the two novels would seem to make ludicrous the suggestion that *Marry Me* (1976) is a forerunner to *Couples* (1968), but such is indeed the case. Updike told me in 1976 that *Marry Me* was "an old manuscript taken out after a dozen years." "The heart of it," he said, "comes from between *The Centaur* and *Of the Farm"* ("Letter"). That would mean that most of it was actually written in 1964. Updike took up the *Marry Me* manuscript again after completing his second collection of essays, *Picked-Up Pieces,* in 1975. He revised the manuscript, seeking to impose "some order upon its plot and decency upon its style" ("Letter").

The bulk of *Marry Me,* then, was written before *Couples,* and this order of composition helps explain why *Marry Me* seems to fit so much more comfortably with *Couples* than with *A Month of Sundays* or *The Coup,* which

are its nearest chronological neighbors in the Updike *oeuvre.*
Aside from the obvious shared characteristics mentioned
above, *Couples* and *Marry Me* have similar structures (each
book is symmetrically shaped into five chapters) and similar
mythological concerns. Whereas *The Centaur* utilized myth
to elevate George and Peter Caldwell, *Marry Me* and *Couples*
use the stories of Jerry Conant and Piet Hanema to
demythologize, to counter any efforts which might seek to
make myths real by making men unreal. Since the "heart" of
Marry Me was written before *Couples,* and since the events it
describes transpire the year before those in *Couples,* we shall
analyze *Marry Me* first, even though it was published eight
years after *Couples.*

Jerry Conant, *Marry Me*'s protagonist, is thirty years
old in the second year of the Kennedy presidency. An
animator of television commercials for a New York advertising firm, Jerry is married to Ruth, a Unitarian minister's
daughter whom he met in art school. In the spring of 1962,
Jerry, a Lutheran, undergoes a spiritual crisis in which his
fear of death aggravates his asthma attacks. He turns to
religion and church-going for help, and he reads Barth,
Marcel, and Berdyaev, but with no measurable relief. When
he begins an affair with Sally Mathias, however, his breathing
improves. After a mid-June tryst in Washington, he and Sally are almost caught because of delays caused by an airline
strike, and Jerry decides to tell Ruth of the affair. What
Jerry does not know—and never finds out—is that Ruth has
recently had an affair with Richard Mathias, Sally's husband.
Ruth has ended the relationship sensibly, with her marriage
still intact, and she thinks that Jerry and Sally will do the
same. She gets Jerry to promise not to see Sally again until
the end of the summer.

Jerry does not keep his promise, although Ruth thinks
he does. Sally goes to Florida in August, hoping Jerry will
come to her. When he stays with Ruth because of the

children, Sally returns home and tells Richard about the affair. Richard, an atheist with one blind eye, insists on divorce and helps Ruth find a lawyer so she can begin proceedings herself. Jerry, however, cannot make up his mind to marry Sally, so the divorces do not proceed. He fantasizes running away with Sally to Wyoming, but actually takes a six-months' leave of absence so the Conants can fly to Nice to paint. The weather is not good and neither is the painting, so they return to Greenwood in February. In March, Jerry flies to the Virgin Islands alone, still dreaming that there may be some time and some place where he might go up to Sally and say, "Marry Me" (303).

ROMANCE

A bare plot summary suggests that the book is superficial, trivial, or even silly. Indeed, these are very ordinary people, and nothing much happens—nobody really changes. And Jerry *is* sometimes silly, with his affected "hip" teenage talk to Sally, his obsessive listening to Ray Charles on the radio, and his running back to get his Medihaler after he has packed up to move out on Ruth. But these are the dots of experience that emerge in the lives of ordinary people, and these are the precise details that can assume a pattern if viewed from proper distance and perspective. In giving his novel the subtitle "A Romance," Updike has suggested the perspective from which to view *Marry Me*. On the lists of Updike's works printed on the flyleaves of his books, each title is carefully labeled as to its genre. *Marry Me* is not, like the other books discussed in this volume, called a novel, but "a romance." Clearly Updike intends *Marry Me* to be considered in a light somewhat different from his other novels. In a television interview in December, 1978, for instance, Updike accepted the description of *The Coup* as his eighth novel, whereas if *Marry Me* were considered a novel, *The Coup* would be the ninth.

What is the significance of the label "romance"? How does it differentiate *Marry Me* from the "novels"? In its common modern usage in reference to fiction, the term "romance" is generally accepted to mean a story that draws largely on the author's imagination and makes very little effort to re-create details of the active world, in contrast to the more realistic "novel." Some critics seek to apply the term "romance" to *Marry Me* in just this sense. For example, Edmund Fuller implies that 1962 is long enough ago that it is almost an Edenic past, while Richard Todd sees Jerry as "an ultimate romantic," "a domesticated Gatsby." Therefore, both critics view the book primarily as an imaginative, fanciful, and unreal work. *Marry Me* is too full of lovingly rendered naturalistic details, however, too full of the daily textures of suburban life in 1962 for this meaning of "romance" to offer convincing entrée into the book's intent. Rather, a somewhat older, longer established meaning of the word seems more fruitful. Romance has for centuries been associated with medieval stories of knights, kings, and damsels in distress. In contrast to the sterner epics which preceded them, medieval romances were full of fantasy and light-hearted, sometimes aimless, adventures. Above all, love, missing or at least of only minor interest in the epics, was supreme in the romances, and reflected the artificial ideals of chivalry (Holman 309). This medieval tradition of romance provides the best handle for grasping the intentions of *Marry Me*.

Images from medieval romantic tradition recur in the novel. For example, as Jerry thinks to himself about Sally, he says, "You were a territory where I went on tip-toe to steal a magic mirror. You were a princess married to an ogre. I would go to meet you as a knight, to rescue you. . ." (33). Actually, he has gone only to a sandy beach with a bottle of warm wine or to a hotel room in Washington, but the chivalric artifice is there. Nor is Jerry the only one to indulge in such medieval imagery. Ruth also employs it as she reflects on her situation after finding out about Sally and Jerry: "There were rules in this mystery, like stairways in a castle; she had mistakenly knocked on the door of the chamber where the lord and lady made love. Before this door she felt small, appalled and ashamed, rebuked and fascinated: a child" (139-140). The unanswered riddle, the mysterious castle stairs, and the locked chamber lead the reader once again to literary motifs of the middle ages.

The appearance of this imagery is not accidental. The whole plot of the novel revolves around Jerry's idealized love for Sally, who is portrayed much like the "Unattainable Lady" of courtly love. Jerry tells Sally:

> I want you and I can't have you. You're like a set of golden stairs I can never finish climbing. I look down, and the earth is a little blue mist. I look up, and there's this radiance I can never reach. It gives you your incredible beauty, and if I marry you I'll destroy it. . . . What we have, sweet Sally, is an ideal love. It's ideal because it can't be realized. (46)

The recurring images and Jerry's references to Sally as his ideal but illicit, unattainable love suggest parallels to one of the most popular of the medieval romances, that of Tristan and Iseult, a story which was attracting much of Updike's attention while he was working on the first version of *Marry Me* in 1964.

In that year Updike published a long essay-review in which he analyzed two works by Denis de Rougemont: *Love Declared,* a 1963 collection of essays, and an earlier monumental study of the Tristan myth, *Love in the Western World.* Updike is obviously fascinated with de Rougemont's locating the explanation of "the inescapable conflict in the West between passion and marriage" in the Tristan myth. De Rougemont sees that in Tristan and Iseult Eros and

Thanatos are combined, and he goes on to affirm: "Passionate love, the longing for what sears us and annihilates us in its triumph—there is the secret which Europe has never allowed to be given away; a secret it has always repressed—and preserved" ("More Love in the Western World" 221). Updike finds de Rougemont's book elegant and "provocative," filled with "aphoristic crackle" and "literary high adventure" ("More Love" 222), but he also admits that it is "imperfectly convincing" (223). He proceeds to list eight cogent objections to de Rougemont's argument, but in the preface to *Assorted Prose,* in which the essay was reprinted in 1965, he says, "My expressed doubts about de Rougemont's theories of Occidental love have faded in importance for me. His overriding thesis seems increasingly beautiful and pertinent" (ix). We shall more carefully examine evidence of Updike's acceptance or rejection of de Rougemont's theories as we turn to a closer analysis of the thematic concerns of *Marry Me.* The point to be made now is that at the time of the novel's composition, Updike was working with at least one medieval romance and its symbolic significance in the development of Western thought. The fact that he would juxtapose elements of medieval romance with the ordinary trivia of daily suburbia should come as no surprise in light of the fact that in *The Centaur*—completed shortly before he began writing *Marry Me*—he had already imposed Olympian gods on Olinger High.

By labeling *Marry Me* a romance, then, Updike alerts the reader to expect a story of forbidden but idealized love. The term, suggesting lightness of tone, also disclaims the responsibilities often associated with the serious novel. So separating *Marry Me* from the rest of the novels, Updike, in effect, disclaims any need to show development from *Rabbit Redux* and *A Month of Sundays,* his two novels immediately preceding *Marry Me* in dates of publication. The ambiguities and ironies with which Updike imbues his "romance," however, necessitate our giving *Marry Me* a significant place among the "novels." In it he does not fully embrace the medieval romance tradition; and as we analyze the ways in which the experiences of Jerry Conant serve to demythologize Tristan, we recognize familiar Updikean themes.

TRISTAN DEMYTHOLOGIZED

According to Updike, de Rougemont finds in the story of Tristan and Iseult that the two lovers are not so much in love with each other as with love itself. Updike summarizes de Rougemont's central point: The essence of the love-myth "is *passion itself;* its concern is not with the possession, through love, of another person but with the prolongation of the lover's state of mind. Eros is allied with Thanatos, rather than Agape; love becomes not a way of accepting and entering the world but a way of defying and escaping it. . . . Passion love feeds upon denial" ("More Love" 222). De Rougemont believes that the "sword of chastity" placed between Tristan and Iseult as they sleep in their love grotto foreshadows the recurring obstructions that inhibit the joining of lovers in most Western plays, novels, and poems. He also finds that this literary tradition encourages attitudes "inimicable to marriage, social stability, and international peace" since its "theory of suffering. . . encourages or obscurely justifies in the recesses of the Western mind a liking for war" (222).

While finding de Rougemont's theory suggestive, Updike is not fully convinced. For example, he suggests that one needs no deep-seated myth of a love-death combination to explain the frequency of unhappy love affairs in literature. "The essence of a story is conflict," Updike says. On the other hand, "happy love, unobstructed love, is the possibility that animates all romances; their plots turn on obstruction because they are plots" (225). The *possibility* of happy, fulfilled love holds the reader's interest, but without obstruction and conflict there is no story; therefore, the frustration of love is merely a plot device used by skillful story tellers. Updike thus suggests that de Rougemont confuses literature and life. Of course literature and life interact, but Updike thinks de Rougemont claims too much for literature because "his thesis at bottom grants 'myths' a ghostly vitality independent of the men who create them, and ascribes to the mirror a magical shaping power" (226).

Concluding his essay on de Rougemont, Updike begins the last paragraph with his characteristic phrase: "Yes, but . . . ." (232). Whatever objections he may have to de Rougemont's sweeping application of his insight, Updike says yes, de Rougemont is "dreadfully right in asserting that love in the Western world has by some means acquired a force far out of proportion to its presumed procreative aim" (232). It is apparently this aspect of de Rougemont's thought that Updike had in mind when he wrote in the foreword to *Assorted Prose* that his doubts about de Rougemont seemed less important and that he now found the "overriding thesis . . . increasingly beautiful and pertinent." The skepticism of *Midpoint,* however, that warned against any "flawless formulas," expresses itself in the "but." Updike insists that we do not need a heresy or a myth to explain the force of sexual love in our society. Instead, he suggests:

> Might it not simply be that sex has become involved in the Promethean protest forced upon Man by his paradoxical position in the Universe as a self-conscious animal? Our fundamental anxiety is that we do not exist—or will cease to exist. Only in being loved do we find external corroboration of the supremely high valuation each ego secretly assigns itself. . . . The heart *prefers* to move against the grain of circumstance; perversity is the soul's very life.
> Therefore the enforced and approved bonds of marriage, restricting freedom, weaken love. (233)

Instead of tracing the Western obsession with the pursuit of passionate love to the elegant but simple Tristan myth, Updike suggests the complex and ambiguous self-world interaction he set forth in *Midpoint*.

Marry Me illustrates this "yes—but" approach to the Tristan myth. On one level, it makes generous use of the devices of the quest for the Unattainable Lady. These devices dominate the first half of the novel, and are generally presented from Jerry's point of view. As Jerry goes to meet Sally on the beach in the book's first scene, he is listening to Ray Charles on the radio. The song is "Born to Lose"—"Every dream has only brought me pain. . ." (3) and the song for Jerry seems filled with Sally. As they meet, the search among the dunes for "the exact place, the perfect place" (4), where they had met before is like seeking Tristan's love grotto; and although they can never find that exact place, whatever place they find becomes "instantly perfect" (6). Since he has idealized Sally, Jerry feels his lovemaking with her is "wonderfully virginal" (15). He even finds "something comic and inappropriate in their living now, in this century" (29), preferring to think of himself as a knight, going to Sally's rescue or climbing the set of golden stairs which will lead to his ideal love which cannot be realized. As the summer wears on, Ruth proves to him that in the realm of the real she is a better wife than Sally, but Jerry's heart perversely streams "away from her, toward the impossible woman" (155). Even after Sally has returned from Florida and the affair is apparently over, Jerry is "still in love; though Sally had been lost she lived within him more than ever" (182).

Jerry's romantic pretensions are generally dismissed by insights and comments from Ruth, from whose point of view most of the book is narrated. Ruth has not turned Richard into a Tristan; rather, in reflecting on their relationship, she discovers that one "can sleep with a person, and have him still be a person, no more" (92). For her there are no golden stairs, no dreams of pain, no perfect place. She has had her affair and there has been no thunderbolt: "Instead, her marriage had stood with the stupid solidity of an unattended church, . . . when she returned to it" (96). She knows from experience that one does get over an affair, and she sees no mythic significance in what Jerry and Sally are doing. "An innocent man and a greedy woman had fornicated and Ruth could not endorse the illusions that made it seem more than that" (143). Ruth sees both Jerry and Sally as exaggerators, and although she recognizes that beauty may be a province of exaggeration, she believes she is standing by the truth. "The truth was," she thinks, "that Sally and Jerry were probably better married to Richard and her than they would be to each other" (143). Although one must always be careful in deciding which—if any—of Updike's characters is speaking for the author, the balance of the novel supports the contention that Updike agrees with Ruth's view of the truth in this instance.

In Chapter IV, for example, even Jerry seems to move toward rejection of the romantic myth, toward giving up his pursuit of forbidden fruit for its own sake. After the confrontation with Richard during which it was agreed that divorces were in order so that Jerry could marry Sally, Ruth and Jerry drive home. Jerry stops the car to relieve a burning desire to urinate, and as he looks into the night, he tries "to make himself conscious, as if of the rotation of the earth, of the huge and mournful turn his life had taken" (231). He would like to feel the high tragic dimensions of his fateful love affair. He is unable to do so, however. Instead, there is only the grass around him, Ruth waiting in the car, and the "diminishing arc of relief" signalled by his emptying bladder (232). When Jerry meets Sally later the next day, he recognizes that his passion was not so great as he had sought to believe. Now he finds that "their love, their affair, had become a great awkward shape, jagged, fallen between them" (257). As he talks to Ruth later, he puzzles: "I don't understand what quite happened. As an actual wife or whatever, she stopped being an *idea,* and for the first time I *saw* her" (284).

As Chapter IV ends, it would seem that Jerry's Tristanlike romance has been demythologized for Ruth, for the reader, and even for Jerry. Yes—but—no, not quite. In Chapter V, Jerry fantasizes running away to Wyoming with Sally and her children. The unsuspecting reader first thinks the scene of the new family descending from the plane at Cheyenne is intended to be real, but five pages later is told that "the desert around them, and they with it, evaporated, vanished, never had been" (292). Tristan is settled with his wife Iseult of the White Hand in Brittany, but his dreams still fly to Iseult the Fair in Cornwall. Jerry has come to see that Sally is not a golden stair to climb, but he has not yet accepted the reality of his ongoing marriage to Ruth. Virtually unable to choose either Sally or Ruth as true wife, preferring to seek the unattainable, he rides the proverbial fence of indecision. When he lands in the Virgin Islands and climbs into a taxi, he cannot even decide whether to go east or west. The taxi driver tells him he must make a decision, but Jerry, at this point predictably, leaves it up to the driver. In the last paragraph of the book, he inhales the Caribbean air and believes that finally he has found the perfect place, away from the mundane, and that perhaps there is still a dimension in which he can ask Sally, with her "downcast eyes" and "gracious, sorrowing face" to marry him (303).

The sensible Ruth and her "truth" dominate the major portion of the book, but the romance opens and closes it. Romance may not be adequate, but neither can it be easily dismissed. One may argue that giving the opening and closing of the book to Jerry, the spokesman for the

Tristan/romance idea, indicates that Updike intends the balance to fall in Jerry's favor. All the commonsense dismissal of romantic claptrap in the middle of the book may be interpreted as the kind of good hedonistic advice the poet gave himself in *Midpoint,* only to reject it in favor of his "otherworldly stand." Jerry, too, has taken an otherworldly stand. He believes in God, fears death, and is very aware of the dualism between body and soul. Ruth, unlike Jerry, is not afraid of death, which Jerry explains means that she has no imagination—no soul (88). Ruth herself feels that as a Unitarian "her soul is one unit removed from not being there at all" (96). Richard, the other male in the quadrangle, is an avowed atheist, and his inability to see the supernatural dimension in life is symbolized by his one blind eye. Jerry tries closing one eye just to see what it would be like to see as Richard does: "Things were just so flat, with nothing further to be said about them; it was the world, he realized, as seen without the idea of God lending each thing a roundness of significance" (225).

There is a pattern of imagery, however, involving not just Jerry and Ruth, but all four of the characters, that swings the final balance of the novel back toward the reality of Ruth, suggesting that however beautiful and pertinent a thesis may be, it cannot adequately fit or explain the world of actual existence. After a long telephone conversation with Jerry, Ruth realizes that she has been doodling, drawing squares interlocking with other squares and shading the overlaps, balancing areas of light and dark (140). The alternating pattern of light and dark squares, literally originating in Ruth's doodling, recurs more significantly and figuratively in four subsequent passages that utilize the elements of chess. The reader learns that Jerry and Richard had often played chess until Jerry began to evade invitations because of his fear of losing. When Richard learns of Jerry's affair with Sally and calls to insist on a meeting, Jerry thinks back to those games and realizes that Richard has caught him in a "knight fork," a two-pronged attack in which whatever move he makes, a piece must be lost (204). In this case, of course, the word "piece" refers to Ruth or Sally, one of whom Jerry must lose, and it carries a rather inelegant and unromantic connotation, even though chess is played with knights, kings, queens, bishops, and castles. Later Richard thinks of the real-life moves the two men have been making as being played out on an "invisible chess board," and finds that Jerry, by his adroit implication that Richard may violently harm Sally, has "daringly . . .castled" (272). Significantly, the castling move in chess is one which protects the *king* by moving him out of the main cross fire of the board, so it would seem that Jerry is more interested in preserving himself than in risking the golden stairs to rescue his lady. In a third reference to chess, Jerry finds Richard applying the knight fork against him once more after he has decided not to marry Sally: Richard calls and makes Jerry say point blank that he will *not* marry Sally even if Richard goes ahead and divorces her. The knight fork is applied; Jerry knows he must lose one woman or the other; and although he recognizes that "life unlike a chessboard is never black or white" (285), he refuses to argue the point and says what Richard wants to hear, thus acknowledging the loss of Sally. Although Jerry comes to know that life is more like Ruth's doodled squares with their interlocking shadings which acknowledge the intersections of two dimensions, he refuses to admit the implications of this insight. In his fantasy of the flight to Wyoming, he sees the "heartland states" unfold below him like a "checkerboard" (289). Even when that vision of Wyoming evaporates, vanishes because it never had been (276), he still holds on to the hope that there is a realm where kings, queens, and knights move on neat black and white squares according to long established rules. He has not fully accepted the ambiguous muddle of human life, but his creator/mentor, Updike, has.

SELF, SEX, WORLD

In tracing varied usages of the Tristan myth in *Marry Me,* we have already encountered a familiar idea from *Midpoint:* skepticism of formulas or social theories as adequate explanations of the complex and ambiguous interaction of self and world. There are three additional *Midpoint* motifs which deserve attention before we conclude our discussion of *Marry Me.* One of the over-arching concerns of *Midpoint* is the question of the existence—or continued existence—of the individual as a discrete ego. The same question is constantly before Jerry Conant, who believes "in choices, in mistakes, in damnation" (45). He thinks choices matter, that choosing makes the individual alive, whereas Ruth and Richard believe that things simply happen (48). This belief explains why Jerry feels in such a quandary when called upon to choose between Ruth and Sally. "I've figured out the bind I'm in," he says. "It's between death and death. To live without you [Sally] is death to me. On the other hand, to abandon my family is a sin; to do it I'd have to deny God, and by denying God I'd give up all claims on immortality" (55). Jerry's dread of death, his fear of the extinction of his own ego, obsesses him. He tries to assuage the fear by going to church, teaching the children bedtime prayers, and reading the theology of Barth, Marcel, and Berdyaev; but the theology doesn't help the dread, which embodies itself in asthmatic attacks that feel like a wall in his lungs. He perceives these attacks as death, and in his irrationality seeks to lay the blame on Ruth, accusing her of trying to smother him. He further berates her for her refusal "to believe in Jesus Christ, the resurrection of Lazarus, the immortality of the soul. . . . After an hour or more, he would tire of abusing her, and God beyond her, and relax, and fall asleep" (142).

The fear of personal annihilation is relieved only when he begins the affair with Sally, thus embodying the paradigm of sex as personal expression and interaction set forth in *Midpoint*. Jerry describes one sexual experience in mystical terms, saying, "I had this very clear vision of the Bodily Ascension, of me going up and up this incredibly soft, warm, boundless sky." Ruth asks if such a metaphor is not blasphemous, but Jerry responds in words that echo a passage in Canto IV of *Midpoint:* "Because it makes my prick Christ? I wonder. They both have this quality, of being more important than they should be. As Christ relates to the universe, my prick relates to me" (153). Jerry furthers this identification of sexuality, individuality, and religion at the conclusion of Chapter IV. He looks out into the darkness and feels the threat of Richard, whom he identifies with darkness and death. He remembers that once Richard chose to antagonize him by using a small statue of Christ to clean his fingernails—a blasphemous act that could emanate only from an agent of darkness. As he reflects on his sexual experiences with Sally, Jerry rejoices "that he had given his enemy the darkness an eternal wound. With the sword of his flesh he had put the mockers to rout. Christ was revenged" (287).

If all this sounds so far-fetched as to be ridiculous, Updike counters with a third *Midpoint* theme: the solid reality of the world. Ruth is the primary spokesman for the ongoing nature of objective forms which give the individual human being patterns within which to function. These patterns, inherent in socio-cultural reality, exist as given entities in which persons interact, but their very existence does not depend on particular human behavior. Ruth ends her affair "in a world of evolving forms" (96). Her son enters first grade; her daughter, the third. Things grow, change, evolve, but continue on ordinary paths. She finds, also, as she and Jerry are sitting in a restaurant and he tells her of his affair with Sally, that other people around them are proceeding with normal conversations—and that their own conversation is proceeding, even through such highly charged emotional subject matter (119). Jerry may feel that his sexual exploits are a personal blow against the forces of darkness and death, but Ruth knows that life will go on much the same. Jerry, too, has some awareness that there is something solid and beyond the midpoint of his own ego that he shares with Ruth. After Jerry has stopped seeing Sally as an "idea," he and Ruth share "intervals of twinned silence." This silence does not pain them, "for they had begun in silence, side by side, contemplating, by fits and starts [in art school], an object posed before them, a collection of objects, a mystery assembled of light and color and shadow" (284). The familiar elements of Updike's bipolar world—objects, light, shadow, mystery—have been shared by Ruth and Jerry, side by side. "In their willingness to live parallel lay their weakness and their strength," Updike adds (284). The boneless ego seeking to live as midpoint of its own circle exists parallel to the solid world of evolving forms. Weakness, yes. But also strength, if the parallel lines can be expanded to include intersecting lines that make overlapping squares, if the questing Tristan can turn his driving Eros from Thanatos to Agape.

A casual reading of *Marry Me* suggests that it is a kind of literary sport in the Updike *oeuvre*. It seems out of place, published, as it was, between *A Month of Sundays* and *The Coup*. When one recognizes the recurrent Updikean motifs beneath its surface of romance, however, and especially when one knows that its original composition pre-dated *Couples,* *Marry Me* assumes a meaningful position in Updike's work. As we shall see in the following analysis, the relatively light-hearted ironic comparison of Jerry Conant to Tristan prepares the way for a much more serious probing of Eros as Thanatos in the lives of Piet Hanema and his friends in *Couples.*

COUPLES

Couples begins as Piet and Angela Hanema return from a party in Tarbox, Massachusetts, on the Saturday night before Palm Sunday in April, 1963—just one month after *Marry Me* had left Jerry Conant still imagining a dimension where his ideal romantic love might be realized. The Hanemas are one of ten couples who gather regularly for parties, word games, basketball, and ski weekends. We are told: "The men had stopped having careers and the women had stopped having babies. Liquor and love were left" (12). For these couples, "Duty and work yielded as ideals to truth and fun" (106).

The Applebys and the Smiths are the first to carry the ideals of liquor and love, truth and fun, to their logical conclusions. In May of 1962, Frank Appleby and Marcia Smith had begun an affair, and Harold Smith and Janet Appleby followed suit. By the time the book opens, the four are already called "the Applesmiths" by the other couples. Eddie and Carol Constantine and Ben and Irene Saltz work out a similar arrangement, and they become "the Saltines."

Although Piet, raised a Dutch Calvinist, attends the Congregational Church and takes the concept of sin seriously, the Monday after Easter finds him with his mistress, Georgene, wife of dentist Freddy Thorne. As spring moves on, Ken and Foxy Whitman, the newest couple in the group, hire Piet, a contractor, to remodel the house they recently bought. Although Foxy is pregnant, she and Piet enter into an affair which lasts until shortly before Foxy's baby is born in October. Both assume the baby's birth has ended their affair, but two months later Piet visits Foxy, supposedly for the last time. Although each thinks this is the end of anything between them, Foxy becomes pregnant. They arrange an abortion through Freddy Thorne, who demands—and gets—as his fee the privilege of spending one night with

Angela, primarily as a way of getting even with Piet for his affair with Freddy's wife, Georgene. Foxy eventually tells Ken the whole story in April. Ken straightway demands a divorce; then Angela decides to divorce Piet who finds himself ostracized by the group of couples. Shortly thereafter, Piet and Foxy spend a sexually exhausting weekend together in Piet's bachelor quarters in the third floor of a remodeled office building, and Foxy leaves for the Virgin Islands to wait out her divorce.

The important action of the book ends with a spectacular lightning-caused fire that destroys the Congregational Church, although the rooster weathervane from its steeple is saved. A final paragraph supplies the information that Angela went to Juarez in July to receive a one-day divorce, and that Piet and Foxy, who were married in September, now live in Lexington, where Piet has an inspector's job arranged by Foxy's naval-officer father, and they "have been accepted, as another couple" (480).

In many ways *Couples* may be seen as an inversion of *Marry Me*. The adultery that could seem romantic in one man and one woman becomes boring when turned into the way of life practiced by a whole group. The myth of illicit love that was comically demythologized through Jerry is brutally destroyed in the story of Piet. Jerry maintains something of his idealism, but Piet loses his as he actually gets the woman he sought. *Marry Me*'s Greenwood, identified as a kind of paradise (*Marry Me* 125), becomes Tarbox, identified as a kind of hell (*Couples* 353). Furthermore, although both books have five chapters, *Marry Me* is much more static than *Couples*. *Marry Me* opens with an idyllic meeting between Jerry and Sally on the beach and ends with Jerry's idyllic dream in the West Indies. The reader must assume that the marriages of both the Conants and the Mathiases are technically still intact and will remain that way. The five chapters in *Couples,* however, trace a distinct change. When I asked about a "shape" for *Couples,* Updike told me,

> The shape is the turn that occurs between the first and last paragraphs, even the first and last sentences, where the Hanemas become a different pair of people. In other words, a couple changes—one couple replaces another. . . . I saw each chapter as steps, in a way. The turn, the revolution that turns Piet and Angela into Piet and Foxy was the shape. ("Interview" 284)

Couples, then, is *Marry Me* turned inside out, a light-hearted examination of individual human foibles turned into a serious evaluation of social trends. Instead of comic overtones, there are tragic undertones, for the outward change of one couple being replaced by another—which, as Updike has pointed out, "occurs within the social network and does not harm it . . . the couples—the group—remain intact" ("Interview" 284-285)—is accompanied by an equally important inner change in the protagonist, Piet Hanema.

AFTER CHRISTIANITY, WHAT?

Despite the notoriety attained by *Couples* because of its explicit sexual scenes, Updike clearly had something more significant in mind than merely an intellectual *Peyton Place.* The seriousness of his intent was indicated in his talk with Lewis Nichols in April of 1968, when he said, "As in *The Poorhouse Fair,* in this novel [*Couples*] I was asking the question, After Christianity, what?" The first of the two epigraphs for *Couples* is from Paul Tillich's *The Future of Religions* and describes the sense of helplessness felt by many individuals. Tillich says the tendency is to consider most decisions as a matter of fate, and points out that this helpless feeling was common in the time of the Roman empire. Such a mood, he suggests, is favorable for the resurgence of religion, but unfavorable for preserving a living democracy.

Updike told me that in the 1960s he felt a new kind of

religion might be emerging, not like the rational, socially engineered welfare state posited in *The Poorhouse Fair,* but rather "a religion of human interplay including sexual interplay" ("Interview" 281). In fact, he said,

> To some extent, in the years since I've written *Couples,* that has happened. There are more formalized ways now of getting together, of touching—T groups, and so on—and all this is foreshadowed in the book. The generation after mine seems to be attempting to find religious values in each other rather than in looking toward any supernatural or transcendental entity. ("Interview" 281)

In probing the question, then, of what might come after Christianity, *Couples* portrays the lives of the inhabitants of a "post-pill paradise" (52). That these couples see themselves as developing a substitute for outmoded Christianity is made clear when Angela tells Piet that Freddy Thorne "thinks we're a circle. A magic circle of heads to keep the night out. . . . He thinks we've made a church of each other" (7). Freddy, the self-proclaimed and willingly accepted high-priest of this church, says that the couples are "a subversive cell. . . . Like in the catacombs." "Only," he says, "they were trying to break out of hedonism. We're trying to break back into it. It's not easy" (148). Later he explains to Angela that it is their fate to be "suspended in . . . one of those dark ages that visits mankind between millennia, between the death and rebirth of gods, when there is nothing to steer by but sex and stoicism and the stars" (372).

The emptiness of the kind of life lived by the "believers" in Freddy's "church" indicates that Updike is not endorsing their attempts to break back into hedonism. For example, after a basketball game, Freddy is dominating the post-game party activities; the couples are described as "courtiers," while Freddy is their "king." But if Freddy is king, he is "the king of chaos" (71), and in a discussion a few paragraphs later, Ken Whitman points out that "Matter isn't chaos. . . . It has laws, legislated by what can't happen" (72). The couples are hesitant to separate on this particular occasion, as they are each time they gather, because they see

> an evening weighing upon them, an evening without a game, an evening spent among flickering lamps and cranky children and leftover food and the nagging half-read newspaper with its weary portents and atrocities, an evening when marriages closed in upon themselves like flowers from which the sun is withdrawn, an evening giving like a smeared window on Monday and the long week when they must perform again their impersonations of working men, of stockbrokers and dentists and engineers, of mothers and housekeepers, of adults who are not the world's guests but its hosts. (73-74)

On occasion the couples themselves recognize the emptiness of their lives, with all the childish games, neat impersonations, and superficial rituals. For example, the Applesmiths find that "much of what they took to be morality proved to be merely consciousness of the other couples watching them" (158). And when the Thornes decide to go ahead with their dinner party even though it is on the night of Kennedy's assassination, all the couples come, even with their uneasiness about the impropriety of such an occasion on the day of national tragedy. When Freddy begins to carve the ham with the words, "Take, eat, ... This is my body, given for thee" (319), Marcia Smith voices disgust and Bea Guerin wistfully suggests that perhaps they should all be fasting. But they don't fast; they all eat, and they drink the burgundy wine, "black as tar in the candlelight" (319).

Earlier Piet has told Foxy that he has only one serious opinion, that "America now is like an unloved child smothered in candy. Like a middle-aged wife whose husband

brings home a present after every trip because he's been un-
faithful to her. When they were newly married he never had
to give presents" (200). When Foxy asks who the husband is,
Piet replies: "God. Obviously. God doesn't love us
anymore. He loves Russia. He loves Uganda. We're fat and
full of pimples and always whining for more candy. We've
fallen from grace" (200). Christianity has been replaced by a
childish hedonism, which Piet sees graphically symbolized as
Foxy drives away with Freddy after the successful abortion.
Piet looks down and sees "a condom and candy wrapper. . .
paired in the exposed gutter" (378).

The second epigraph for *Couples,* a little quatrain by
Alexander Blok, gives further clues to Updike's opinion of
the "new religion." It reads:

> We love the flesh: its taste, its tone,
> Its charnel odor, breathed through Death's jaws. . .
> Are we to blame if your fragile bones
> Should crack beneath our heavy, gentle paws?

Although Updike explained that he and his wife had just
come back from a trip to Russia and the use of a Russian poet
was in part meant to be a personal touch, he said in 1976 that
his main purpose in using the quatrain was to "convey the
sense of sex as something brutal, crushing, barbaric, even"
("Interview" 281). What starts out as fun and games in a magic
circle to keep out the night through love of the flesh soon
leads to a charnel odor and the cracking of fragile bones.

Updike does not suggest, either, that the modern love of
the flesh might be tempered or improved by the revival of the
romantic love-myth of Tristan and Iseult. In *Marry Me* there
was at least a playful suggestion that the pursuit of love might
add an extra dimension to a mundane life, but in *Couples* the
only "yes" given to the myth is the recognition that it has
come to dominate American society in a polluted, perverted

way. The ultimate identification of Eros with Thanatos, of the pursuit of sex for its own sake with the death-wish, is openly shown. Tristan is thoroughly demythologized in the life of Piet Hanema.

Angela, whom Piet calls Angel, is always associated with the stars, the heavenly. She should, in terms of the myth, be the "Unattainable Lady." In fact, however, she is Piet's wife, not the woman whom he must seek to obtain against the obstacles set by society and convention. Foxy, on the other hand, is the illicit love, the one whom society's rules would deny to Piet. Foxy's animal name suggests her earthiness, however, and she hardly makes a good representative of the ideal. In truth, Piet does not idealize her. He simply enjoys her—and finally marries her, in direct contradiction to the myth. The Tristan myth that was clear behind the modern dress of *Marry Me* has undergone radical alteration.

As the summer of Piet's affair with Foxy comes to a close and the approaching birth of her baby brings an end to their meetings, Piet feels the urge to confess his "fornication with Foxy" (273) to Angela. Instead, he goes outside, looks at the stars, and goes back inside satisfied that "a crisis in his love for Foxy has passed, that henceforth he would love her less" (273). In the dentist's chair "beneath the red blanket of her closed eyelids, Foxy saw that she must soon break with Piet, and felt no pain" (293). Certainly neither Tristan nor Iseult nor Jerry nor Sally would have so easily given up their loves. The myth has degenerated and lost force.

In fact, of course, Piet and Foxy do still feel something for each other, and in an often-remarked-upon scene at the Thorne's party on the night of the Kennedy assassination, they enact an outrageous parody of one (or two) of the Tristan-myth's most vivid incidents. During the party, while Foxy is in the upstairs bathroom, Piet joins her there and asks her to nurse him. Foxy reluctantly agrees, but they are interrupted by Angela's knocks on the door. The only escape Piet sees is to jump from the window, which he does, much to the amusement of Ben Saltz and Bea Guerin, who are outside looking for a satellite that Ben helped produce (not the stars of nature). Later Foxy tells Piet that it was silly to jump, that even if they had been discovered it would not have been the end of the world, for she could have made up some explanation. She observes that he was "clearly in love with the idea of jumping" (316). Whereas Tristan was, as de Rougemont says, in love with love itself and Jerry Conant was in love with the *idea* of Sally, Piet is in love with neither love nor Foxy, but with the idea of jumping—and out of a bathroom window, at that. The jump, of course, suggests Tristan's leap from his bed to Iseult's in King Mark's castle, necessitated by the suspicious king's having spread flour on the floor so that footprints would provide evidence of Tristan's guilt. The jump may also suggest Tristan's leap from the chapel on the coast of Cornwall when he was cornered there with no apparent way out. Both of these leaps, however, are dignified by passion, athleticism, and genuine danger, whereas Piet's leap is neither really dangerous nor even necessary. Piet himself sees his act less in terms of a heroic leap than as simply a fall (314). The credibility of the Tristan myth has also fallen, far below the level to which one may be expected to maintain the suspension of disbelief necessary to accept its viability in modern dress.

When Piet visits Foxy in her home after the birth of her baby, he feels that they must not see each other any more. What they had together had been good, but now it would be wrong. He thinks: "They had been let into God's playroom, and been happy together on the floor all afternoon, but the time had come to return the toys to their boxes, and put the chairs back against the wall" (323). He has not sought Foxy in a castle with golden stairs; rather, they have been children with toys that should now be put away. Although Piet does go to see Foxy again—the fateful visit that produces her pregnancy—he finds the experience "disappointing" (331) and tells her he thinks they should stop seeing each other; she agrees that he is right (334). Glad that this final sexual encounter together was not really satisfying, he leaves with no emotion except exhilaration "once again at not having been caught" (335).

Actually, of course, they *have* been "caught." Foxy becomes pregnant (as Iseult conveniently never did), and Freddy Thorne arranges the abortion. It is through Freddy that the identification of love and death suggested by de Rougemont is made most explicit in the novel. Freddy, clearly the most anti-romantic figure in the book, the high priest of "sex, stoicism, and the stars," has no room for any mythic idealism. He is the foil for Piet, who believes in the supernatural. Piet tells Angela that he is afraid of Freddy because, he says, "he threatens my primitive faith" (304). Freddy talks at length with Angela during their night together, which was his price for arranging the abortion, to avoid facing the fact of his impotence. Angela tells Freddy that he really would like to be a teacher, and Freddy admits that he used to want to teach, but "then I learned the final thing to teach and I didn't want to learn any more" (370). The final thing that he has learned is that "We die. We don't die for one second out there in the future, we die all the time, in every direction . . . . Death excites me. Death is being screwed by God. It'll be delicious" (370). When Angela objects that he doesn't believe in God, Freddy replies, "I believe in that one. Big Man Death" (370). For Freddy, de Rougemont's secret has become apparent. Worship of sex is really worship of death. In this case the seeking of sex for its own sake leads to the very death of sex itself, since Freddy's impotence prevents his realizing either his desire for Angela or the achievement of his revenge on Piet through her.

Piet's expression of fear of Freddy is justified, for Piet gradually loses his own belief and succumbs to Freddy's teaching. Talking to Foxy from a phone booth after the abortion, Piet feels that he is "a droll corpse upright in a bright aluminum coffin" (380). Despite earlier resolutions that their affair was over, Piet feels that "of course he must go to her" now. "Death," he reasons, "once invited in, leaves his muddy bootprints everywhere" (380). He goes to Foxy not out of idealism or even passion, but simply in recognition that in choosing to abort the unborn child they have not only accepted death but also invited it in.

Georgene Thorne's discovery of Piet with Foxy leads to Ken's finding out about the affair, and when the Hanemas and the Whitmans face each other, Ken suggests that Freddy's arranging the abortion was a criminal act. Piet defends Freddy, saying he did it out of love for his friends. As Piet says these words, he feels "his heart vibrate with the nervousness of love, as if he and Freddy, the partition between them destroyed, at last comprehended each other with the fullness long desired" (398). After Piet has moved out of his house and is living alone in the converted office building, he feels that "he has been redeemed from Freddy Thorne's spell; the old loathing and fascination were gone. Freddy's atheism, his evangelical humanism, no longer threatened Piet" (407). The underlying reason Freddy no longer threatens Piet is that Piet has accepted Freddy's gospel. After he and Foxy spend a weekend of almost constant sex together, Foxy says, "It's good to have enough, isn't it?" Piet replies, "Sex is like money; only too much is enough." When Foxy points out that that sounds like Freddy Thorne, he replies, "My mentor and savior" (437). Piet is no longer a questing knight in even a marginal sense.

Although the above examples are more than adequate to illustrate that the Tristan myth has been effectively shown to be inadequate, Updike adds a few more touches. During the conversation with Ken Whitman, "Piet's itch was to clown" (395) rather than to indulge in the high-sounding tragic posturings of Tristan or even of Jerry Conant. He thinks also of Foxy, who in the myth should be the ideal love, "that her underwear was not always clean" (396). He tells Angela later that he is "scared to death of that woman [Foxy]" (404). If Tristan had been frightened of Iseult, he certainly would never have said so. The weekend Foxy and Piet spend together might at first glance be likened to Tristan and Iseult's idyllic days in their hidden love grotto. Unlike the scene in the grotto where Tristan and Iseult sleep peacefully, however, Foxy "snuffled, and restlessly crowded him toward the edge of the bed, and sometimes struggled against nightmares" (434). The sating of his sexual appetite leads Piet to groans which seem "to be emptying his chest, creating an inner hollowness answering to the hollowness beneath the stars" (437). Piet realizes the world has gone its way during their love tryst, not caring as much about lovers as he had imagined (438). Love becomes, for Piet, "real and leaden" (438), rather than light and airy like Jerry Conant's bodily ascension. Piet has no illusions of a romantic dimension where his ideal love may be realized. He doesn't *dream* of asking Foxy to marry him; he marries her. She is not and never was Iseult. Piet was the best candidate for a modern Tristan that Tarbox had to offer. Before the book ends, however, he has resigned all claims to the title, and it is clear that, for Updike, a romantic idealization of love is not a viable contemporary alternative.

If neither the religion of human sexual interplay nor a revival of medieval myth provides a viable successor to Christianity, then one might suppose that Updike is advocating a return to traditional Christianity. The church as presented in *Couples,* however, hardly offers more promise than Freddy's substitute or the failed Tristan. Pedrick, the pastor of the

Congregational Church that Piet attends, is much less interesting than Freddy, and poorly articulates the faith. For example, in his Palm Sunday sermon, "the palms spread across Jesus' path . . . become greenbacks and the theft of the colt a troubled disquisition on property rights" (22). After the church has burned, Pedrick sees Piet and is interested only in the contractor's opinion as to how much in dollars and cents it will take to replace the building (444). When Piet first began attending the church, he was impressed by the quality of its workmanship. Like Hook in *The Poorhouse Fair,* he thinks the old carpenters were the best and "that none of their quality had been born to replace them" (18). The church is thus presented as a solid institution, but representative of the past. After the church has burned, Piet again comments that "the carpentry can never be duplicated" (444). Actually, however, when the building is inspected, it is discovered that "the old church is not only badly gutted but structurally unsound: a miracle it had not collapsed of itself a decade ago" (457). Thus not only does the church represent a dead past, but it has also been merely a facade of false solidity for a long time—like the apparently solid wall in *The Poorhouse Fair* which collapsed to reveal the rubble inside.

Perhaps the most telling comment on institutional Christianity, however, is found in the image of the rooster weather vane that tops the church steeple and dominates every view of the town. Although the church has been rebuilt three times since the colonial era, the old gilded weathercock has been salvaged each time. It serves as a landmark for fishermen and is the single most important symbol associated with the church. In fact, "children in the town grew up with the sense that the bird was God. That is, if God were physically present in Tarbox, it was in the form of this unreachable weathercock, visible from everywhere" (17). The eye of the rooster is an old English penny, "and if its penny could see, it saw everything" (17). When the church burns, the weathercock is saved once more. Updike scholars Alice and Kenneth

Hamilton believe that the rooster suggests God with his all-seeing eye, and find in the rooster/God association a "link with St. Peter and the cock who announced the disciple's denial of his Master. Piet is a Peter who does not repent of his denial" (238). If we accept the Piet-Peter-rooster-denial association, however, we also have to admit that when the bird is examined it is found that "his eye was tiny" (457), and that there is no resurrection appearance to Piet, to whose ears the cheering at the rescue of the cock seems "a jubilant jeering" (457).

It is even more difficult to see the weathercock symbol as a positive endorsement of institutional Christianity when one considers two other associations it strongly suggests. Although Updike uses the word "cock" sparingly, turning instead more often to "rooster" or "gilded bird," the phallic suggestions of the word are inescapable, considering the numerous sexual exploits and constant sexual concerns of the ten couples. The tiny-eyed cock seems to suggest that the God of Christianity has been replaced by the god of sex. The church is gone, but the cock remains. In addition, it is the very nature of a weathervane to point in a different direction with each shift of the wind. It is hard to see how such an easily-turned "god" could provide a valid alternative to the admittedly unsatisfactory emerging religion of human sexual interplay or the exhausted Tristan myth. The answer to the question "After Christianity, what?" seems to be "Nothing."

THE GOODNESS OF REALITY

Nihilism and despair, however, do not set the dominant tone of the novel. Even these hedonistic couples have not completely lost their capacity to marvel at something beyond self and sex, as evidenced by the pleasure they take in a new game Freddy proposes: "Wonderful." Each participant is to name the most wonderful thing he or she can think of. Carol Constantine suggests a baby's fingernails, explaining that "a lot of *work,* somehow, ingenuity, *love* even, goes into making each one of us, no matter what a lousy job we make of it afterwards" (238). Piet thinks of a sleeping woman, "because when she is sleeping, . . . she becomes all women" (239). Terry Gallagher proposes the works of J. S. Bach, explaining that what made Bach so wonderful was that "he didn't know how great he was. He was just trying to support his seventeen children with an honest day's work" (240). Foxy finds the Eucharist her most wonderful thing, although she can't offer an explanation. For Angela, the stars are wonderful because "they're so fixed. So above it all. . . . I know they move but not relative to us, we're too small" (241). Freddy imposes his usual cynical point of view on the game by insisting that the most wonderful thing he knows "is the human capacity for self-deception." He sees this capacity as the thing that "keeps everything else going" (240). Despite the somewhat sour note Freddy inserts, all of the "wonderful" things proposed move beyond a simplistic view of man as an animal and suggest an added dimension to human life. Even these adherents of the religion of human sexual interplay have not completely surrendered to nihilism.

Piet is often the spokesman for this positive urge toward a life-giving force beyond the self. At the Thornes' party, for instance, he responds to the pain caused by his mouth cankers by feeling that "a maze of membranes never could have evolved from algae unassisted. God gave us a boost" (311). Further, although he insists that Foxy abort their baby, he finds "amid the terror pleasure that she had proved doubly fertile, that she had shown him capable of bringing more life to bud upon the earth" (340). While he waits for Foxy to have the abortion, even realizing that he has literally invited death in, he finds as he watches the passersby in the park that "all people seem . . . miraculous" (376). In his isolation after leaving Angela, Piet finds that "in loneliness he was regaining something, an elemental sense of surprise at everything, that he had lost with childhood" (423). As he walks alone on the beach after visiting his dying friend John Ong in the hospital, he finds that "nothing is too ordinary . . . to notice" (429). He feels the power of the waves beating on the shore "with energies that could power cities." Somehow he finds that "the great syllable around him seemed his own note, sustained since his birth, elicited from him now, and given to the air" (429). He finds a "companionship in the motion of the waves," and decides that "the world was more Platonic than he had suspected" (429). He does not receive nearly so clear a word as Caldwell did in *The Centaur,* but he at least finds "one great syllable" that seems to be his own, and his recognition that the world is more Platonic than he had suspected suggests an acceptance of a life of polar interaction.

Piet may have urges toward another dimension, and he may recognize the existence of an ideal reality beyond himself, but he does not successfully develop his "one great syllable" into a meaningful word. During his last weekend with Foxy, he tells her he doubts that he is a Christian any more (454), and as he watches the rooster being salvaged from the top of the burned church, he recognizes that "his life in a sense had ended" (457). He is glad that he will marry Foxy; he has what he wants. As Updike pointed out in his *Paris Review* interview, Piet "divorces the supernatural to marry the natural." He is "relieved of morality, can move out of the paralysis of guilt into what after all is a kind of freedom" ("One Big Interview" 504). On one level, then, there seems to be a happy ending to the novel.

If, however, the ending is indeed a happy one, the reader might assume that Updike is advocating the hedonistic advice that was labeled "all wrong" in *Midpoint*. Therefore, the reader must look past the surface and see that the happiness of the ending is also, in a sense, "all wrong." Piet may be happy—or better yet, not *un*happy—but as Updike has pointed out, he has become

> insignificant. He becomes merely a name in the last paragraph; he becomes a satisfied person and in a sense dies. In other words, a person who has what he wants, a satisfied person, a content person, ceases to be a person. Unfallen Adam is an ape. . . . I feel that to be a person is to be in a situation of tension, to be in a dialectical situation. A truly adjusted person is not a person at all—just an animal with clothes on. So . . . it's a happy ending, with this "but" at the end. ("One Big Interview" 504)

The "but" suggests that although there is no endorsement of a dogmatic traditional Christianity, the commitments of *Midpoint* stand firm. Just as William Faulkner described doom, decadence, perversion, and despair, yet insisted in his 1950 Nobel Address that he had always been dealing with "the old verities of the heart"—"pity, pride, compassion, honor," etc. (929)—so Updike affirms the mystery of life by exposing the multiplicity of patterns formed by the dots of daily existence.

THE WITCHES OF EASTWICK

Just as *Marry Me* was published eight years after *Couples,* it was in turn followed eight years later by *The Witches of Eastwick,* the third of Updike's small town New England novels dealing with deteriorating marriages and deteriorating innocence. Like its predecessors, it is set in the 1960s, but at the end of the decade while Nixon is in the White House and the Vietnam war drags on. Also like its predecessors, it probes American culture's attempts to find a replacement for an abandoned Christianity and demythologizes popular attempts to locate sources of ultimate meaning.

The novel opens in September of an unspecified year in the late sixties. Updike usually fills his novels with details of specific events that enable one to pinpoint the exact dates of his fictions, but this time we are told on the dust jacket only that "the action consumes a year during the national *Walpurgisnacht* of the Vietnam era." In the small village of Eastwick, Rhode Island, three divorcees, Alexandra Spofford, Jane Smart, and Sukie Rougemont, having shed their husbands, discover the power of femininity and sisterhood by forming a coven of witches. When Darryl Van Horne, whom Margaret Atwood finds to be "part Mephistopholes . . . and part Miltonic Satan" (40), moves to town and buys the old Lenox mansion, each of the witches seeks and receives his favors, but he ultimately chooses the much younger Jennifer Gabriel for his wife. The witches make a poppet and stick it full of pins, conjuring the girl's death. When she dies of cancer, neither they nor the reader knows whether the death results from their curse or the more general curse of human susceptibility to disease. Van Horne, invited to preach in the Unitarian Church during Jennifer's illness, raises the age-old problem of the terrors of suffering and makes the claim that he himself could have made a better creation.

Van Horne does not choose one of the three witches to replace his young bride; instead he slips away with her brother. The three witches find their solidarity broken and their powers fragmented. They use their powers to attract new husbands: Jane marries a prim and prissy scion of an old Boston family; Sukie marries a word processor salesman; and Alexandra marries an art instructor who takes her back to Taos with him. Just as Jerry and Ruth and Sally and Richard stay married, suggesting the solidity and validity of traditional moral arrangements, and just as Piet and Foxy marry, move to a new town and become once more a couple in a group of couples, so Alexandra, Jane, and Sukie return to solid married life. The novel's final passage includes these words: "The witches are gone, vanished; we were just an interval in their lives, and they in ours" (307). But Updike has used this interval and these characters to "dramatize issues and tensions" ("Response"), "to hold up to the light" ("Response") feminism, the impotence of evil, and the price of self-absorption that denies an objective, ordered, natural world.[1]

FEMINISM HELD UP TO THE LIGHT

Because the witches become disenchanted with casting spells and playing with the devil and because each seeks out a new conventional husband and marriage, many readers have thought that Updike is seeking to point out the weakness of contemporary feminism. As Peter Prescott points out, "the witches, of course, are feminists. Updike didn't invent the metaphor—feminists have applied it to themselves—but he expands it" (92). Craig Raine believes that among the most important aspects of the book is that "Updike shows that the feminist myth of the gentler sex—the idea that women would exercise power more responsibly than men—is simply sentimental." Although there certainly is satire on aspects of the women's movement, Updike told me that his "intention was not to put down feminism but to hold it up to the light" ("Response"). He also admitted to Andrea Stevens that he was aware of being criticized "for making the women of my books subsidiary to the men." "Perhaps," he said, "my female characters have been too domestic, too adorable, too much what men wished them to be." This novel, he told Stevens, like witchcraft itself, is "about female power, a power that patriarchal societies have denied while trying to retain the 'wonderful male power' of killing people." Furthermore, he told me that he found that "this kind of coven, of divorced women, is a small-town (and maybe big-town) phenomenon and that is why [he] wrote about it" ("Response"). Thus the motivation for writing the novel is more complex than a simple desire to satirize feminism.

Once more, then, we have the familiar "yes—but," the turning of things over to see what can be said on both sides. On the one hand, Updike has succeeded in imagining himself into the lives of his three women protagonists. In portions of *Rabbit Redux* Updike undertook the feminine point of view as he narrated sections through Janice's consciousness. Again in *Marry Me,* as we have noted, he used Ruth's point of view for much of the central section. But telling this story from the point of view of three women and using no male center of consciousness is a departure for Updike, a serious attempt to investigate what it means to be a woman. Despite his confessing that for any man women can be "something *other* . . . . elusive, strange and frightening to a degree. . . . full of menace and magic and strangeness" (qtd. in Stevens), Updike has identified with Alexandra, Jane, and Sukie completely enough to make them convincing when they reveal their central beliefs about themselves as women.

Alexandra is the first to explain that "many of her remarkable powers had flowed from [the] mere reappropriation of her assigned self, achieved not until midlife. Not until midlife did she truly believe that she had a right to exist, that the forces of nature had created her not as an afterthought and companion" (14). Now she recognizes that she is not just "a bent rib" (14) but a vital part in the chain that links DNA to its very source of life in the heat of the sun. She speaks with conviction that seems to come from her creator/author when she affirms that as a woman she is "the mainstay of Creation, . . . the daughter of a daughter and a woman whose daughters in turn would bear daughters" (14). Sukie proclaims that when "sheer womanhood had exploded within her," "she realized that the world men had systematically made was all dreary poison, good for nothing really but for battlefields and waste sites" (135). And Jane voices the philosophical basis for this dreary world: "Men are violent," she explains. "It's biological. They're full of rage because they're just accessories to reproduction" (157).

One is tempted to dismiss this high-flown feminist rhetoric as deft irony since the three witches do not seem to capitalize on or profit from their newly-discovered feminine ties to nature, motherhood, and creativity. Instead, they use their power for spiteful tricks such as bringing a thunderstorm to clear the beach of young people who called Alexandra a hag, breaking an old woman's string of pearls, causing feathers to come from the mouth of an annoying liberal do-gooder, turning tennis balls into bats and toads, killing innocent puppies and squirrels, and, ultimately, casting the death curse on young Jennifer Gabriel. They seem to dabble in magic merely as a means to indulge personal whims.

On the other hand, when we look at the empty men around them, we see that whatever irony may suffuse feminists' claims, male magic—busily napalming innocent peasants in Vietnam—seems even less attractive than the witches' tricks. When Ed Parsley makes a fool of himself, for example, blowing himself up while dreaming of glory in a "movement" that doesn't even exist, his wife, Brenda, successfully takes over the Unitarian Church, running it more efficiently than he ever did. Alexandra, Jane, and Sukie—and Brenda—are certainly as capable as any men in this story, and are as interesting and effectual as Piet Hanema in *Couples* and more interesting and effectual than Jerry Conant in *Marry Me*.

There is, then, clearly appreciation for the feminist position. Van Horne, diabolical as he is and therefore suspect as spokesman for any point of view, seems to be representing some of the careful research Updike did for this book when he says:

> the whole witchcraft scare was an attempt—successful, as it turned out—on the part of the newly arising male-dominated medical

profession, beginning in the fourteenth century, to get the childbirth business out of the hands of midwives. That's what a lot of the women burned were—midwives. They had the ergot, and atropine, and probably a lot of right instincts even without the germ theory. When the male doctors took over they worked blind, with a sheet around their necks, and brought all the diseases from the rest of their practice with them. (109)

Here is a specific example of what Updike meant when he said that both his novel and witchcraft are about female power that patriarchal societies sought to deny and repress (Stevens).

Ultimately, however, it is clear that Updike takes Alexandra, Jane, and Sukie seriously because they move beyond discussing or playing roles in a game of power between the sexes. They move beyond male/female issues to become representatives of concerns that the poet expressed in *Midpoint*. The titles of the three parts of the novel suggest a progression in understanding on the part of the three protagonists. Part I, "The Coven," describes the exhilaration they feel when they gather for their regular Thursday trysts and feel the "cone of power" (33) above their heads. As they become entangled with Van Horne, however, they move into Part II, "Malefica," in which genuine evil and wickedness begin to bring discord and dissatisfaction. Part III, "Guilt," finds each woman feeling guilty about Jennifer's death, and such guilt feelings contribute to their decisions to leave the coven and seek new lives in new marriages. Like the *Midpoint* poet, they have reached a time in their lives when they feel that things are "ALL/ wrong, all wrong" (*Midpoint* 23).

The three witches also come to terms with death as Jerry, Piet, and Harry do. As Alexandra wades across the causeway at high tide after her first visit with Van Horne at the old Lenox mansion, she reconizes not only her part in the passing on of creation but also her share in the mortality of all living creatures. She feels the "mindless flow" of the sucking tide and thinks, "The coldest thing about this pull was that it would be here whether she was or not. It had been here before she was born and would be here when she was dead" (95). Alexandra later confesses to Sukie that she feels guilty about Jennifer's illness and that she is afraid, afraid of death. When Sukie points out, "But it isn't *your* death," Alexandra replies, "Any death is your death, in a way" (284). Sukie herself has felt this fear of death as she looked at the beauty of early fall around her in Eastwick: "*Such beauty!* Sukie thought, and felt frightened that her own beauty and vitality would not always be a part of it, that some day she would be gone like a lost odd-shaped piece from the center of a picture puzzle" (76). Like the *Midpoint* poet, she realizes that although she is the center of the puzzle of herself, there is an earth beyond that will have her for its own all too soon.

It is Jane, however, who most fully comes to understand and accept the reality of death as she plays an extremely difficult Bach suite on her cello during a sleepless night. In a tour de force of technical musical description, Updike explains how Jane comes to understand the recurrent theme, "the matter under discussion," to be death (275). In the final movement of the suite, there are two voices which strike against each other, "the last revival of that . . . receding, returning theme, still to be quelled" (277). As she plays the difficult music almost flawlessly, Jane thinks:

> So this was what men had been murmuring about, monopolizing, all these centuries, death; no wonder they had kept it to themselves, no wonder they had kept it from women, let the women do their nursing and hatching, keeping a bad thing going while they, *they,* men, distributed among themselves the true treasure, onyx and ebony and unalloyed gold, the substance of glory and release. Until now Jenny's death had been simply an erasure in Jane's mind, a nothing; now it had its tactile structure, a branched and sumptuous complexity, a sensuous down-pulling . . . . (277-278)

197

Through the three witches, Updike holds feminism up to the light, but not for propagandistic purposes. Instead, he presents for the first time in his fiction three women whose full humanity suggests that however the balance of power may fall in the ongoing struggle between the sexes, neither can claim exemption from the limits of the human condition.

SATAN DEMYTHOLOGIZED

Part of the enjoyment of reading *The Witches of Eastwick* lies in the recognition of bits of traditional devil-lore casually worked into the presentation of Darryl Van Horne. When we first meet him, for instance, we notice that his trousers "bag . . . at the backs of his knees somehow" and that he wears "on his feet incongruously small and pointy black loafers" (34). The devil's cloven-hoof feet and goat or satyr legs have always provided him problems in appearing fully human. Darryl paints the door to his new home black, and the sheets and couches are also black, as if he is deliberately contradicting the command in Genesis, "Let there be light." When Alexandra first goes through the black door, she is greeted by a "sulphurous chemical smell," but "Van Horne seem[s] oblivious to it, it [is] his element" (84). Van Horne is posing as an inventor, so there is rational explanation for the smell from his laboratory, but Updike's recurring references to the fumes remind us that Faust's innocent Gretchen could smell the devil when he had been in the room. Updike's witches, however, recognize the smell but do not sense its significance. Sukie, although she feels a "sulphurous pillow of heat hit her in the face" (180) when she enters Darryl's house after a tennis game, and although she recognizes that "the whole house [is] like a stage set, stunning from one angle but from others full of gaps and unresolved shabbiness. . . . an imitation of a real house somewhere else" (181), nevertheless willingly submits to Darryl, even to the point of kissing him on the anus.

This particular act of obeisance is also part of traditional satan/witch lore, as indicated in one of the epigraphs Updike has used for Part I, a quotation from the witch Agnes Sampson in 1590, in which she describes the devil coming out of his pulpit and causing "all the company to com and kiss his ers, quhilk they said was cauld lyk yce." Darryl also has this distinctive coldness. The first time he touches Alexandra, she feels "a chilly tingle" (34), and after their first big orgy around the hot-tub on Halloween, the witches all agree that his semen "was marvellously cold" (119). Alexandra reflects that "Darryl's potency had something infallible and unfeeling about it, and his cold penis hurt, as if it were covered with tiny scales" (208). After disillusionment has set in, Sukie wonders how Jenny can stand to share a bed with Darryl: "That body so cold and clammy under the fur. He was like opening a refrigerator with something spoiling in it" (240).

Darryl also shares other traditional Satanic traits. He denies the reality of guilt (134), he has "a voracious appetite for immaterial souls" (203), he is depressed by spring in general and Easter in particular (82, 221), he insists on being called king (118), and he is an expert at "getting people to sign pacts" (300). But all these traditional items of devil-lore are less important than several deft strokes by which Updike demythologizes Satan as effectively as he demythologized Tristan in *Marry Me* and *Couples*.

When we first meet Darryl, we are made aware that his features make a "strange, slipping, patched-together impression" and that there is an "artificial element somewhere in his speech apparatus." His voice does "not quite go with the movements of his mouth and jaw" (35). The blankness of his eyes gives Alexandra the "sensation of looking down a deep hole" (47). As we and the witches come to know more about

Van Horne, we are shown that there is no solid reality behind the show he puts on. He is supposed to be rich, but he does not pay the plumber who put in his fancy hot-tub and spa, and the town threatens to turn off the water to the mansion for nonpayment of the bills (197). Jenny suggests that the name Van Horne sounds made up, and Alexandra notes that his cups are monogrammed with an "N" ("old Nick"?) instead of a "V" or an "H," and his towels are monogrammed with an "M" (Mephistopholes?).

Darryl's pretense and emptiness are suggested when Alexandra says that "For all his talk of glories still to be unpacked, the rooms were badly underfurnished; Van Horne had the robust instincts of a creator but with only, it seemed, half the needed raw materials" (85). Actually, it turns out that he has *none* of the raw materials and is incapable of any kind of creation. When he performs on the piano, he plays two of his own compositions. The first is "The A Nightingale Sang in Berkeley Square Boogie" and the second is "The How High the Moon March." Neither is really something Darryl has himself created; rather, each is merely an unexpected and ingenious combination of elements created by others. It is "wizardry," Alexandra sees, "of theft and transformation, with nothing of guileless creative engendering about it, only a boldness of monstrous combination" (224).

When Darryl is invited to give a lay sermon at the Unitarian Church during Jennifer's losing bout with cancer, he chooses the topic "The Terribleness of Creation." He cites tape worms, tarantulas, round worms, and lung flukes as examples of basic nature—parasites, not the dancing daffodils and soaring skylarks of Romanticism. The lung fluke is his favorite example because although it matures in the intestines of dogs, the huge larvae grow in the lungs of man. "Man," Darryl charges, "allegedly made in the image of

God, . . . is just a way station on the way to the intestines of a dog" (292). He insists that these loathesome parasites are as lovingly designed as human beings, and concludes:

> You got to picture that Big Visage leaning down and smiling through Its beard while those fabulous Fingers and Their angelic manicure fiddled with the last fine-tuning of old *Schistosoma*'s ventral sucker: that's Creation. Now I ask you, isn't that pretty terrible? Couldn't you have done better, given the resources? I sure as hell could have. So vote for me next time, O.K.? Amen. (293)

This sermon sounds surprisingly like the arguments of Conner and Buddy in *The Poorhouse Fair*. They argued against God from the basis of the cruelty of creation, just as Darryl does. But we have already seen that Darryl cannot create, so could *not* do a better job if given the chance. As Updike told me, "Darryl's sermon shows that the Devil is good at criticism but can't make anything himself. Much the same point as the book of Job" ("Response").

After Jennifer's death, Darryl disappears with her brother, Christopher. When she first heard about the rich man from New York with no wife or family who was buying the old Lenox place, Alexandra, sure that he was a homosexual, had said, "Oh. One of those" (3). Now Jane tells her, "You were right in the first place. He was one of those" (297). The witches suspect that Darryl's marriage to Jenny was all along just a way to get to Chris and to Jenny's share of the money from the sale of their parents' house. Alexandra, however, doubts that Darryl was capable of such an elaborate plan. She says:

> I really doubt . . . that Darryl was ever organized in that way. He had to improvise on situations others created, and couldn't look very far ahead. . . .He couldn't create, he had no powers of his own that way, all he could do was release what was already there in others. Even us: we had the coven before he came to town, and our powers such as they are. (299)

The devil, then, is shown to be the master of lies, manipulating but incapable of creating, empty and sterile at the core. He is not the source of the feminine powers of the witches, even though he would like to use those powers to his own ends and pretend that he was their source. He trades on the self-focused illusions of a society that does not have a firm grasp of the objective reality of created nature. And Updike's comments on the American society that allows the devil into the pulpit without ever knowing it are what make *The Witches of Eastwick* much more than just a black comedy.

SELF VS. WORLD

Although most of *The Witches of Eastwick* is told from the point of view of one of the three witches, there are occasional intrusions of an objective narrative voice. This voice speaks for the other citizens of the town, and, thus, as Margaret Atwood suggests, serves "as a collective chorus" (40). Toward the end of Part II of the novel, as winter is passing, this choric voice comments on the scruffy band of teenagers who hang out in front of the Superette waiting for the drug dealer from Providence. Waiting outside in the bitter cold of winter, "these children," we are told, are

> Martyrs of a sort . . . risking nightly death by exposure; martyrs too of a sort were the men and women hastening to adulterous trysts, risking disgrace and divorce for their fix of motel love—all sacrificing the outer world to the inner, proclaiming with this priority that everything solid-seeming and substantial is in fact a dream, of less account than a merciful rush of feeling. (201)

Like Harry Angstrom in the first two Rabbit novels, both youth and adults of Eastwick (read America) solipsistically deny the substantial and solid outer world of phenomena and social forms to seek meaning in momentary feelings.

The witches, seeking to mold outer circumstances to their own inner wants, are only representatives of the culture at large. In fact, there is a strong suggestion that the witches are actually imaginative projections of the common psyche. The choric narrative voice comments:

> Insofar as they were witches, they were phantoms in the communal mind. . . . [with] a certain distinction, an inner boiling such as had in other cloistral towns produced Emily Dickinson's verses and Emily Bronte's inspired novel. . . . We all knew there was . . . something . . . about them, something as monstrous and obscene as what went on in the bedroom of even the assistant high-school principal and his wife, who both looked so blinky and tame as they sat in the bleachers chaperoning a record hop with its blood-curdling throbbing. (209-210)

The witches, then, are really no different from most of the community's childish "Me Generation," who secretly seek to find fulfillment in a "momentary rush of feeling." The witches, who have "left their children behind" to enter Van Horne's realm, have become "children themselves" (207). They are emblematic of the type of hedonism presented in *Couples* when the adults did not want to leave their games to face up to the fact that they were "not the world's guests but its hosts" *(Couples* 74).

The witches represent another deep and hidden desire of the community, too. There is always in Updike that turning over to see the other side. If the witches are really dream projections of the communal mind, dreams are "our way . . . into the nether world," experiences that

> help us to believe that there is more to life than airbrushed ads at the front of magazines, the Platonic forms of perfume bottles and nylon nightgowns and Roll-Royce fenders. . . . the fact of witchcraft. . . offered the consolation of completeness, of rounding out the picture, like the gas mains underneath Oak Street and the television aerials scraping *Kojak* and Pepsi commercials out of the sky. (210)

The witches, then, are "phantoms of the communal mind" that project the solipsistic rejection of "everything solid-seeming and substantial" but at the same time embody the basic need to be in touch with a transcendent and mysterious world beyond the magazine ads. The struggle of the *Midpoint* ego to balance its individuality, the objective world, and its sense of the transcendent finds continued expression in the experiences of the witches and in the community's experience of the witches in its midst.

In *Marry Me, Couples,* and *The Witches of Eastwick,* Updike has presented stories of deteriorating marriages and deteriorating innocence in the America of the 1960s. He has examined a variety of attempts to find a meaningful successor to a Christianity that once provided the blueprint for the lives of most Americans but now seems largely abandoned. In each of these novels the "new" fashions are found wanting. To the question, "After Christianity, what?" Updike suggests that the attempt to find a successor to Christianity is futile. There is no dogmatism, however, only the points and dots of experience presented in their rich variety. But significant patterns emerge for the perceptive reader. These three novels, then, provide an example of Updike's faith, which, he has said, "urges [him] to tell the truth, however painful and inconvenient, and holds out the hope that the truth—reality— is good. Good or not," he adds, "only the truth is useful" ("Interview" 304).

NOTE

[1]The movie version of *The Witches of Eastwick,* unlike the earlier movie of *Rabbit, Run,* was immensely successful financially and received considerable critical praise as well. Jack Nicholson was especially praised for his performance in the role of Van Horne. The movie, however, bore little resemblance to the novel discussed here. Jennifer and Christopher Gabriel, for instance, were not included among the characters, and the ending found the three witches each the mother of a son by Van Horne and living comfortably in his mansion.

WORKS CITED

Atwood, Margaret, "Wondering What It's Like to Be a Woman." Review of *The Witches of Eastwick* by John Updike. *New York Times Book Review* 13 May 1984: 1; 40.

Fuller, Edmund. "Updike at the Top of his Form." Review of *Marry Me* by John Updike. *Wall Street Journal* 7 Dec. 1976: 22.

Hamilton, Alice, and Kenneth Hamilton. *The Elements of John Updike*. Grand Rapids: Eerdmans, 1970.

Holman, C. Hugh. *A Handbook to Literature*. Indianapolis: Odyssey, 1972.

Nichols, Lewis. "Talk With John Updike." *New York Times Book Review* 7 Apr. 1968: 34.

Prescott, Peter. "Updike's Three Weird Sisters." Review of *The Witches of Eastwick* by John Updike. *Newsweek* 7 May 1984: 92.

Raine, Craig. "Sisters With the Devil in Them." Review of *The Witches of Eastwick* by John Updike. *Times Literary Supplement* 28 Sep. 1984: 1084.

Stevens, Andrea. "A Triple Spell." *New York Times Book Review* 13 May 1984: 40.

Todd, Richard. "A Ladies' Man." Review of *Marry Me* by John Updike. *Atlantic* Nov. 1976: 116.

Updike, John. *Couples*. New York: Knopf, 1968.

--. "Foreword." *Assorted Prose*. Greenwich, CN: Fawcett, 1966: vii-ix.

---. "Interview Conducted by Jeff Campbell, Georgetown, MA, 9 Aug. 1976." Published as Appendix to this volume.

---. Letter to Jeff Campbell, 8 Nov. 1976.

---. *Marry Me*. New York: Knopf, 1976.

---. "More Love in the Western World." *Assorted Prose*. Greenwich, CN: Fawcett, 1966. 220-223.

---. "One Big Interview." *Picked-Up Pieces*. New York: Knopf, 1975. 491-519.

---. Response to Written Questions Submitted by Jeff Campbell. 25 May 1987.

---. *The Witches of Eastwick*. New York: Knopf, 1984.

CHAPTER 6

"THE PRINCIPLE OF AMBIGUITY":
A MONTH OF SUNDAYS, THE COUP, AND *ROGER'S VERSION*

A Month of Sundays (1975), *The Coup* (1978), and *Roger's Version* (1986) form the final group of Updike's novels for consideration in this study. Although the three are not so closely related to each other in subject matter as were *The Centaur* and *Of the Farm,* the three Rabbit books, and the three New England novels set in the 60s, they share several characteristics that make them different from Updike's other works and which encourage their joint treatment. Each of these novels uses first-person narrators, a technique previously used by Updike only in *Of the Farm* and in portions of *The Centaur.* The narrators of these later novels are unlike their earlier counterparts, however, for each is aware of himself as the narrator of a fiction to be read by others. These novels, then, are departures from Updike's usual conventional naturalistic and psychological realism into experimentation with the "self-conscious" techniques more commonly associated with James Joyce, Vladimir Nabokov, John Barth, John Hawkes, and Thomas Pynchon. Furthermore, both *A Month of Sundays* and *Roger's Version* deal overtly with theological themes which, although present, have been less obvious in the other novels; and both are freighted with allusions to *The Scarlet Letter.* Finally, *The Coup* and *Roger's Version* required the use of extensive research materials (the sources of which are acknowledged in the preliminary pages of each novel) as none of Updike's other books have.

For these reasons, these three books have more in common with each other than with the balance of the Updike canon. They do not, however, signal a basic change in Updike's approach to his craft or a rejection of his previous techniques and subject matter; *A Month of Sundays* and *The Coup* were followed by *Rabbit Is Rich* and *The Witches of Eastwick,* both of which returned to familiar themes, settings, and techniques. But *A Month of Sundays, The Coup,* and *Roger's Version* do signal the continual breaking of new ground by an author who as a young man began his novelistic career by imagining himself into the lives of a group of old people in the future, daringly attempted the use of cinematic present tense in his second novel, then sandwiched Greek mythology with the mundane affairs of a Pennsylvania high school in his third. As we shall see, the *Midpoint* commitments remain firm in these later novels, but Updike continues to experiment with new ways of viewing and interpreting the patterns created by the emerging dots of experience.

A MONTH OF SUNDAYS

Updike's eighth novel, *A Month of Sundays* (1975), is crucial to an understanding of his novelistic *oeuvre* for two fundamental reasons: in it for the first time he overtly treats several substantive themes that have been only implicit in earlier novels; and, as Updike said in 1976, this book, along with *Midpoint,* is among his "franker" books because Marshfield, the book's protagonist, to some extent speaks for Updike himself ("Interview" 300). Despite its importance, *A Month of Sundays* has received almost no scholarly attention. It was widely reviewed, but most critics have taken a sociological rather than literary approach, tending, as George

Hunt has pointed out, to "see the book as an updated version of *Couples*" (59, note #2). Hunt himself provides one of the few serious and sensitive treatments of the book, recognizing that it "capsulizes . . . much thematic material found in Updike's previous fiction" and that "its fictive and psychological structure . . . is somewhat unique in Updike's work and well rewards close analysis" (47). Hunt aptly points out some of the capsulized thematic material, and his Jungian reading of the book's structure is incisive and helpful; but he does not adequately probe the ways in which *A Month of Sundays* sums up earlier Updike themes. Furthermore, a Jungian analysis does not fully explicate the basic commitments Updike sets forth in *Midpoint*. As we shall see, applying Updike's professed *Midpoint* commitments demonstrates that *A Month of Sundays* is, in effect, a fictional restatement of the philosophical position of the autobiographical confessional poem.

The novel's structure is unique among Updike's works in that it takes the form of a diary, specifically the diary of the Rev. Thomas Marshfield, a disgraced Protestant minister who has been sent by his bishop to spend a therapeutic month in a motel in the desert southwest. The other occupants of this motel are also troubled ministers. Marshfield spends thirty-one days from mid-November to mid-December of 1973 in the motel-sanatorium, where his therapy is to spend the mornings writing about whatever interests him most, his afternoons playing golf, and his evenings playing poker with the other guest/patients. His morning writings, then, become the novel.

Marshfield does not name either his denomination or the location of his parish, but the details he offers suggest that his denomination is Episcopal (he has a bishop and a recurring church debate concerns the merits and dangers of a common chalice for communion) and that the parish is somewhere in the Midwest (the land is flat, the winters snowy). He is forty-one years old in 1973 (exactly the age of Updike himself). The incidents he relates center on events occurring from shortly after Easter of 1972, when he begins an affair with the church organist, Alicia Crick, through the end of that affair in February of 1973, and his subsequent involvement with numerous women—most notably Frankie Harlow, the wife of the chairman of the board of deacons[1]—to early November of 1973 when he fires Mrs. Crick and she reveals, to Mr. Harlow, Marshfield's affairs with her and all the others. This revelation leads to his banishment to the desert motel.

Through Chapter XXII, Marshfield dwells on events and involvements of the eighteen months prior to his "fall" and banishment. He talks about his wife, Jane, daughter of Dr. Wesley Augustus Chillingworth, Marshfield's seminary ethics professor; he tells of visits to his elderly father (also a minister, as was his father before him) in a nearby rest home; he describes his associate minister, Ned Bork, a bearded young "liberal" strongly influenced by Paul Tillich and Rudolph Bultmann and a stark contrast to Marshfield's own Barthian theological conservatism; and he details his affair with Alicia and his involvement with Frankie Harlow, with whom he is frustratingly impotent. By Chapter XXIII, however, these figures have faded in importance to him, and he writes about fellow minister-inmates and becomes increasingly concerned with addressing Ms. Prynne, the manager of the motel.

Although he has been denied access to a Bible (part of the therapy), he keeps count of the days, and on each Sunday he writes a sermon, taking his text from memory. The first sermon is a deliberately blasphemous polemic on the "sacrament" of adultery. The second sermon is a somewhat less heretical discussion of the miracles of Christ. The third, addressed now specifically to his fellow ministers-in-exile and indicative of the fading importance of the people and events left behind, is an almost orthodox probing of the meaning of the desert in Biblical terms. Marshfield has been eagerly looking for evidence that his pages are being read by someone, and at the end of this third sermon he discovers an "N" that has been penciled in and then erased. He wonders if Ms. Prynne has been reading his words and has started to write that the sermon was "nice." The final sermon, again addressed to his fellow ministers, is an affirmation of the reality of the resurrection, a call to ministers to witness to the impossibility that makes life possible. The therapy is nearing its close; only four more days are left in the month of exile; and, when he returns to his writing the morning after the last sermon, Marshfield discovers the words "Yes—at last, a sermon that could be preached" penciled in at the end (212).

The last four chapter/entries are addressed specifically to Ms. Prynne, whom Marshfield assumes is his reader, and whom he desperately wants to come to him, believing that sexual union with her will be the final step in his cure. For three days there is no response, no evidence that anyone is reading his words, but the brief two-page final chapter records the coming of Ms. Prynne and the ecstasy of their union.

As always with Updike's novels, a superficial recounting of the plot line gives little indication of the thematic depth of meaning conveyed. It is not the dots of apparently insignificant experiences which are important, but the patterns which emerge when those dots are sifted through the screen of experience and viewed from the proper perspective. Tom Marshfield is much more than an oversexed preacher who could not resist temptation; and the book's ending is not a shallow affirmation that good sex is the answer to man's problems of faith. Examining the implications of the book's epigraphs, its structure, and its re-echoing of the *Midpoint* commitments will underscore the significance of Updike's achievement in *A Month of Sundays*.

THE EPIGRAPHS

Like *Couples, A Month of Sundays* has two epigraphs, one of which is a quotation from Paul Tillich. The first of the two epigraphs is drawn from the Bible—the first Biblical epigraph Updike has used since his first novel, *The Poorhouse Fair,* in 1959. The temptation to over-interpret the significance of this Biblical quotation from Psalm 45—"my tongue is the pen of a ready writer"—is a distinct possibility just as it was with the quotation from Matthew in *The Poorhouse Fair.* The Matthew quotation used in the earlier novel came from an eschatological utterance of Jesus, and, given the future-oriented nature of the novel, one might take the epigraph as an invitation to read an apocalyptic message from the book. Updike, however, denied any such intentions, insisting that he had not been aware of the broader context of the verse, but merely intended to draw on the intrinsic meaning of the statement as it stood by itself ("Interview" 278). Psalm 45, source of the quotation used in *A Month of Sundays,* was originally written to celebrate the marriage of a Hebrew king to a foreign princess and was later interpreted allegorically to suggest the union of Christ and the Church. Therefore, one might be tempted to utilize the quotation as suggesting the unification of religion and sexuality, as George Hunt, in fact, does (48). Once more, however, Updike denies any such intentions. He said in 1976 that he was unaware of the background and context of the Psalm and that the particular quotation was intended as "a little joke" on himself, appearing as it does just below the dedication of the book to his editor at Knopf, Judith Jones. "I've often been accused," Updike said, "of being much too ready a writer, and Marshfield is himself. . . in the book a very ready writer" ("Interview" 283-284).

Therefore, the second epigraph, Tillich's assertion that "This principle of soul, universally and individually, is the principle of ambiguity," assumes prominence in suggesting Updike's intentions for the novel. "I think the book is somewhat ambiguous," Updike said in 1976, "even more than the others, and maybe to some extent Tillich's remark [makes] sense of the ambiguity; I think I came upon it later and couldn't resist appending it in the hope that it would somehow be helpful. I like the idea of the principle of the soul being ambiguity; it's a very neo-platonic, I suppose, notion" ("Interview" 284).

The book is, indeed, full of ambiguities. On the most obvious level, the ending of the book leaves Marshfield's future ambiguous. Has he in any sense been "cured" by his "therapy"? Could the book appropriately be subtitled *Marshfield Redux?* Or will he return to pick up his life much as he left it, repeating the same adventures and misadventures in a new parish now that the recent scandal has been forgotten? In addition to not clarifying the nature of Tom's future, the book's final chapter raises other ambiguities. Just who is Ms. Prynne? What does her union with Marshfield signify? From the outset, Marshfield has been aware of writing his diary for someone to read. At first he refers in general terms to an apparently abstract "Ideal Reader," but by the end of the book he is writing directly to Ms. Prynne—whom he now also addresses as his "Ideal Reader." Are we, Updike's readers, really all Ms. Prynne? Does Marshfield's union with this woman suggest something about the union of writer and reader? Updike's initial intention was to leave this ending even more ambiguous than it now stands. "My original plan," he says "was to have chapter thirty-one blank. The trouble [was], being the end chapter, it didn't look blank. That is, it just looked like the book had ended. But then I wrote it as you read it." The intention was, he said, to convey "in this blankness some kind of merger of I-Thou" ("Interview" 301).

The suggestion of "some kind of merger of I-Thou" provides a clue to understanding, if not resolving, the book's ambiguities. The book is, in fact, the psycho-machia or soul-wrestling of Marshfield. The ambiguities he faces in wrestling with the relationships of soul to self, ego, body, and world are common to all mankind, as are his struggles with good and God, transparency and opacity, abstractions and particulars, love and freedom, fluidity and stasis. The seriousness with which Marshfield assumes the role of clown also points up the ambiguity which Updike sees as the condition of mankind in the "middle" or "muddle" of life "in between times." A tracing of Marshfield's progress through his month of diary writing will indicate that Updike's celebration of ambiguity is not a mere nihilistic acceptance of confusion and hopelessness, but a deliberate and thoughtful restatement of his philosophy as presented in *Midpoint*.

STRUCTURE

Just as the primary epigraph points to ambiguity, the novel's structure suggests complexity. There is, however, the temptation to a false simplicity. Marshfield makes much at the outset of the shape of the motel. He says it "has the shape of an 0" (4). Knowing Updike's penchant for utilizing geometrical shapes as metaphors for his novels, one is tempted to assume the shape underlying this novel must be a circle. After all, the 0 is often used as a vaginal symbol, and it is Marshfield's sexual adventures that have brought him here—and he ends his stay with the penetration of one more circular orifice. A month represents the ever-recurring cycle/circle of the moon, always the same, and Marshfield seems to end the month not really much different from the way he began it. The 0 also may suggest a zero or nothing, relevant if "month of Sundays" has its common popular meaning of an indefinite period of time or no real time at all. The motel almost seems a magic circle to which Marshfield withdraws from reality to rest and recuperate, only to go back to where he began. Yes—but.

The closed circle will not adequately serve as shape for the novel because it does not allow for the multiplicity of ambiguities. Marshfield offers us a better option by qualifying his original description of the motel. He says that it is not quite an 0, but "more exactly, an omega" (4). The omega, with its two discrete feet, suggests a polarity, a sense of movement from one point to the other. The points may be close together, but they are not the same. Furthermore, the omega is the end point of the Greek alphabet. If it is the end, there must have been a beginning, a process, a development rather than a meaningless recurrent cycle. Also, omega brings to mind the familiar appellation of God, found in the Book of Revelation, as "Alpha and Omega," the beginning and the end. In contrast to the classical Greek idea of history as recurring cycles, the Hebrew-Christian view of history has always been one of linear progress, moving from a given point toward some ultimate future. Updike shares this sense of change and development. "Nothing is ever the same twice," he said in 1976.

> What does Heraclitus say? We never put our foot in the same stream twice. Marshfield goes to the motel; it is a kind of end point. He is pretty thoroughly disgraced and out of it and yet still obstinately alive, kind of the way Beckett characters are. They are reduced to nothing yet keep talking and refuse to be crushed or dismissed. Of course it is true the motel is a self-enclosed bubble and Marshfield does return and possibly to much the same. . . . Well, I doubt it; I don't think he will repeat those exact same adventures. ("Interview" 286-287)

Marshfield is the same man after his month in the desert, just as Harry Angstrom was the same man after his trial by fire in *Rabbit Redux*. But Marshfield has come to an end and a new beginning, just as Harry had.

The omega shape, then, suggests the looping quality of Marshfield's exile and return while maintaining an openness, a polarity, and an ambiguity not allowed by the circle. It also suggests the necessity of endings for new beginnings, both for Marshfield as representative human being and for Updike as an author developing his *oeuvre*.[2] Only through a tracing of the novel's recapitulations of the *Midpoint* commitments, however, can we fully grasp the meaningful ambiguity of *A Month of Sundays*.

THE *MIDPOINT* COMMITMENTS

The Centrality of the Self

Just as the autobiographical form of *Midpoint,* with its opening assertion that the poet will speak of "nothing but me, me" (3), affirms the centrality of the self, so does the form of *A Month of Sundays.* Although Updike used first-person narration in *Of the Farm* and for portions of *The Centaur,* Marshfield is the first Updike hero to be as self-consciously self-centered as the narrator of *Midpoint.* Marshfield is instructed to write of what interests him most, and what interests him most is himself. The first image he calls to mind is the ludicrous one of his bare-bottomed self, clad only in a pajama top, spying on Alicia and Ned Bork in Bork's converted carriage house behind Marshfield's parsonage. Thus Marshfield sets the tone of self-indulgent clowning that will dominate the book—Updike's first comic novel[3]. As Updike utilized his own persona in *Midpoint* to indulge his own cleverness, he here uses the persona of Marshfield to do the same. Marshfield never lets us forget that *he* is the center of the narrative. He does not correct his own typographical errors but inserts footnotes to comment on their possible Freudian significance, and it is always clear that the people and scenes he describes are important only in their relationship to *him*. There is only one scene in the novel in which Marshfield himself is not the central character, and that is the episode in which Alicia reveals their affair to Jane. Of course, Marshfield is the center of interest in this conversation even though he is not physically present, and he tells us that he has imagined the scene by taking the two versions he heard later from Alicia and Jane and setting it down as *he* imagined it.

The central ego of *Midpoint* is clearly suggested when Marshfield imagines himself the center of a circle in which all the various affairs of his life are arranged (39). Solipsism, acknowledged in the first canto of *Midpoint,* is also expressed by Marshfield. He refers to "these pages' solipsism" (167), and on the golf course admits that "I can't believe the world will go on spinning without me" (187). Marshfield affirms, "I am all, I am God enthroned on the only ego that exists for me" (189). Furthermore, utilizing the first-person diary form implies a centrality and importance of the self; Marshfield's specific statements make those underlying implications explicit.

The Reality of the World

As in *Midpoint,* however, the giant solipsism of the central ego is tempered by recognizing the reality of an external material world. The child presented in the pictures in *Midpoint* is part of a network of relationships, and Marshfield similarly presents himself in relation to other selves. Unlike young Rabbit Angstrom, he is aware of himself as son, husband, father, parish priest—involved with and responsible to a complex social network. Furthermore, like the poet in *Midpoint,* Marshfield often addresses the reader directly, thus acknowledging the reality of and the need for a self outside his own ego.

The child in *Midpoint* came to realize the external world as he was met, dot by dot, by concrete entities beyond himself. Marshfield, too, affirms the reality of an objective, concrete world as he recalls the pleasure he took as a child in the solid furniture which surrounded him, the patterned carpets, and the cracked and discolored ceilings beyond his head (22-23). He finds particular pleasure in recalling the experience of repairing broken sash cords in windows. "What an interlocked, multi-deviced yet logical artifact. . . a window . . . is!" he says. "And how exciting, all the screws unscrewed and stop strips removed, to pull forth from decades of darkness the rusted sashweight, such a solid little prisoner, and fit him with a glossy new noose and feel him, safe, once again in his vertical closet, tug like life upon the effortlessly ascendant sash!" (115).

Updike affirmed in *Midpoint* that the writer must begin by seeking to describe the seemingly random dots of experience, and this is precisely what Marshfield does. As Updike said in 1976, Marshfield is "trying to talk about experience as it . . . first arrive[s]—dot, dot" ("Interview" 30). As he does so, he moves beyond solipsistic egoism to affirm an objective reality—the "scramble" of dinosaur bones (179), the importance of "small hard perceptions" (193), "the something gritty, practical, mortised, functional in our lives, something olfactory and mute, which eludes our minds' binomial formulations" (203).

This last quotation suggests another way in which Marshfield's monologue echoes *Midpoint*'s affirmation of the external world. The phrase "olfactory and mute" recalls Archibald MacLeish's phrase in "Ars Poetica" which affirms that a poem should be "palpable and mute/ As a globed fruit." Just as Updike's use of the traditions of

Dante, Spenser, Whitman, and Pope in *Midpoint* affirmed the existence of a literary tradition beyond the author's own centered ego, so do this allusion and numerous others in *A Month of Sundays* point to a broad network of relationships. As we have seen, *A Month of Sundays* is Updike's first departure from psychological realism into the techniques of the "self-conscious" novel more often associated with Joyce, Nabokov, Barth, Hawkes, and Pynchon. Thus when Marshfield comments: "This is fun. First you whittle the puppets, then you move them around" (12), or when he writes: "Spent an hour now rereading . . . the pages we (you and I, reader; without you there would be the non-noise of a tree crashing in the inhuman forest) have accumulated" (202), Updike is addressing not only the reader but "the literary tradition of the self-conscious novel" (Hunt 50).

The most obvious allusions to literary tradition, however, are those to *The Scarlet Letter.* Both stories deal with ministerial adultery, and the ministers' names are certainly similar in symbolic implication. Tom is a marshy field, Arthur a dim valley, both in need of a clear path. The parallels to the 19th century novel, however, are generally intended more to call attention to differences between 20th century and 17th century America (and 19th century America, too) than to suggest similarities, just as Marshfield's omega stands at the opposite end of the alphabet from Hester's *A*. One must admit that Hester would make an "ideal reader" for the confessions of an adulterous minister and that therefore using the name Ms. Prynne is appropriate and suggestive in the novel. Unlike Hester, however, Marshfield's mistress, Alicia, publicly reveals the name of her partner in sin and precipitates his disgrace. And unlike Arthur, Marshfield himself immediately proclaims and celebrates his union with Ms. Prynne. In fact, Updike makes clear that Marshfield's situation is an inversion of Arthur's Puritan dilemma: rather than suffering from excessive sexual repression, Marshfield is "a poor Wasp stung by the new work-ethic of sufficient sex, sex as the exterior sign of interior grace" (218). Hawthorne's Chillingworth, unlike his Updikean namesake, was on fire with hatred and revenge. The modern Chillingworth is dry, rational, and Deistic, but perhaps he, too, is an unpardonable sinner—not because he has forcibly violated another human heart, but because his self-satisfied naturalism "chills" the possibility of true belief in both his student and his daughter.

Other parallels and inversions will doubtless occur to every reader, but such overt allusions to Hawthorne's 19th century classic of American fiction clearly, if ambiguously (and Hawthorne, himself a master of ambiguity, would most assuredly appreciate the ironic implications), reminds the reader that he is reading a novel, an objective artistic artifact—which exists in a world of countless similar experiential dots.

One other way in which *A Month of Sundays* recognizes the reality of an objective world beyond the boneless ego is through the affirmation of the physical body and its sexuality. Marshfield comments that he and Jane had become more and more alike. Jane, then, instead of representing the reality of an external other, has become a "twinned impression," "a parallel spindle" of himself (49). The affair with Alicia, however, awakens something. Marshfield is again aware of his physical body as separate from his ego: "What fun my forgotten old body turned out to be—the toy I should have been given for Christmas" (35). As he becomes involved with even more women, he is aware of the "monstrous and gorgeous otherness . . . which . . . the female and male genitals meet in one another" (135). Sex, then, which serves also as a paradigm for both dualism and mystery, at this point reminds Marshfield that the ego is confronted with an external reality quite other than and separate from itself.

Dualism

Updike's "gut-level" dualism emerges most clearly in *A Month of Sundays* in Marshfield's first two sermons. The first sermon, despite its defiant and blasphemous celebration of adultery as a new sacrament, concludes with what must be taken as a genuine expression of Marshfield's underlying belief in the dual nature of reality. Before Jesus, he says, "reality was monochromatic." Since the incarnation, however, "truth is dual, alternating, riddled." He suggests images like the chessboard and tilled fields (important in *Marry Me)* and the Romanesque zigzag (the shape suggested by *Rabbit, Run)*, and concludes that Christ represents "another light . . . the shadow of another sun, a shadow brighter than worldly light" (48). The second sermon asserts that "His way is not ours" (104), and that "he came not to revoke the Law and Ground of our condition but to demonstrate a Law and Ground beyond" (105). Marshfield, then, despite his having apparently fallen away from the faith it is his vocation to profess, speaks from the "otherworldly stand" of *Midpoint.*

In addition to these two sermons, there are two other specific affirmations of dualism in the novel. On the night before he writes his fourth and final sermon, Marshfield steps out of the "omega-shaped shelter, testing [his] impending freedom" (204). As he looks up at the stars, he feels that they are both close and yet immutably fixed in the dome of the night. In words that reiterate the assertion from the final canto of *Midpoint* that "I am another world, no doubt; no doubt/ We come into this World from well without" (43), he records his feelings:

> I felt, for an instant—as if for an instant the earth's revolution had become palpable—that particle or quantity within myself, beyond mind, that makes me a stranger here, in this universe.

A quantity no greater than a degree's amount of arc, yet vivid,
and mine, my treasure. (204)

In addition to his physical and mental self and the various
concrete realities which he can write about cleverly day by
day, a quantity of something else exists in him, beyond mind.
However small that quantity may be, it is vivid, and he will
treasure it.

The final affirmation of dualism, found in Chapters
XXVIII and XXIX, assumes additional substance because it
comes immediately after his fourth sermon (the one which
finally elicits Ms. Prynne's positive response) in the course of
chapters which indicate the completion of his therapy and his
readiness to return home to the "reshouldering of
ambiguity" and "daily grits" (213). At the end of Chapter
XXVIII, he records that as he was sitting on the toilet it occurred to him that his situation with Jane belonged "to the
province of works, purely, and works without faith are constipation" (218). The comment and its context seem at first
only self-consciously clever scatology, but the comments that
follow, coupled with a related passage in Chapter XXIX, indicate that here is a veiled but serious allusion to the dualism
inherent in the theology and experience of Martin Luther.

The key insight that turned Martin Luther from a monk
who was afraid of God and despairing of his own ability to
achieve righteousness into a bold, self-confident reformer
was his so-called "revelation in the tower" when he came to
the full understanding of Paul's words in Romans 1:17:
"The righteous shall live by faith." Luther describes the impact of this experience:

> Day and night I tried to meditate upon the significance of these
> words: "The righteousness of God is revealed in it, as it is writ-
> ten: the righteous shall live by faith." Then, finally God had
> mercy on me, and I began to understand that the righteousness of
> God is that gift of God by which a righteous man lives, namely,

faith, and that . . . the merciful God justifies us by faith. . . . Justification does not take place through works, but by faith alone, without any works and not piecemeal, but completely at once. . . .(qtd. in Lee 117)

The exact time and place of this "revelation" or new insight is still debated by Lutheran scholars since Luther often referred to the experience in later years, but made no record of it when it occurred. The most widely accepted current scholarly opinion is that the revelation must have happened at some point during his series of lectures on the Psalms in 1513. The location of the "tower" where the revelation occurred may have been Luther's study, but Luther's own testimony as recorded in one of his "Table Talk" comments in 1532 suggests another place, somewhat troubling to those of squeamish piety. He said:

These words "righteous" and "righteousness of God" struck my conscience as flashes of lightning, frightening me each time I heard them. . . . But by the grace of God, as I once meditated upon these words in this tower and C1 . . . there suddenly came into my mind the thought that . . . . (qtd. in Lee 118)

Rorer, considered to be the most reliable of the original reporters (Erikson 204), unhesitatingly transcribed the abbreviation *Cl.* as *cloaca* or toilet. Although as Erik Erikson points out, "no other reported statement of Luther's has made mature men squirm more uncomfortably, or made serious scholars turn their noses higher in contemptuous disbelief" (204), such earthy evidence of a great man's humanity is the kind of confession that Tom Marshfield—and John Updike—would appreciate. Furthermore, as Charles M. Lee, Jr., points out:

Luther was plagued by fear and doubt and the Devil, by his own anger, his hostile feelings toward God, his rebelliousness— and by constipation. And somehow, getting rid of one problem was linked to getting rid of them all. . . . For one whose theology was that of the "whole man" it was as appropriate an occasion as could be imagined; the fusion of humanity and spirit that he saw in Christ, he lived himself. . . . Although Luther would be troubled by his digestion all his life, at this moment he evidently won a decisive battle against the Devil. (118)

Marshfield is not "troubled by his digestion," but his insight while sitting on the toilet that "works without faith are constipation" is similar to Luther's "revelation" that "jusification does not take place through works, but by faith alone." After recording his insight, Marshfield goes on to reflect on the importance of accepting God's grace:

> I must cease, it seemed to me, as my happily growling guts sustained their seemingly endless process of emptying, cease regarding any lives other than my own as delivered into my care; they, and mine, are in God's care. Most of what we have is given, not acquired; a gracious acceptance is our task, and a half-conscious following-out of the circumambient lode. This century's atrocious evils have stemmed from the previous century's glorification of the Will. (218)

One will immediately recognize here the parallels to the concluding canto of *Midpoint,* which asserted that "Nothing has had to be, but is by Grace" (40) and condemned an "easy Humanism" (38).

Chapter XXIX picks up the constipation theme as Marsh-field recalls his one and only physical religious experience, which occurred while he was in college. He was desperately constipated, and day after day, six times a day, he would "sit on the hopeful porcelain oval and wait; nothing" (222).

> Then, one morning, sweating over all my body, I pushed out perhaps an inch of dry compacted turd, knobby as a narwhal's tusk, and stalled; my eyes filled with tears; how could I waddle to class with this extrusion? I bent forward as far as my torso would go, driven to home-made yoga in this extremity, and in my soul confessed my desperation to whatever powers there be. And a great force as if manually seized my bowels, and my body, like a magnificent animal escaped from its keeper, savagely and so swiftly the dilation of pain passed in a flash thrust out of itself a

great weight of waste. It was a thrust from beyond, a release into *trans*; a true Lutherian experience, and my only. (222)

The dualism expressed here lies in the feeling that the release was a thrust from *beyond* and that he felt released into *trans*— a different realm of reality and experience. The comment that this was a true Lutherian experience adds seriousness to the comedy of the situation.

The parallel between Marshfield and Luther is obvious— fear, doubt, anger, hostile feelings, rebelliousness. The parallel has its ambiguities, though, since Marshfield informs us that after his one serious bout with constipation and the ensuing sense of being freed from beyond, he has "remained regular" (222). Nevertheless, his recollection of the experience reminds him that "works without faith are constipation" and that "most of what we have is given, not acquired" (218).

Erik Erikson finds Luther's experience psychologically crucial for his developing personality. Bodily functions, he says:

> are related to the organ modes of retention and elimination—in defiant children most obviously, and in adults through all manner of ambivalent behavior. There can be little doubt that at this particular time, when Martin's power of speech was freed from its infantile and juvenile captivity, he changed from a highly restrained and retentive individual into an explosve person; he had found an unexpected release of self-expression, and, with it, of the many-sided power of his personality. (205)

Since college, Marshfield has had no trouble with retentiveness—he has by Chapter XXVIII adequately demonstrated that indeed he is a "ready writer" who regularly daily releases the contents of his mind, his memory, and his "growling guts." But his recollection near the end of the therapy of his one "physical" religious experience reminds him that he has allowed himself to suffer the "chilling" effect of the modern age's glorification of the human will, forgetting gracious acceptance of the thrust which comes from beyond. He even thinks, for instance, that his impotence with Frankie Harlow was probably due to an over-emphasis on will: "My impotence with Frankie seems now a product of over-management. . . . " (218).

At the end of Chapter XXX, Marshfield goes out under the desert stars and finds that he is both afraid and not afraid "to be born again" (226). He recognizes the uncertainty and ambiguity of his position, but anticipates a rebirth as the gift of a force beyond rationality and will. His final words in the chapter reinforce, again ambiguously, the implicit dualism. He says, "Even so, come" (226). The words are most obviously addressed directly to Ms. Prynne, whom he is imploring to come to him, and in this context clearly call to mind the polar dualism of sexuality—male/female. But the words are also an allusion to the final verse of the Book of Revelation, addressed to Jesus, and therefore, allude to the ultimate dualism of the universe, of which sexuality is only a human paradigm.

Mystery and Faith

The multiple ambiguities of the dualism engendered by a concurrent insistence on the centrality of the self and the objective reality of a concrete universe are no more eliminated in *A Month of Sundays* than they were in *Midpoint* or in any of Updike's other works. Those ambiguities, however, are made acceptable by recognizing the mystery or secrecy of reality and by affirming a faith in which man's apparently gratuitous existence floats in the "permanently hopeful-making" fact that the void was breached at all ("Interview" 299). We have already noted in Chapter One Updike's comment concerning his "sense of the mystery and irreducibility of one's own indentity mixed with fear of the identity being an illusion or being squelched" coupled with his "philosophical obsession that there is a certain gratuitousness in existence at all" ("Interview" 303; 299). These concerns recur throughout *Midpoint* and find their most cogent development in *A Month of Sundays* in Marshfield's third and fourth sermons.

The third sermon takes its text from the thirty-second chapter of Deuteronomy: "He found him in a desert place." The verse refers to Jacob, but Marshfield says that it might just as well refer to any of the Old Testament's "God-chosen men" (161). He points out that the desert is ever-present in the Bible, always surrounding the special "oasis world" of God's promise (161). Marshfield, somewhat like Mim in *Rabbit Redux,* finds that in the modern world, the desert seems to be growing and spreading, both literally and figuratively. It is in the desert—God's wider creation beyond the oasis of his special favor—that modern man lives. Unlike Mim, however, Marshfield adds: "And yet, and yet . . . ." (164), just as Updike says "yes—but." The Spanish name for Death Valley is *La Palma de la Mano de Dios*—the Palm of God's Hand—and Marshfield affirms that even in the desert we are in God's hand: even the desert, when one looks closely, abounds with life.

The lesson Marshfield draws from this meditation on the desert is: "Live. Live, brothers, though there be naught but shame and failure to furnish forth your living" (166). He concludes the sermon with these words:

> Brothers, we have come to a tight place. Let us be, then, as the chuckwalla, who, when threatened, *runs* to a tight place, to a crevice in the burning rock of the desert. Once there, does he shrink in shame? No! He puffs himself up, inflates his self to more than half its normal size, and fills that crevice as the living

soul fills the living body, and cannot be dislodged by the talon or
fang of the enemy.
We *are* found in a desert place.
We *are* in God's palm.
We *are* the apple of His eye.
Let us be grateful *here,* and here rejoice. Amen. (166)

The fear of identity's being squelched and the suspicion of
the emptiness of existence are springs from which these words
flow; but the insoluble mystery at the root of self-identity is
cause for celebrating the self, not for relinquishing it, and the
inexplicable gratuitousness of existence is met by gratitude,
not despair.

Sermon number four takes its text from the fifteenth
chapter of Paul's epistle to the Romans, in which Paul insists
upon the bodily resurrection of the dead. Marshfield affirms
that "Paul is right in his ghoulish hope," and that

> all those who offer instead some gaseous survival of a personal
> essence, or one's perpetuation through children or good deeds or
> masterworks of art, or identification with the race of Man, or the
> blessedness of final and absolute rest, are tempters and betrayers
> of the Lord. . . . Is not the situation in our churches indeed that
> from the pulpit we with our good will and wordy humanism lean
> out to tempt our poor sheep from those scraps of barbaric doc-
> trine, preserved in the creed like iguanadon footprints in
> limestone, that alone propel them up from their pleasant beds of a
> Sunday morning? (209)

But he must add an "and yet": "Yet the resurrection of the
body is impossible" (209). No one, he admits, can believe it.
"We can only *profess* to believe. . . . It is our station to be
visible and to provide men with the opportunity to profess the
impossible that makes their lives possible" (210). Is Marshfield thus urging hypocrisy on himself and his fellow
ministers? No, not hypocrisy, but the grateful acceptance of
hard roles given, though not chosen. These roles, he says,
"still stand though we crumple within them. We do not invent ourselves, and then persuade men to find room for us;

rather, men invent our office, and persuade us to fill it" (211).

But why should men like Marshfield—and his fellow inmates Amos (whose parish has been engulfed by urban sprawl), Woody (who cannot tolerate Mass except in Latin), and Jamie Ray (a homosexual)—be given such roles? Recalling the Pascal he read as part of Professor Chillingworth's ethics course, Marshfield remembers the cry *"Qui m'y a mis? Who has set me here?"* (211) and concludes his sermon:

> *Qui m'y a mis?* Can the mystery, frightening and astonishing, of our existence be more clearly posed? The old mysteries erode; Henri Bergson, that graceful fellow-traveler of our rough faith, spoke of the three creaky hinges, or inexplicable gaps, in the continuum of materialism: between nothing and something, between matter and life, between life and mind. The last two have since silted in with a sludge of atomic information, and even the imposing first may, eventually, reveal an anatomy: already radio telescopes have picked up a cosmic hum that apparently originates at the very rim of time.
>
> But what could explicate and trivialize the deepest and simplest mystery, that I find myself here and not there, in the present rather than the past or future? *Il n'y a point de raison pourquoi;* there is not a particle of reason why. So those of us who live by the irrational may moderate our shame. Who has set us here, in this vocation, at this late date, out of due time? To ask this question is to imply an answer; there is a *qui,* a Who, who has set; we have not accidentally fallen, we have been placed. As of course we already know in our marrow. (211-212)

The ultimate mystery of "Why am I me?" with which Updike wrestled in *Midpoint* is explicitly raised again in *A Month of Sundays.* The mystery remains a mystery, but those who "live by the irrational"—*Midpoint*'s "otherworldly stand" that "the world belittles"—may moderate their shame by recognizing that asking the question implies an answer, felt in the marrow. Although no attributes are described, there is a

"Who"—or, as *Midpoint* affirms, "Deepest in the thicket, thorns spell a word" (44).

These two sermons, then, forcefully echo *Midpoint*'s insistence on the grateful acceptance of mystery at the heart of existence. The final four chapters of *A Month of Sundays* reinforce this affirmation while moving beyond both the sermons and *Midpoint* by describing the mystery and acceptance on a more experiential level. In Chapter XXVIII, written the Monday after the fourth sermon, Marshfield recalls Ms. Prynne's being confronted by a drunken Indian on their earlier tour to Sandstone. Marshfield is appreciative of Ms. Prynne's eagerness to get the Indian out of the way so her charges can board the bus while at the same time not depriving the Indian of his dignity. He says that as he watched her, he "moved through" her, and it came to him "that love is not an emotion, an assertive putting out, but a *trans*-motion, a compliant moving *through*" (217). One should note here the Lutheran joining of passivity and activity. Luther insisted that in justification man is first passive—God acts, while man only accepts (compliantly) the gift; then, however, man is free to move through God's grace into a life of active good works on behalf of others. Indeed, after recording this insight about a "compliant moving through," Marshfield records his insight about works without faith being constipation, and in the next chapter records his Lutheran experience concerning a different kind of "moving through."

At this point, however, Marshfield claims that since he has "moved through" Ms. Prynne as she compassionately dealt with the drunken Indian, he has seen through her and therefore presumes to claim her as his (217). It would be more spiritual if the I-Thou merger which is the paradigm of the mysterious dualism at the heart of reality could be adequately expressed through such empathic mental telepathy. But as the doctrine of the incarnation (the "indignity of the

230

incarnation'' Marshfield calls it on p. 135) proclaims that God himself entered the messy muddle of humanity, and as Luther finds grace in the relief of his constipation, Marshfield seeks physical confirmation of his mystical communion with Ms. Prynne. ''You are yet the end, the *intelligens entis,* of my being, insofar as I exist on paper,'' he says. ''Give me a body. Otherwise I shall fall through space forever'' (220). There must be a concrete physical experience, else the self is really nothing but ''some gaseous . . . personal essence'' (209). The self must have a body as well as a boneless ego, and so the final physical union with Ms. Prynne takes place.

Both during and after the sexual union, Ms. Prynne remains mysterious and unknowable. Marshfield acknowledges, however, that she has brought him to an edge, ''a slippery edge,'' and that there is nothing for him to do ''but slip and topple off, gratefully'' (228). There is once more, then, a ''compliant moving through,'' and a grateful acceptance of something given by a mysterious other. ''What is it, this human contact, this blank-browed thing we do for one another?'' Marshfield asks in the final paragraph. Addressing Ms. Pryne, whom he has once more just called his ''dear Ideal Reader,'' he says:

> There was a moment, when I entered you . . . when your eyes were all for another, looking up into mine, with an expression without a name, of entry and alarm, and of salutation. I pray my own face, a stranger to me, saluted in turn. (228)

The human sexual experience is thus presented as a paradigm of duality and mystery, unexplainable but experienceable. When one understands love as a ''moving through'' rather than an ''assertive putting out,'' sexual experience, the most intimate expression of human love, denotes the uniqueness of the individual, recognizes the otherness of the objective world, and provides palpable participation in the mystery of existence through joining the duality of male and female.

Although sex becomes a paradigm for experiencing and celebrating the mystery of human existence, it is not therefore the only means to such experience and celebration. Marshfield has earlier found that despite his intolerance for homosexuality, he has to some extent "moved through" Jamie Ray, so that the two have become "a bit less opaque to one another, fumbling and shrugging" (200). More significant, however, is the Marshfield-Updike and Ms. Prynne-Ideal Reader conjunction. Marshfield knows from the outset—as does his creator Updike—that someone will be reading what he writes. He asks in his first entry, "Who are you, gentle reader?" and then immediately adds, "Who am I?" (6). The questions of identity and *qui m'y a mis* are seen to be questions we as readers must answer along with Marshfield. Although Marshfield progressively more specifically identifies Ms. Prynne as his reader, we know that Updike himself is aware of a much wider group of readers, unknowable and mysterious to him in ways beyond those in which even the enigmatic Ms. Prynne is unknowable and mysterious to Marshfield. If Updike was, as he has said, seeking in the final chapter to convey "in this blankness some kind of merger of I-Thou" ("Interview" 301), then surely he is suggesting that in the blankness which exists between author and reader there may also be some kind of merging. Obviously there can be no such physical joining of the polarities of author and reader as there is of the polarities of male and female with Marshfield and Ms. Prynne, but the possibility of such actual, physical, yet mysterious union provides us the qualitative basis for affirming that there is a "human contact," a "blank-browed thing we do for one another," and these moments enable us to accept and affirm the principle of ambiguity that pervades human existence.

As our analysis has demonstrated, *A Month of Sundays* definitively sums up the themes that have dominated Updike's novels since 1959. Moreover, these themes are treated more openly and directly in this book than in previous novels, as Updike himself has indicated. For one thing, ministers have figured as important secondary characters in most of the earlier novels—Hook in *The Poorhouse Fair* (technically a layman, but a preacher nontheless), Eccles and Kruppenbach in *Rabbit, Run,* March in *The Centaur,* the unnamed minister in *Of the Farm,* and Pedrick in *Couples*—but this is the first time that Updike has utilized a minister as the central character. Since Marshfield is exactly the age of Updike himself, and since Updike in a television interview once suggested that the roles of novelist and minister are similar in many ways, the choice of Marshfield as protagonist suggests a direct and explicit treatment of concerns implicit but more or less covert in the earlier novels. In addition, as the almost point-for-point reaffirmations of the confessedly autobiographical *Midpoint* commitments demonstrate, Updike means it when he says, "Marshfield to some extent is speaking for me" ("Interview" 300).

Yet the omega of *A Month of Sundays* suggests not only the end point of summation, but also an end point which implies a new beginning, a change of direction, or, as Updike says, "a trying to . . . move on to something else" ("Interview" 31). This book, as we have seen, is Updike's first comic novel. Furthermore, it is his first to be set outside the narrow radius of Pennsylvania/New York/New England. And although Marshfield speaks for Updike, he is the first Updike hero who does not depend upon Updike's own experience for many of the details of his life. Marshfield is truly an imaginative creation; he is not modeled on Updike's grandfather, father, mother, schoolmates, or neighbors. The fourth important departure of the novel, its deliberately self-conscious technique, has already been noted as a change from

Updike's previous exclusive use of traditional psychological and/or naturalistic realism.

Marshfield leaves the desert ready to reshoulder ambiguities, realizing that he has been prepared "for a return to the world and not a translation to a better" (213). But Updike says that he doesn't "think [Marshfield] will repeat those exact same adventures" ("Interview" 287). He has changed; he will probably seek new directions. *A Month of Sundays* also signaled that Updike, although he, too, would continue to shoulder the ambiguities of human existence, was ready to explore new territory. As we shall see, his next novel, *The Coup,* does explore new ground, but we shall also find that we recognize familiar characteristics and concerns in the explorer.

THE COUP

The Coup (1978), Updike's ninth novel, quickly introduces the reader to the distinctive personality of its first-person narrator, as did *A Month of Sundays.* The narrator of the earlier novel identifies himself immediately as belonging to a class of characters quite familiar to readers of Updike—an American Christian minister. *The Coup*'s narrator, however, is a departure from the usual Updike *dramatis personae:* he is Colonel Félix Hakim Ellelloû, the black President-dictator of the imaginary African nation of Kush. Born in 1933 as the result of the rape of a Salu woman by a Nubian raider in what was then the French territory of Noire, Hakim at seventeen joins the French Foreign Legion and serves in the ill-starred final French campaigns in Indo-China. Reassigned to Algeria, he deserts rather than fight against fellow Africans, and manages a four-year stint of liberal arts studies at McCarthy College in Franchise, Wisconsin. When De Gaulle grants freedom to Noire, the former Lord of the Wanjiji tribe becomes King Edumu IV of the re-named land of Kush. Hakim is thus able to return to his native land and become an aide to the king.

It is the king who suggests to Hakim the addition of the name Ellelloû—the Berber word for freedom. A revolution in 1968 overthrows the king, who is kept prisoner although most of the officials of his regime are executed. Ellelloû becomes the Chairman of the Supreme Counseil Revolutionnaire et Militaire pour l'Emergence (SCRME), Commander-in-Chief of the Armed Forces, Minister of National Defense, and President of Kush. The form of government in Kush, then, is "a constitutional monarchy with the constitution suspended and the monarch deposed" (7). The SCRME makes its decisions based on "the pure and final socialism envisioned by Marx" and "the theocratic populism of Islam's periodic reform movements" (7).

Ellelloû was married to Kadongolimi, a Salu woman, before he left home to join the military, and he brings home from America a second wife, the white Candace Cunningham. As a Moslem, he is entitled to four wives, and he fills his quota by adding two more: Sittina, daughter of a Tutsi chief and a graduate of a small all-black Alabama college, whom he marries after she wins his heart as she competes in the Pan-African Games in 1962; and Sheba, a beautiful young girl he finds wandering the streets of Kush's capital city of Istiqlal, stoned on kola nuts and listening to rock music on a transistor radio.

Ellelloû makes clear from the start that he is writing from a place of exile, that he is no longer the president of Kush. His memoirs, then, describe the events which lead to the coup that displaces him in 1974, as his own coup had displaced Edumu in 1968. The capital city of Istiqlal is located on the Grionde River, which forms the country's southern border. Most of Kush's territory, however, is comprised of the "delectable emptiness" (4) of the southern reaches of the Sahara Desert, the area of central Africa desperately stricken by drought in the early 70s. It is Ellelloû's feeling of responsibility for and efforts to do something about the drought that precipitate the events which lead to his downfall.

Ellelloû hates the United States, and his Marxist ideology has led him to consider the Russians his natural allies and to allow them to conceal a huge missile installation in the barren northwestern section of his country. The United States, however, moved by pictures of hunger and starvation caused by the persistent drought, ignores ideological differences and sends a literal mountain of food—boxes and boxes of Korn Kurls, Kix, Trix, Chex Pops, and Total. Ellelloû's first symbolic effort to end the drought is to destroy this useless gift from America—"that fountainhead of obscenity and glut" (3)—by inciting a crowd to set fire to the boxes sitting barely over the border in neighboring Sahel. A frustrated American functionary, who had been climbing over the pile trying to point out its genuine food value, is immolated in the process.

The heroic ideological purity of Ellelloû's rejection of American aid does not bring an end to the drought. Seeking another symbolic act which may induce the rains to fall again, Ellelloû decides he must execute the old king, who is a "Blot upon Our Flag" (67) and whose crimes have led to "Widespread Shortages, Dislocations, and Suffering" (66). This decision is reached with the advice of Kutunda, an illiterate but imaginative Sara woman he brought back to Istiqlal as his mistress after having met her while he disguised himself as a beggar during his trip to the border. She tells him that "one must look for the center of unhealth," but she also adds: "This center lies not, I think, within the king . . . but within your mercy toward him" (51). Ellelloû himself

236

takes the ceremonial scimitar and beheads the king, but the occasion does not draw the great crowd of people he had anticipated, and the ceremony is interrupted when a troop of muffled Tuareg ride swiftly into the square and carry off the newly severed head. Ellellou immediately suspects a CIA-engineered plot, but cannot help noticing the smell of vodka on the breath of the man who snatches the head.

Once more, despite Ellellou's claim that "By the sword in my hand I shall clean the land!" (73) the rains do not come. Soon there is a cable from America asking for information on the fate of the State Department official who was to deliver the food. Ellellou insists that Michaelis Ezana, his Minister of Interior, ignore the request and make no reply. When Ezana tells Ellellou of rumors that the head of the deposed king is speaking prophecies from a cave deep in the mountains, Ellellou is again suspicious of American interference and "tricknology," and knows that he must make another journey. He delays the trip long enough to find out that Ezana has been communicating with the Americans despite his orders to the contrary, and that even Kutunda, who has not yet learned to write, has been talking on the telephone with officials in Washington. Ellellou orders Ezana's imprisonment, appoints as interim minister a former police spy whose name he does not even know, and sets out for the mountains with his fourth wife, Sheba.

The trip by caravan is long and dangerous. It takes three months, and both Ellellou and Sheba are near death when they finally arrive at the site of the cave. It turns out to be not an American creation but a Russian one. The ingeniously wired head of Edumu has become a sensational tourist attraction, complete with refreshment stands, parking lots, a slide show, and busloads of foreigners brought in by travel agencies in Zanj, Kush's "neo-capitalist" neighbor to the east, near whose borders the cave is located. Edumu's head

237

blames the drought on Ellelloû's defection from the "People's Revolution so vividly blueprinted by our heroic Soviet Allies" (213). While pretending to hate capitalism, the head says, Ellelloû has brought "an entire American boom town" (213) into existence. Both the town and Ellelloû must be destroyed, the head says. Ellelloû, still clad as a desert wanderer from the caravan, snatches the head loose from its wiring, which is apparently what the Russian colonel in charge has expected. The ruse with the head was intended to bring Ellelloû to the area so that the Russians could inform him of Ezana's recent devious accomplishments and of the American incursion into Kush.

Ellelloû discovers that there is a broad and easy highway down the eastern side of the mountains—quite different from the perilous ascent he made from the west—and he is soon driven to the new city in the state Mercedes. The city, located on a geological formation called the Ippi Rift, where great quantities of both water and oil are trapped deep beneath the sandstone, has all the accoutrements of its American counterparts—lawn sprinklers, used car lots, drug stores, a McDonald's, and an oil refinery. Its name is, ironically, Ellelloû, but no one in the town knows or recognizes the honored man when he appears among them.

Ellelloû rallies the citizens at the gates of the oil refinery and tries to get them to set fire to it as he had earlier incited the crowd to burn the cornflakes. This time, however, he is unsuccessful, and the crowd happily tramples over him to accept the American offer of free beer for all. Ellelloû has failed to convince the crowd of his identity as their president; his wallet (containing Brezhnev's unlisted telephone number and other such items) has been stolen; his driver and body guard and the familiar Mercedes have deserted him; Ellelloû has, in effect, ceased to exist. But all is not bleak. As the crowd turns from him to go for the beer, "a little cloud covers the sun" (256), presaging the rains which return now and continue steadily for months. Apparently, Ellelloû thinks, he himself "was the curse upon the land" (261).

For five months in the city bearing his name, Ellelloû works as a short-order cook and parking attendant, saving enough money to return to Istiqlal disguised as a beggar. In his absence, Ezana has escaped and been given an "emeritus" position in the new administration of the former police spy, who has now adopted the name Dorfu, a Salu term with the double meaning of "solidarity" and "consolidation" (265). Dorfu has elevated Kutunda to the position of Minister of Interior and Protector of Female Rights. Americans have been welcomed with open arms, and the widow of the man immolated on the cornflakes has fallen in love with Ezana and is converting to Islam. Rain continues to fall, and Istiqlal is bustling with economic activity. Ellelloû convinces Dorfu that the state of Kush will profit more from a mysteriously disappeared hero than from another dead ruler, and is granted a comfortable pension contingent upon his silence. Kadongolimi has died in his absence; Candace is getting a divorce and returning to America; and Sheba disappeared in the confusion at Edumu's cave. That leaves only Sittina, the third wife, to accompany Ellelloû into exile to the south of France, where they live comfortably while Ellelloû writes these memoirs.

NEW DIRECTIONS

When Tom Brokaw asked Updike in a television interview in 1978 why he had chosen Africa as the setting for his recent novel, Updike replied that he felt it was high time that he "move out" and "move on" to try different things. "Africa," he said, "is the only continent left for imaginary countries." When asked if this moving out in new directions meant that he was bored with his earlier subject matter, Updike replied that it did not, but that this new direction might be seen as a move to lay the more familiar material to rest for a while.

There are obvious ways in which *The Coup* represents an effort to "move out" and "move on." The action is more complex, with more incidents, more people, and more literal ground covered than in the earlier novels, which, in contrast to *The Coup*, seem to be concerned with a quite insular, suburban, American middle-class world. Furthermore, as Updike pointed out to Dick Cavett in another 1978 television interview and as the full page of acknowledgements following the copyright page in the novel documents, the geography involved and the anthropological background of Islam and tribal Africa called for extensive research that had not been necessary for any of the earlier novels. In addition to these obvious and relatively superficial differences, *The Coup* represents three other significant departures for Updike.

Although Updike has explained that Ellelloû was "based on people [he] glimpsed in college—the exotic foreigners who come for a few years to share our American way and then go back to unimaginable circumstances" ("Response"), Ellelloû is the first Updike hero with no parallels in Updike's own experience. In *Bech: a Book* (1970) and *Bech Is Back* (1982), collections of short stories about an imaginary American Jewish intellectual author, Updike created a non-Wasp protagonist whose family background is quite different from his own. In imagining Bech, however, Updike was able to draw heavily on his own experiences as a successful author— including a trip to Russia and eastern Europe and visits to college campuses. In *Rabbit Redux* Updike created his first fully-realized non-white character, the black militant, Skeeter. But Skeeter is an American product, and all Updike had to do to bring him to life was to be sensitive to various spokesmen of black power familiar to contemporary Americans of whatever race. Marshfield in *A Month of Sundays,* as we have seen, represents Updike's first substantive move away from his own specific experience to create a protagonist for a novel, but Marshfield differs from Updike only in external details, not in basic cultural background or in philosophical position. Ellelloû, then, represents a genuinely new direction in that he is a protagonist whose background, motivations, and day-to-day experiences must be imagined and then validated by careful research. That Updike enjoyed this venture into more exotic realms is indicated by his telling Katherine Stephen in 1987 that, along with *The Centaur,* he is especially fond of *The Coup* among his novels. Both of these books, he said, he "wrote along somewhat eccentric lines to please [him]self" (4).

Second, *The Coup* is unique among Updike's novels in that it deals directly with and centers around events and matters of world-wide historical significance. The earlier novels make vivid the particular historical setting in which they occur by including incidents and details that keep the reader aware of broader events surrounding the stories: *Rabbit, Run* is specifically a book of the 50s; *Couples* takes place in the year of the Kennedy assassination; *Rabbit Redux* is a 60s book, filled with counter-culture rhetoric and deliberately set in the summer of the American moon shot; and Marshfield's diary entries occupy a month during Nixon's unraveling after Watergate. In each of these novels, however, the historical setting only provides a backdrop to highlight the basically personal story being told. None of the characters in these earlier novels has any important role in the events which swirl around them. Characters may have political opinions and argue them, but none of them is in a position to effect any real difference in the outward sweep of events, and the concerns of the novels are basically a-political. Ellelloû, however, is the ruler of his country. His decisions affect thousands of his own people and are also important in the struggle for world power between America and Russia. *The Coup,* then, is overtly political as none of the previous novels has been, using the emergence of third-world nations as a vehicle for satirical attacks on both of the two super-powers.

Finally, *The Coup* represents a new direction in novelistic technique. We have seen that *A Month of Sundays* was Updike's first venture into the form of the self-conscious novel. It is written in such a way that the reader is constantly aware that its first-person narrator is creating a fictional construct—and that the narrator is a fictional construct of Updike himself. *The Coup* goes a step further by combining the use of first- and third-person narration. Ellellou lets us know that he is self-consciously recalling the events described from his exile, but he moves beyond Marshfield in *A Month of Sundays* by explaining that

> there are two selves: the one who acts, and the "I" who experiences. The latter is passive even in a whirlwind of the former's making—passive and guiltless and astonished. The historical performer bearing the name of Ellellou was no less mysterious to me than to the American press. . . . Ellellou's body and career carried me here, there, and I never knew why, but submitted. (7)

Thus we have not only a narrator who is conscious of the problematic relationship between himself and his readers, but also a narrator who is conscious of the problematic relationship between his sense of self and his actions in an outer world. Thus he can describe his inner feelings at the beheading of Edumu and confess: "The very ink in my pen coagulates at these memories" (74). But he must add:

> So it seemed from the truck—. . . . From the vantage of the crowd, it looked far otherwise. Ellellou's neat brown figure, sunglassless, stepped forward and with a leverlike stroke altered the quality of the smallest of the puppets posed on the makeshift stage. (75)

The stylistic technique of the novel, then, is a departure for Updike, forcing the reader to be aware not only of an author utilizing the persona of a narrator, but also to recognize the complexities of the subjective, experiencing "I" (whether Ellellou or Updike) and the mysterious historical performer who bodies-forth that "I" in concrete acts (whether beheading the king and writing memoirs or writing a novel about a man who beheads a king and writes his memoirs).

YES—BUT. . .

The Coup's new directions seem to suggest that the critic must say, *"Yes,* this novel marks the beginning of a distinct change in the development of Updike's *oeuvre."* The familiar Updikean ambiguities persist, however, and the critic must add, *"But* although Updike is exploring new territory, the explorer still has the same basic concerns." Updike has launched out in this novel to trace a different aspect of reality, but we find that, like the Möbius strip, his original circle of concern is integrally interlocked with the new one. In fact, Updike admitted to Tom Brokaw in the previously cited interview that the book is really "about America wearing an African mask." Analysis reveals three important continuities which lead us to recognize that, despite his differences from George and Peter Caldwell, Harry Angstrom, Piet Hanema, and Tom Marshfield, Ellellou is, finally, the familiar Updike hero.

The first of these continuities emerges when one considers the epigraph Updike chose for the novel. Although the source of the quotation—the Koran—suggests a departure from the more familiar material of Western intellectual tradition used in earlier epigraphs, the implications of the quotation call to mind a recurring Updike theme present since *The Poorhouse Fair* and carefully articulated in *Midpoint.* Taken from sura 76, the epigraph reads: "Does there not pass over a man a space of time when his life is a blank?" Blankness and emptiness provide dominant striking images which recur throughout the novel, with the land of Kush itself as the source. Ellellou tells us that Kush is "a land of delicate, delectable emptiness, named for a vanished kingdom" (4). He also says that its shape on the map suggests "an angular skull whose cranium is the empty desert" (6). In order to reach the far northwest border where he instigates the burning of the American cornflakes, Ellellou must cross the vast, empty Hullul Depression, "an evaporating pan out of which all things human rise into blue invisibility" (23). The trip to the northeast in search of Edumu's cave takes him across the wastes of Balak, where even the sky is white, and "the earth . . . only dreary varieties of gray" (128). The blankness of the geography of the land is reinforced by recurrent references to the artificiality of the nation as a political entity. Its boundaries were created by European bureaucrats with no reference to the numerous tribes who inhabited its various regions, and Ellellou says that he is apparently the only person who "has within himself an idea of Kush" (11). The country, then, as well as the countryside, is a blank, and Ellellou's efforts to establish the viable reality of his idea of Kush are at the same time efforts to establish the reality of his own identity.

The emphasis on blankness and emptiness recalls the arid future envisioned in *The Poorhouse Fair* when "the wood is dry," the emptiness of Rabbit Angstrom's peddling Magipeelers, the empty jumble of Peter Caldwell's inept abstract paintings, the lapse into apelike innocence of Piet Hanema, the "big round nothing" of the moon in *Rabbit Redux,* and the Death Valley desert of Tom Marshfield.

Although Ellellou is Muslim, not Christian, his concern with blankness, emptiness, and nothingness is similar to that of the earlier protagonists in that it roots in one of the central questions raised by *Midpoint,* the question of the possibility that one's sense of irreducible identity may be merely an illusion. Ellelloû raises the question by suggesting that the ultimate law of the universe may be entropy. He reflects:

> It may be . . . that in the attentuation, desiccation, and death of religions the world over, a new religion is being formed in the indistinct hearts of men, a religion without a God, without prohibitions and compensatory assurances, a religion whose antipodes are motion and stasis, whose one rite is the exercise of energy, and in which exhausted forms like the quest, the vow, the expiation, and the attainment through suffering of wisdom are, emptied of content, put in the service of a pervasive expenditure whose ultimate purpose is entropy, whose immediate reward is fatigue, a blameless confusion, and sleep. (91)

Ellelloû thus entertains the possibility that the struggle for identity is an illusion, that the ultimate end for humankind is merely fatigue, confusion, and, finally, death. Although he entertains the possibility, however, he cannot and does not finally accept it. (Updike himself refuses to accept entropy as the determining factor in human lives, as we have already seen in our discussion of *Rabbit Is Rich,* which was published three years after *The Coup.*) When Ezana tries to convince Ellelloû that the world has changed, that suffering no longer has any purpose or meaning because "the units of race and tribe, sect and nation, by which men identified themselves" no longer attract loyalty, Ellelloû replies: "These units you disparage. . . were mankind's building blocks. If they dissolve, we have a heap of dust, of individual atoms. This is not peace, but entropy" (117). He goes on to suggest the possibility of a principle opposite to the emptiness of entropy: "Is it possible . . . that some principle of contention is intrinsic to Nature, from the first contentious thrust of bare existence against the sublime, original void?" (117).

Reflecting the *Midpoint* beliefs in the hope-creating fact that the void was breached at all and in matter itself as a reflection of the dynamic nature of the universe, he adds:

> The serene heavens, as witnessed by astronomers, shine by grace
> of explosion and consumption on a scale unthinkable, and the
> glazed surface of marble or the demure velvet of a maiden's eyelid
> are by the dissections of particle physics a frenzy of whirling,
> and a titanic tension of incompatible charges. You and I,
> for additional example, have long been at odds, and the govern-
> ment of Kush has been born of the dialectical space between us.
> Out of the useful war between us, a synthesis has emerged; a syn-
> thesis, for a while at least, does package the conflicting energies
> that met within it. (117)

Ellellou, then, like the earlier Updike heroes, seriously
entertains the possibility that his sense of the reality and importance of his own identity may be an illusion in a universe
of slowly increasing emptiness, but, also like the others, he
refuses to accept this possibility. Perhaps things "like the
quest, the vow, the expiation, the attainment through suffering of wisdom" are empty, but Ellellou persists in the quest,
performs the vow, assumes the suffering of his people.
Although the coming of the rains suggests that Updike intends his readers to infer that Ellellou's insistence on these
old-fashioned undertakings is not blank and empty, more important is Ellellou's own growth toward recognizing that
although there may "pass over a man a time when his life is
is . . . blank," time does indeed "pass over." There may be a
time when life is blank, but life itself is *not* blank, even
though it remains ambiguous and mysterious.

Updike's familiar insistence upon a self-world bipolar
dualism is the second significant thread of continuity that
binds *The Coup* to the earlier novels. This dualism is
underscored by the already noted technique of utilizing both
first- and third-person narration. We are thus constantly
reminded of the duality of the "I" who experiences and the
"he" who acts in the world. Three of many specific rein-
forcements of this duality will suffice to illustrate the novel's
continuation of this central *Midpoint* theme. When Ellellou

visits Sittina, his third wife, he recognizes that she is eager for him to leave, "so she can proceed with that life of uncomplicated curves that amuses her" (62). This recognition, Ellelloû says, underlines "the desolation known only to those who live between two worlds," and then adds the following rhetorical question: "But who, in the world, now, does not live between two worlds?" (62).

When Ellelloû is later being ushered to the cave where Edumu's head is speaking with the aid of modern technology, he feels "uncaught up" with himself: "the physical half hurried along to expectancy's accelerated heartbeat, while the spiritual man loitered behind in a fog, groping for the reason for his shadowy, guilty sensation of something undone, of something disastrous due" (190). And when he rips the head loose from its wiring, he holds it to his breast, recognizing that the king had been the "closest approximation to a father the barren world had allowed him" and that he and the king were two of a kind, "small, cool men more sensitive than was efficient to the split between body and mind" (216).

It is Sittina, whose actions reminded him that he and every man live between two worlds, who accompanies him into exile. He tells her that Candace, his white wife, has divorced him, explaining that "mixed marriages have a lot of extra stresses" (295). Sittina responds that "any marriage is mixed" (296), bringing the physical-spiritual dualism back down to the experiential male-female level, as Marshfield did in *A Month of Sundays*. Ellelloû's life with Sittina in exile, he tells us in the penultimate paragraph of the novel, is "middling," again affirming an existence between two worlds.

The third and most significant continuity that suggests Ellelloû's kinship with his predecessors in Updike's fiction is a grateful acceptance of the mystery of life. As he visits the little Mosque of the Clots of Blood in a remote section of Istiqlal, he is struck by the presence of a limestone fountain that has continued to flow with fresh water all through the years of the drought. He wonders about the source of the water, and thinks gratefully of "the unknown men, their names and bones now lost as thoroughly as grains of sand underfoot in Istiqlal, who had dug down to this undying spring, where so few choose to come" (111). Few may choose to come to this undying source of water, with its inscription honoring the "Creator, who created man from clots of blood," as few choose to look to the heavens to seek out the constellation of the Centaur, but Ellelloû seeks out this fountain, even as George Caldwell chooses to take up again his centaur-life on the boundaries of heaven and earth.

On the long trip in search of Edumu's cave, Ellelloû finds the sands of the Balak "strange, black and white like salt and pepper, and at moments it seem[s] an immense page of print too tiny to read" (131). He is unable to find a pattern because the dots are too numerous and too small. He has not achieved the proper perspective. Once he has reached the new American city in the Ippi Rift, however, he points out that the rift is clearly visible to astronauts in orbit, running from northern Europe all the way to Johannesburg. "Those who live in it do not see it at all" (234), he adds—they, like Ellelloû himself with the grains of sand, are too close.

Ellelloû has earlier sensed that his journey to seek Edumu's cave has an element of mystery to it beyond the mere uncertainty of its geographical location. When Sheba asks him, "When do you think we will reach our destination?" he replies, "When there is no farther to go" (150). And he recognizes that the discovery of Edumu's head is not yet the end of his journey. He must continue the quest to the new American city. As he starts down into the rift, he feels "the weariness of the destined, who must run along a track to arrive at what should have been theirs from the start: an identity, a fate" (219).

Ironically, it is in the American-built city, where he fails to convince the crowd of his identity and in the eyes of the outside world ceases to exist, that Ellelloû finds his identity, his fate. In the middle of the city's emptiness (even the city streets are as empty as the desert), he finds a bronze statue of himself erected within a fountain whose inscribed rim carries the words for freedom in each of Kush's twelve languages. Ellelloû—"freedom"—stands in the middle of this fountain, unrecognized and unknown, and the fount itself, Ellelloû now sees, symbolizes "the universe, that so dazzlingly and continuously pours forth something into nothing" (242). Ellelloû has pursued the quest, sought to certify his own identity by taking on the burden of guilt and expiation. All of his efforts seem to fail until that identity is swallowed up by the mindless forces of historical flux which apparently lead only to entropy. Yes—but. The rains come. Ellelloû's quest is successful in that sense. And by losing the identity he has been seeking to assert, by giving up the "assertive putting out" that Marshfield mistakenly thought was love, Ellelloû relaxes and begins to find his true self. The blankness passes over the man who has apparently become a blank in the eyes of his country. He has become, in a sense, a passover sacrifice who frees his people from the scourge of the drought. He returns to Istiqlal disguised as a beggar and finds that Kadongolimi, the wife of his youth, is dead. His daughter tells him, however, that before Kadongolimi died she told her children that their "father had succeeded" (273). The daughter, who will now go forth to become either an agronomist or a pediatrician, insists that her mother told her that her father would give her a blessing. Ellelloû asks why he should bless the unavoidable, and the daughter replies, "It is just that . . . which needs to be blessed" (275). "In the disappearing accent of the Amazeg," Ellelloû gives her his blessing (276).

Ellelloû's disguise prevents the common people of Istiqlal from recognizing him, but his former associates know him immediately. Kutunda tells him, "You have run out of masks" (279), and she would have him tortured and killed, much as she earlier recommended the execution of Edumu. Dorfu, however, recognizes that "a live man far away is less of a presence than a dead man underfoot," and that it is better to leave things as they stand. Ellelloû died, he says, "as President, in the city that bears [his] name" (280). After quoting from the Koran the passage, "Let him that will, take the right path to the Lord. Yet you cannot will except by the will of Allah," Dorfu says to Ellelloû:

> Strange. . . . You took the name Freedom, and have been captive, until now, of your demons. Our capital is called Independence, yet our polity is an interweave of dependencies. Even the purity of water is a paradox; for unless it be chemically impure, it cannot be drunk. To be free of hunger, men gave up something of themselves to the tribe. To fight against oppression, men must band in an army and become less free, some might say, than before. Freedom is like a blanket, which, pulled up to the chin, uncovers the feet. (290)

Ellelloû then responds:

> You are saying, perhaps, . . . that freedom is like all things directional. . . . Even the universe by which we measure the separate motions of the earth and the sun itself moves, through some unimaginable medium, toward some unimaginable destination. How delicious it is, my President, to pause in movement, and to feel that divine momentum hurtling one forward! (290)

Like Marshfield, Ellelloû has found the necessity of recognizing that "most of what we have is given, not acquired" *(Month of Sundays* 218). His task is not the aggressive pursuit of proof of his own identity through the realization of his idea of Kush, but a "half-conscious following out" *(Month* 218) of the "divine momentum" hurtling him forward. Only in the paradox of losing his self-identity does Ellelloû achieve his long-sought dream of the creation of a viable nation.

As Marshfield's month led him to see all those for whom

he felt responsible fade in importance, so Ellelloû as he writes finds that "the crush of present reality"—his simple life of exile in the south of France—makes the hints of his life in Kush "no more than fragile scraps of wreckage that float to the surface, fewer and fewer as the waves continue to break, to hiss, to slide, to percolate through the pebbles" (229). "All yesterdays," he says, "are thus submerged." But he continues to write his memoirs, for the words he writes are "long tendrils like the tendrilous chains of contingency that have delivered us, each, to where we sit now on the skin of the world, waterlilies concealing our masses of root"(299).

Ellelloû is thus not very different from Harry Angstrom, Piet Hanema, or Tom Marshfield, who also sat on the "skin" of the same world, concealing, as all persons do, the "masses of root" that suggest the mysterious interpenetration of inner and outer poles. Although the Muslim Ellelloû quotes the Koran, the quotation and his comment which follows apply almost equally well to all of Updike's novelistic protagonists: *"Those who have gone before them also plotted, but Allah is the master of every plot: He knows the deserts of every soul. The man is happy, hidden"* (299).

ROGER'S VERSION

Roger Lambert, narrator/protagonist of *Roger's Version,* is similar to Tom Marshfield of *A Month of Sundays* in that he is a minister whose sexual straying has brought disgrace. Unlike Marshfield, however, Lambert has limited his extramarital encounters to the one affair which led to his dismissal from his Methodist parish, has been uneventfully married to the "other woman" for fourteen years as the story opens, and is comfortably settled into his career as a professor at the Divinity School of a large university in an unnamed eastern city that suggests Boston. Roger's specialty is teaching seminars in early Christian heresy, and he has found some satisfaction in the "spiritual fatigue" of middle age, recognizing that "the flares of ambition and desire that had lit [his] way when [he] was younger and had given [his] life the drama of fiction or of a symbol-laden dream had been chemical devices, illusions with which the flesh and its percolating brain had lured [him] along" (224-225). But Roger is not destined to remain comfortably on the plateau of middle-aged satisfaction that Harry Angstrom enjoyed in *Rabbit Is Rich.*

Into Roger's study one afternoon in late October of 1984 comes Dale Kohler, a twenty-eight-year-old graduate student in computer science. Dale seeks Roger's help in gaining a grant from the Divinity School to assist him in proving the existence of God via the computer. Dale has chosen Roger as a starting point for his request for a grant because of his acquaintance with Verna Ekelof, the daughter of Roger's half-sister from Cleveland. The mother of a half-black illegitimate baby, Verna has been disowned by her pious father and has come east to live in a housing project in her uncle's city, although Roger does not know of her presence until Dale tells him. Dale is convinced that "God is showing through" (10). "It's what science has come to," he says. "Everywhere you look, . . . there are these terrifically finely adjusted constants that have to be just what they are, or there wouldn't be a world we could recognize, and there's no intrinsic reason for those constants to be what they are except to say *God made them that way"* (14). Roger is appalled by the whole idea of the project, finding it both "aesthetically and ethically repulsive. Aesthetically because it describes a God Who lets Himself be intellectually trapped, and ethically because it eliminates faith from religion, it takes away our freedom to believe or doubt" (24). Nevertheless, Roger agrees to let Dale use his name on the grant application, admitting that "it *would* be a relief to underwrite something. . .

other than black or feminist studies . . . or . . . pathetic papers on 'street religion' " (25).

Roger's wife Esther, at thirty-eight, is fourteen years younger than he, and their once-torrid affair that ended Roger's ministerial career has settled into dull, academic routine. Roger feels boredom wafting "from [Esther] like the scent of stale sweat" (35) as he enters his home after his initial interview with Dale, and he realizes that without their twelve-year-old son, Richie, they "would have almost nothing to talk about" (39). The story of Dale's proposed project and the news of Verna's presence in the city arouse Esther's interest, however, and she suggests that Roger invite both of them over for tea some time. In early November Roger goes to visit Verna and her daughter, Paula, in the housing project. He invites her, not to tea, but to Thanksgiving dinner. During their second interview, in which they discuss gaps in the theory of evolution, Roger asks Dale to join them as well. At the dinner Roger notes Esther's vivacious reaction to Dale as she arranges to have Dale come to the house to tutor Richie in math. Roger also takes on the tutor's role as he visits Verna again in early December to encourage her to study for a high-school equivalency test.

Events of January fill the central chapter of the book (third among five). Roger ponders the words of Tertullian, presents his vision of the sexual involvement he is sure is now in full swing between Dale and Esther, argues problems of the mind-body split with Dale in their third interview, discovers that Verna is pregnant again and helps her arrange an abortion, attends the meeting of the Divinity School grants committee and by speaking against Dale's proposal as a committed Barthian ironically sways the committee to approve $2500 to underwrite Dale's research.

In April Dale spends a disappointing night crunching figures into the computer. He finds a ghostly hand on the screen at one point, but when he commands the computer to *repeat,* the "hand has vanished, unless its shape has been reduced and transformed into the single green scale at the lower right of the screen, in the position of an artist's signature" (250). The night is over and "Dale feels wasted," but consoles himself (as Roger pictures him) that "Zero is information also" (251). That same night Verna interrupts Roger's peaceful reading of Tillich by her desperate call for help. She has become so frustrated and angry at little Paula that she has struck the child and broken her leg. Roger takes the two to the hospital, where Paula's leg is set and she is kept overnight until a social worker can clear up any questions of child abuse the next day. When Roger takes Verna home, she invites him into her apartment and into her bed. Despite his fear of the "many new kinds" of VD and of AIDS, Roger succumbs to the lust he has felt for Verna since his first visit. His memory of this experience is "less distinct in [his] refractory mind than . . . [Esther's] . . . many pictured infidelities with Dale" (280), and the reader is surprised that Roger's own adultery (and, as he says, incest and child abuse as well) receives only one paragraph instead of the many lyrical and graphic pages devoted to his visions of the couplings of Esther and Dale.

In the final chapter of the book, Roger describes events from the second week of May through the second week in June 1985. Esther helps smooth things over with the child welfare people, promising to look after Paula while Verna seeks counseling. The Lamberts give their big annual cocktail party just before the end of the spring term. Dale comes to this party, knowing that he is not going to succeed in his project and that Esther is ready to end their affair. His arguments for the necessity of God are systematically destroyed by the Lamberts' neighbor, Myron Kriegman, a chemist. The next day Roger has lunch with Verna and gives her money to go home to Ohio and promises to call his half-sister to pave the way for Verna's homecoming. Verna tells him that Dale, too, is returning to his home in Akron, having lost his faith. Roger's story ends on a Sunday in the middle of June as he looks after little Paula (who will soon follow her mother to Cleveland) and Richie while Esther dresses to go to church. "Why would you do a ridiculous thing like that?" Roger asks. Esther, "in her gorgeous rounded woman's voice," replies smilingly, " 'To annoy you' " (328).

This brief summary of the events Roger recounts in the novel does not indicate either the length or the complexity of the discussions of technical scientific information that take place between Roger and Dale and between Dale and Myron Kriegman. Updike carefully researched the technical material (as indicated by the twenty-two people thanked on the copyright page of the book) and has presented it in terms that a layman can follow and understand if he is willing to put forth the effort, although Paul Gray has complained that sometimes the science-talk "sounds like intelligent speech turned up to a volume of impenetrable noise" and that "it is hard to tell at such moments whether Updike is parading knowledge or satirizing it." What Gray calls "this dazzling and sometimes maddening display of talent and erudition" comes as no surprise, however, to readers of the third canto of *Midpoint,* which demonstrated Updike's concern with and mastery of current developments in science.

Updike told Katherine Stephen that the wealth of complex information in *Roger's Version* was in part a deliberate retort to some of his critics: "I've been accused of writing novels without ideas, so I thought I'd write a book with a few ideas in it" (1), he said. Elaborating on his motives for writing the novel, he added, "I was sitting at my word processor one day, and I noticed this scramble of numbers that it throws up. The notion of there being a magical secret in that code of numbers occurred to me, being a superstitious sort of person" (1). As we shall see, however, despite breaking some new ground in dealing directly with complex ideas and in pursuing possibilities of revelation on a computer screen, *Roger's Version* is a further probing of familiar Updikean concerns that have been held up to varying lights and viewed from different perspectives through almost thirty years of developing a novelistic *oeuvre*. The choice of epigraphs indicating a continuing "otherworldly stand," the use of the I/eye combination in juxtaposition with a world of objective reality, and the sifting of pointillistic dots through varying grids in order to seek a meaningful pattern all give clues to the persistence of the *Midpoint* commitments.

EPIGRAPHS

The failure of Dale's humanistic attempts to reduce God to the size of a computer screen is predicted for the alert reader by the epigraphs Updike has chosen. As he pointed out in our 1976 interview, Updike chooses epigraphs carefully, meaning them to offer the reader important clues ("Interview" 277). The four epigraphs for *Roger's Version* suggest a basic philosophical position inimicable to the success of undertakings such as Dale's

The first epigraph, taken from Matthew 26:8, is the third Biblical epigraph Updike has used for a novel. He used a comment from Jesus in the Gospel of Luke on the dryness of the wood for his first novel, *The Poorhouse Fair* (1959), and he used a portion of a verse from Psalm 45 as one of the epigraphs for *A Month of Sundays*. In neither of these cases, however, was the context of the verse of particular importance. Instead, the Luke verse was chosen for its relevance to the dryness the young author felt to be common to the Eisenhower era, and the selection from the Psalm ("My tongue is the pen of a ready writer") was intended as a joke on himself ("Interview" 277, 283). The Biblical epigraph for this twelfth novel, unlike the other two, does require some knowledge of its context if one is to grasp the clue it offers to the book's meaning.

"To what purpose is this waste?" is the question that Updike pulls from the twenty-sixth chapter of Matthew (KJV). The question is asked by the disciples after a woman has poured a jar of very expensive ointment on Jesus' head at the house of Simon the Leper. The disciples are indignant because the ointment could have been sold and a large sum of money given to the poor. Such a judgment is sound from a humanistic, materialistic point of view. But Jesus rebukes the disciples for misunderstanding the meaning of the woman's act. "She has done a beautiful thing to me," he says, for she has, in effect, anointed his body for the burial he will soon face. Jesus takes the "otherworldly stand" that there are acts which are not always justifiable on rational grounds but that are appropriate and even necessary because they meet some special need of human beings to acknowledge something greater than themselves. As Roger tells Dale, "There is surely more at stake in theology than this. . . mechanical-statistical approach of yours. . . . There is a whole realm of subjective existential questions you are ignoring. . . . People don't turn to God because He's likely or unlikely; they turn out of their extremest need, against all reason" (86-87).

The fifth and concluding canto of *Midpoint* opens with the poet's rejecting of an "easy Humanism" and choosing instead the "Archimedean point" of "an otherworldly stand" (38). Prominent among the Updikean heroes and champions of such a stand listed in subsequent lines are Soren Kierkegaard, nineteenth century Danish existentialist theologian, and Karl Barth, Swiss theologian and primary spokesman for the "neo-orthodox" movement in theology in the mid-twentieth century. His choice of these two *Midpoint* heroes as the sources for the second and third epigraphs for *Roger's Version* is further evidence that two decades have not altered Updike's basic philosophy. The Kierkegaard quotation is from one of his journals: "O infinite majesty, even if you were not love, even if you were cold in your infinite majesty I could not cease to love you, I need something majestic to love." Kierkegaard here expresses much the same idea that Roger used in arguing with Dale in the passage quoted in the previous paragraph. Updike told me in 1976 that part of what attracted him to Kierkegaard was his "insistence on the importance of the individual," his sense of the "radical jump between one's individual sense of me—I—and any other kind of reality." Kierkegaard, he added, "almost says that God is there because I so much want him to be there" ("Interview" 296). Or, as Roger reflects in the novel, "the longing for God. . . is, when all is said and done, our only evidence of His existence" (67). God, Roger insists, "will *not* be deduced . . . ." He cannot be reduced "to the status of one more fact" or "made subject to statistics and bits of old bone and glimmers of light in some telescope" (88).

The third epigraph is from Karl Barth's *The Humanity of God:* "What if the result of the new hymn to the majesty of God should be a new confirmation of the hopelessness of all human activity?" We have noted that the theology of Barth has been important to Updike since he first began reading it seriously in 1960 or 1961 ("Interview" 302). The Barthian epigraph here confirms Updike's continuing rejection of "an easy Humanism" and his continued commitment to the basically Barthian position held by Tom Marshfield in *A Month of Sundays.* Roger Lambert, too, is a confessed disciple of Barth, unfashionable as such discipleship is in his seminary in the 80s. His quoting of Barth throughout the book confirms the suggestion of the epigraph that God is "totally other," always beyond the scope of any human endeavors.

Roger tells Dale during their initial interview that "The

God we care about in this divinity school is the living God, Who moves toward us out of His will and love, and Who laughs at all the towers of Babel we build to Him" (22). He recognizes that he is "echoing Barth," but he must wait until he gets home before he can find time to locate the exact quote and its source. He picks up Barth's *The Word of God and the Word of Man,* searching for the passage that had particularly impressed him thirty years earlier. He finally finds it, unexpectedly, in the chapter entitled "The Problem of Ethics Today": "There is no way from us to God—not even a *via negativa*—not even a *via dialectica* nor *paradoxa.* The god who stood at the end of some human way—even of this way— would not be God." He recognizes that Barth has given him the clue to the impossibility of proving God via computer or any other human means: *"The god who stood at the end of some human way would not be God"* (41).

Roger sums up his Barthian version of the proper human position in relation to God as he speaks against Dale's project before the divinity school grants committee:

> Barth, I fear, would have regarded Dale's project as the most futile and insolent sort of natural theology. . . . His objectivity must be of a totally other sort than that of these physical equations. Even if this were not so, there are additional problems with provability. Wouldn't a God Who let Himself be proven— more exactly, a God Who can't *help* being proven—be too submissive, too passive and beholden to human ingenuity, a helpless and contingent God, in short?. . . . Facts are boring. Facts are inert, impersonal. A God Who is a mere fact will just sit there on the table with all the other facts: we can take Him or leave Him. The way it is, we are always in motion *toward* the God who flees, the *Deus absconditus;* He by His apparent absence is always with us. . . . As Barth himself says somewhere. . . "What manner of God is He Who has to be proved?" (218-219)

As it turns out, Roger's bringing of Barth, "the scornful enemy of religious humanists and accommodators" (219), into the argument swings the committee against him and in favor of Dale, and $2,500 is proffered to underwrite Dale's efforts. Roger's version of theology, however, sets forth Updike's own "otherworldly stand" which dictates the futility and failure of all attempts to reduce God to the level of phenomena analyzable by the human mind.

The final epigraph is from Jane Miller's poem "High Holy Days": "god the wind as windless as the world behind a computer screen." This final epigraph relates more directly to the plot line of the book while maintaining the sense of the paradoxical nature of the God who is behind both the wind of nature and the windless technology of the computer. Taken as a whole, the four epigraphs clearly predict the inevitable outcome of any human attempt to bridge the gap between man and God.

I/EYE

The use of the first person narrator and the announcement by the very title of the book that this is *Roger's* version of the story suggest the familiar *Midpoint* theme of the centrality of the individual, of the importance of the ego as the interpretive center of its own universe. In this case, Roger is not only the subjective I who tells the story; he is also the voyeuristic eye who sees and reports the adulterous activities of Esther and Dale and at times the omniscient eye who sees into Dale's very consciousness. He is always careful, when reporting actions or thoughts not his own, to remind the reader that these are *his* views or intuitions of others, but he nevertheless presents them as factual. Like Marshfield, he is aware that someone is reading his version of the story, and he never pretends that it is anything but his own view. Like Ellelou, he knows that there is a difference between the acting, observable self—the divinity school professor his students know—and the subject Roger Lambert. Thus

Roger's Version is the third of Updike's experiments with "self-conscious" fiction. But with Roger the reader has problems not associated with either Marshfield or Elleloû. With each of them one was aware of a fictional artifice, of an implied author/reader contract, but there was never a question about their trustworthiness. With Roger, however, we can't help wondering whether all the things he intuits or imagines about Dale and Esther are simply products of his own resentment at Esther's boredom and Dale's youth. He even confesses in a footnote (a practice also frequently indulged in by Marshfield) that at his age "the best sex is head sex—sex kept safe in the head" (190). We rather expect the revelation at the end of the book that Dale and Esther were innocent, that Roger's version has taken place only in his own head. Instead, however, Verna gives objective confirmation to Roger's intuitions when she tells him (and the reader) at their concluding luncheon interview that Dale has been having an affair with an older, married woman in Roger's neighborhood. It is usual for the first person narrator to share his author's poetic and stylistic sensibilities; it is not usual for the narrator to share the author's omniscience. So we are left with ambiguity: exactly how true is Roger's version?

One way of justifying the validity of Roger's uncanny intuitions is to recognize the allusions in his story to *The Scarlet Letter*. Just as Marshfield's story was in a sense a re-telling of what Updike has called Hawthorne's "strange little fable" (qtd. in Stephen 4) from the point of view of the adulterous minister, *Roger's Version* is the same story told by the cuckolded husband. Dale Kohler replaces Arthur Dimmesdale, Esther replaces Hester, and Roger himself parallels Roger Chillingworth of the original novel. Updike told me that the allusions to *The Scarlet Letter* in *A Month of Sundays* and *Roger's Version*—and in his next novel, scheduled for publication in late 1987 and told from Hester's point of view—"are meant to be more than playful; they mean to show how things have changed since 1640, or 1850" ("Response"). As we have seen, Marshfield's story is almost an exact inversion of Dimmesdale's. Lambert's story also surely shows "how things have changed," although the inversion is not quite so neat. The adulterous couple is not exposed to shame or ridicule—even the husband seems not too disturbed by their affair. Dale does suffer from inner guilt and torment as Arthur Dimmesdale did, so that by the time of the Lamberts' cocktail party he looks "terrible" (as Roger sees him), "terrible from within: the inner worm was gnawing lustily" (291). Dale's inner torment comes from a sense that he is too small to undertake and succeed at his project, from guilt over his continued affair with Esther, and from frustration that he knows that that affair is at an end. But Dale does not make public confession of his guilt and thereby earn redemption for himself. Furthermore, although Verna tells Roger that he is evil in contrast to Dale's naive faith (324), there is no really serious suggestion that he, like the original Roger Chillingworth, is to be identified with the old black man of the forest. In fact, the one time that Roger mentions the Devil, it is to ridicule Dale's naive belief that the Devil is doubt. No, Roger says, "The Devil is the absence of doubt. He's what pushes people into suicide bombing, into setting up extermination camps. Doubt may give your dinner a funny taste, but it's faith that goes out and kills" (81).

Although Lambert is not, like Chillingworth, identified with the Devil, nor does he, like Chillingworth, seek revenge on his wife's lover, he does share one of his namesake's abilities. As Chillingworth was able to see into Dimmesdale's inmost soul and know his secrets, so can Roger Lambert get inside the sensibility of Dale Kohler. The intuiting of Dale's consciousness begins immediately after the first interview in Roger's office. "In one of those small, undesired miracles that infest life," Roger says, "my disembodied mind empathetically followed Dale Kohler down the hall" (28). Next

Roger imagines Dale's feelings as he walks to Verna's apartment, following the route he knows Dale must also follow. "I was taking this walk in the steps of another," he confesses, "and I felt his spirit invading mine" (54). Later, sitting in Verna's apartment, Roger has "a sense of being Dale Kohler" (66-67). By incrementally building such moments of empathic identification, Updike is able to let Roger believably present Esther's and Dale's couplings (including details of Dale's room with its plastic cross that Roger has never actually seen) and Dale's long night of the soul struggling with the computer on the seventh floor of "The Cube" (the giant computer building into which Roger has never ventured). Although we can never be absolutely sure that Roger's version of things outside the realm of his own consciousness is trustworthy, Chillingworth's uncanny ability to see into Arthur's heart provides a parallel that inclines us to believe Roger. At any rate, *Roger's Version* certainly affirms the *Midpoint* commitment to the centrality of the individual while still presenting that central ego in ambiguous but inescapable involvement with an objective, phenomenal world presenting dots of experience which require sorting and interpreting.

POINTILLISM

In *Midpoint,* the poet asserted that "The Truth arrives as if by telegraph:/ One dot; two dots; a silence; then a laugh," and that the dots of truth were governed by rules which could not be imposed by any human plan or scheme (38). In *Roger's Version* the metaphor has been updated: the dots now arrive not one or two at a time by telegraph, but as 262,000 pixels at once on a video monitor (116). Nevertheless, Dale finds that no matter how he crunches the figures through the computer, he is no more able to impose his pattern upon those hundreds of thousands of dots than were those before him who worked for similar humanistic or rationalistic goals with fewer dots. Dale can take a "roundish pool of dots" and turn them into a tree, which he can then print out in various combinations on a dot-matrix printer (237). But "the black dots dart and swarm from one edge of the screen to the other like midges above a summer pond" (240), and Dale cannot discover any meaningful configuration. At one point he does seem to see "a mournful face" staring "out of the instant ionic shuffle," but it is only "a ghost of a face" which in "a matter of milliseconds" is gone (244).

Dale does succeed in isolating the image of a hand, but "the printout is disappointing. . . . The hand hardly shows—a dim mottled ghost flat on the paper" (249). When he tries to repeat the process, the screen is filled with ripples, stripes and concentric tunnels which then subdivide into "geometrical fish scales. The hand has been folded in, has vanished, unless its shape has been reduced and transformed into the single green scale at the lower right of the screen, in the position of an artist's signature" (250). When Dale asks the machine to repeat once more, "the screen goes a cool gray, saying in unanswerable black letters *Insufficient heap storage*" (251). Dale has been wrestling with the computer all through a night in the middle of Lent; tonight he has anticipated a climax, "an atonement, atonement in its root sense of *at one*" (243). Now, though, the night is over, the moon is gone, and no atonement has occurred. Dale looks out the window and sees "only a few windows . . . lit—bright slots spelling, in binary code, a word here and there. But of course, actually, a row of dead windows, of empty slots, spells words just as well. Zero is information also" (251). Whether on the computer screen with its hundreds of thousands of dot/windows or in the phenomenal world with its more limited dots of information, Dale finds that he cannot successfully impose his own explanation of the ultimate mystery of reality but must accept the pattern as it emerges.

There is a structural pattern that emerges from the varied dots of Roger's story. Roger and Dale have three formal interviews. In the first of these they discuss cosmology, basically the Big Bang theory of the origin of the universe and the difficulties of believing that the many close adjustments required for life as we know it could have been a result of mere chance. In the second they discuss Darwin's theory of evolution and the many gaps it leaves as a satisfactory explanation for the development of life. In the third they discuss problems raised by the mind-body split. Each of these interviews is paralleled by Roger's preparation for one of his seminars on ante-Nicene heresies. Immediately following the first interview, Roger is to lecture on Marcion (fl. A.D. 139), the first of the early heresiarchs. The pairing of Marcion with a discussion of cosmology is appropriate because Marcion's heresy involved a rejection of the Old Testament God, creator of the world, in favor of a God of mercy, newly revealed in Jesus, thus denying the orthodox Christian affirmation that the God who breached the void and brought matter into existence is the same God whose love became incarnate in Jesus Christ. In fact, Marcion denied the reality of the incarnation, holding that Christ really did not have a fully human body, but only *appeared* to be human and to die a real death upon the cross. His new God of mercy would not contaminate himself with the messy trappings of the flesh. By his own admission, Dale's attempts also will have nothing to do with the Incarnation or the Trinity. All he hopes is to prove "the absolute basics—the bottom line, as it were" (25), thus, like Marcion, splitting the traditional Christian affirmation apart. For Roger, such a provable God is just as heretical as Marcion's, for it seeks to make God "un*int*eresting" and "pat." "Whatever else God may be," Roger says, "He shouldn't be pat" (24). Rather, he must be "a God Who acts, Who *comes to us,* in Revelation and Redemption" (22).

The discussion of the many unexplained gaps in evolutionary theory—which Dale believes can only be filled by demonstrating a God who created matter in the specific way He did—comes as Roger is preparing to discuss Pelagius (fl. c. A.D. 400), whose belief in the freedom and basic goodness of the human will was ardently attacked by Augustine. Pelagius' general position is summed up by the phrase "If I ought, I can," but Augustine—and subsequent Christian orthodoxy—found that Pelagius' position erred by not acknowledging original sin, by denying the necessity of infused grace for salvation, and by affirming human power to live without sin. Pelagius' confidence in the ability of man to achieve virtue by developing his own capacities parallels Dale's hope to show God at work through the gradual development of life processes.

It is the third discussion, however, that is most crucial to the overall meaning of *Roger's Version*. This discussion of the mind-body split is paralleled by Roger's rather full discussion of the thought of Tertullian (b. ca. A.D. 150-155) and his description of the encounters between Dale and Esther. These three interrelated incidents—the explication of Tertullian, the description of Dale's sexual activities, and the facing of the problem of the mind-body split—form the core of the third chapter of the book, the central and pivotal chapter among five.

As Chapter III opens, Roger is translating Tertullian's *Of the Resurrection of the Body [Flesh]*. Tertullian, who lived and wrote most of his life in Carthage, was a trained lawyer with the Roman sense of order and authority; his writing showed such clarity and precision that, although he was not primarily a speculative theologian but an interpreter of others, he is known as the father of Latin theology. Tertullian wrote actively in defense and explication of Christianity from 197 to 220, but about 202 he joined the heretical

Montanist sect which proclaimed the imminent end of the world and the necessity for strenuous asceticism—celibacy, fastings, and abstinence from meat—as preparation for the end. As Roger points out, *The Resurrection of the Body* was written in 208, several years after Tertullian had "fallen away from orthodoxy," but Roger, though a trained heretic-hunter, cannot "sniff out" anything unorthodox in this particular book (149). So although Tertullian is considered a heretic to be studied in Roger's seminar, his thoughts as presented here in Chapter III are not heretical, but are presented as bench marks to interpret the meaning of Dale's involvement with Esther and the relationship of mind to body.

As Roger explains, Tertullian argues that "the flesh cannot be dispensed with by the soul" because the body provides the bases for all the senses; even the power of speech—the word, the Logos—is dependent upon the bodily tongue. It is through the body that the soul's life is derived. The flesh is thus not only the "soul's minister and servant," but also "its consort and co-heir" (150-151). Thus Tertullian argues that the soul and the flesh must be united eternally through the resurrection of the body. Tertullian insists, Marcion and pagan Gnostics alike to the contrary, that the Christian view is that "the flesh is man" (152).

This meditation on the centrality of the flesh and the dependence of the soul upon it is abruptly cut off as Roger closes his eyes and pictures Dale and Esther together in the third-floor room of the Lambert home. Hilton Kramer finds that "it is only in the pages devoted to [Dale and Esther's] lovemaking, depicted here with the author's customary pornographic precision, . . . that *Roger's Version* comes to life. This is John Updike at the old stand, so to speak, worshipping at the shrine of sexual intercourse and lavishing all of his well-known powers of description on its physical details." Frederick Crews also strongly objects to "Roger's depictions of Esther and Dale," for, he says, they "constitute pornography proper, the close-up representation of sex without reference to the mind and heart, without antecedents or consequences" (14). Mr. Kramer, Mr. Crews, and many other critics fail to grasp the connection between flesh and spirit, between sex as at once an expression of individuality and interrelatedness, and fail to understand sexual intercourse as a paradigm of duality and mystery. But Updike, by juxtaposing excerpts from Tertullian throughout the chapter, has provided the screen through which to view these particular dots of experience properly. Roger's references to Tertullian's *Of the Resurrection of the Body* open Chapter III, but later in the chapter, both during the sex scenes involving Dale and Esther and during the interview with Dale in Roger's office, excerpts and ideas from *Of the Body [Flesh] of Christ* and *Of the Soul* (generally credited to be the first book of Christian psychology) are also brought in. All three of these works come from Tertullian's second period, shortly after he had become a Montanist but before he had actually left the church. Roger explains that the significant point in *Of the Body of Christ* is "shame, embarrassment" (168):

> But what is more unworthy of God, Tertullian asks, more likely to raise a blush—being born or dying? What is in worse taste, being circumcised or crucified? Being laid in a manger or in a tomb? It's all something to be ashamed of. But "Whoever is ashamed of Me," God says, "of him will I be ashamed."
> "I am safe," Tertullian says, "if I am not ashamed of my Lord"—not embarrassed, that is to say, by the incarnation and all the awkwardness that goes with it. The son of God died, Tertullian says: it is absolutely to be believed, because it is out of place, in poor taste—*ineptum*, the Latin adjective is. And was buried, and rose again; it is certain, because it is impossible. (168-169)

The awkwardness, poor taste, embarrassment, and shame involved in accepting the full humanity (flesh-ness) of Christ is highlighted as Roger suggests to Dale:

Think of being Jesus Christ at age fifteen, back home in Nazareth after Your impish behavior in the Temple has been forgotten and everybody thinks You're going to be just another carpenter like Your dad. Do You masturbate? Do You go out behind the stack of wood scraps with the little Canaanite girl next door? Do You have wet dreams that not even old Yahweh at His most forbidding could hold against a boy? Don't be embarrassed. (174)

Roger insists that the only way to overcome the embarrassment and shame—not only of considering such delicate questions as the sex-life of Jesus but also of facing the implacability of physical matter in general—is through "some huge effort of swallowing shame such as Tertullian outlines" (170). Like Tertullian, Roger believes that "it"—the presence of God in the very flesh—"is certain, because it is impossible." The only salvation is to not be ashamed.

In *Of the Soul* Tertulian expands on his insistence that one must not be ashamed. Roger explains it to Dale:

You know what Tertullian said? He said, "There's nothing to blush for in Nature; Nature should be revered." *Natura veneranda est, non erubescenda.* He goes on in rather interesting detail about men and women. He says when they come together the soul and the flesh discharge a duty together; the soul supplies the desire and the flesh the gratification. That the man's semen derives its fluidity from the body and its warmth from the soul. He calls it, in fact, a drip of the soul. . . . Nothing to be ashamed of, in short. *Non erubescenda.* (175)

With this background from Tertullian, we can see that Hilton Kramer is mistaken in being embarrassed or offended by the precision with which the love-making is described, and that Frederick Crews has completely missed the important references not only to "mind and heart" but soul as well. In addition to anatomical precision, these passages include interpretive comments which suggest that the sex act is a fleshly *(per carnem)* expression of a soul *(anima)* which cannot know or be known apart from its fleshly consort. We are told, for instance, that by the flesh *(per carnem)* the love-making allows "care on one side and trust on another" to emerge (152), and that Esther "wraps" her joint climax with Dale "with her *anima*" (156). Dale sees Esther as "a sensual field in which his incarnation has room at last to run and roam" (159). As Roger mentions the lovers' "interfaced *pudenda* (the plural of *pudendum,* 'that of which one ought to be ashamed,' a grammatically neutral form whose onus has been patriarchally shifted onto the female genitals alone)" (157), we are reminded of Tertullian's insistence that there's *nothing* to be ashamed of in nature. And if one takes the time to translate the Latin comments from Tertullian interspersed throughout the scene (and Updike provides the translations on preceding pages for those who care to look back to decipher their meanings), he finds that he is quoting the squeamish heathen who are embarrassed by the origin, substance, causality, and uncleanness of the flesh, the ones *against* whom Tertullian was arguing. *"Frivolae, infirmae, criminosae, onerosae, molestae. . . . immundioris deinceps ex seminis sui limo.. . . inprimis pabula atque potacula . . . pudendis non pudendum"* (157, 159, 161)—paltry, infirm, guilty, burdensome, troublesome . . . uncleaner still from the slime of its semen . . . especially food and drink . . . not being ashamed of the shameful organs. But for Tertullian—and Roger and Updike—there are no shameful organs, nothing in nature to be ashamed of. Or, as Roger puts it directly to Dale: "Don't be afraid of the Earth. The flesh" (175).

The Tertullian acceptance of the shame of the inexplicable inseparability of soul and body also underlies the discussion of the mind-body split that Dale thinks his computer project can throw some new light on. Dale points out that comparing the brain to computer hardware and the mind to software is a false analogy because "software can exist without hardware. Or, rather, it can function with a variety of hardwares" (164). The brain, which Dale insists is "just a mass of electrochemical jelly" (166), may be compared to a computer, but the computer has no sensation, no emotion, no will, no self-reference. The brain has none of these things, either, but Dale insists that human experience posits a subjective world of mental events, some of which set up electrical signals that move our bodies" (167). Quantum physics now says that consciousness is "intrinsic to matter: a particle doesn't become actual until it's observed," Dale insists (167-168). Particle physics, he goes on, adds "that reality is intrinsically uncertain and in a very real way dependent upon observation. There's this physicist named Wheeler down in Texas who says the entire universe had to wait for a conscious observer before it could be real. Not just subjective-real, but real in a very real way. . . .Mind really does affect matter in this sense" (169).

Roger is unimpressed with the pressing of physics into the service of philosophical idealism. "This is very charming," he says:

> but isn't it, honestly, rather stretching it? The reason people don't make too much of their minds is that they see how totally at the mercy of the material world the mind is—a brick drops on your head, your mind is extinguished no matter how indeterminate are the motions of the atoms composing the clay of the brick . . . there is no way around matter. It's implacable. It doesn't give a damn about us one way or another. It doesn't even know we're here. And everything we do, from looking both ways when we cross the street to designing airplanes with huge safety factors, acknowledges this, this heartless indifference in things. (170)

The only way Roger can see to solve the mind-body split is Tertullian's "swallowing shame," refusing to be embarrassed, accepting the messy muddle of life as it is given. Or as Updike put it in *Midpoint,* "Our Guilt inheres in sheer Existing, so/ Forgive yourself your death, and freely flow. . . ." since "Nothing has had to be, but is by Grace" (42, 40).[4]

Updike is still searching deep in the thicket of the flowing bits and pieces of human existence, confident that the thorns there spell a word. As he has been in all of his novels, he is much more ready to expose false words—including in this novel computer technology, quantum and particle physics, the anthropic principle applied to cosmology, and other newly fashionable discoveries and theories—than he is to identify any word he may have found. The *Midpoint* voice which warned against false gods, flawless formulas and bandwagons, and which announced its determination to continue "knocking on the doors of days" (44) while continuing to laugh and believe in the absurd still speaks strongly through Roger Lambert.

A hint of some familiar words, if not *a* definitive word, is found, however, in the novel's conclusion. Verna tells Roger that through her therapist she has learned that all she really wants is to be normal, to have some structure to her life. As Piet and Foxy find peace and acceptance by returning to the normal, structured world at the conclusion of *Couples,* and as the three witches eagerly return to normalcy and structure at the end of *The Witches of Eastwick,* so Verna outgrows her "Girls Just Want to Have Fun" understanding of life. As Jerry recognizes the impossibility of his mythical pretensions in *Marry Me* and learns to live side by side with his wife, so Dale recognizes he met only a passing need for Esther and that his hope of forcing God to show Himself through the computer screen was a task beyond human undertaking. He, like Verna, returns to Ohio, to heartland America. Roger, like Harry Angstrom, is "brought back" from a life of cynical academic routine and forced to resurrect his "hot Barthian nugget" of belief which he had kept "insulated within layers of worldly cynicism and situation ethics" for years (180). Esther, who had used Dale to assuage her own fear of approaching death, ends the affair still comfortably married (as did Ruth in *Marry Me*), and concludes the book by going to church for the first time in years. Although she says that she is going simply to annoy Roger, one suspects that Esther's return to church may parallel Verna's desire for normalcy and structure, Dale's return home from the alien, urban East, and Roger's dredging up of beliefs he had thought were carefully buried.

Updike told Katherine Stephen that he had "written maybe all to much about religion here and there," but admitted, "I don't see anything else around really addressing one's basic sense of dread and strangeness other than the Christian church for me" (1). Yes—but, he added:

> I must have a certain amount of hostility, too, toward organized religion. I notice when I write about it that it comes out kind of acid. It is basically an amazing phenomenon among us. You could give a reason, I suppose, for the existence of gas stations. But it would be very hard to explain to a Martian what all these churches are doing. They're a little like books, in a way; a little like fiction. It would be very hard to explain to a Martian why novels exist. (4)

American earthlings, however, need no explanations for the existence of the novels of John Updike. They are the perceptive siftings of the grains of our commonplace lives by one who continually seeks a meaningful pattern in the seemingly random phenomena of emerging experience. Although he most often exposes the emptiness of what passes for meaning in most lives, the ambiguity and muddle of man's existence as a thinking animal have not stopped his seeking for the thorns that spell a word.

NOTES

[1]Since Episcopalian churches do not have boards of deacons, Updike may be inserting terminology more appropriate to Baptist or Presbyterian church organization to raise questions about a too-quick identification of Marshfield as an Episcopalian, thus avoiding possible charges of belittling the clergy of any one specific denomination.

[2]George W. Hunt's essay, cited above, has an elaborate and quite different explication of the significance of the omega shape.

[3]In 1970, Updike published *Bech: A Book* which comically creates a fictional Jewish contemporary writer. Since this book is a collection of short stories centering around one character rather than a novel, it has not been included in this study.

[4]Frederick Crews, in his review of *Roger's Version,* quotes this same passage from *Midpoint,* but with a quite different interpretation. He says the lines indicate "that Updike would not feel bound by standard notions of sin" (7). Obviously, I believe that Crews has misinterpreted the intent of these lines as well as several other passages from the poem which he cites without setting them in the context of the poem as a whole. Updike himself has said that Crews "misread . . . several lines from the poem" ("Response").

WORKS CITED

Crews, Frederick. "Mr. Updike's Planet." Review of *Roger's Version* by John Updike. *New York Review of Books* 4 Dec. 1986: 7-14.

Erikson, Erik. *Young Man Luther.* New York: Norton, 1962.

Gray, Paul. "Theology and the Computer." Review of *Roger's Version* by John Updike. *Newsweek* 25 Aug. 1986: 67.

Hunt, George W. "Updike's Omega-Shaped Shelter: Structure and Psyche in *A Month of Sundays. Critique* 19 (1978): 47-60.

Kramer, Hilton. "A High-Tech Shrine to Sex and Society." Review of *Roger's Version* by John Updike. *Wall Street Journal* 24 Sep. 1986.

Lee, Charles M., Jr. *White Robe, Black Robe.* New York: Putnam's, 1972.

Stephen, Katherine. "Prolific John Updike Still Finds Things to Say About Life, Sex, and Religion." *Los Angeles Times* 4 Jan. 1987:VI. 1;4.

Updike, John. *The Coup.* New York: Knopf, 1978.

---. "Interview Conducted by Dick Cavett." PBS, 15 Dec. 1978.

---. "Interview Conducted by Jeff Campbell, Georgetown, MA, 9 Aug. 1976." Published as Appendix to this volume.

---. "Interview Conducted by Tom Brokaw." *Today,* NBC, 7 Dec. 1978.

---. *Midpoint.* New York: Knopf, 1969.

---. *A Month of Sundays.* New York: Knopf, 1975.

---. *Roger's Version.* New York: Knopf, 1986.

APPENDIX

INTERVIEW WITH JOHN UPDIKE

Conducted by Jeff Campbell

Georgetown, Massachusetts, 9 August 1976

Campbell: How important do you see the epigraphs as suggesting the meanings or the shapes of the novels?

Updike: Quite important, really, and I've read very few reviews or critical articles that seem to me to take the clues that the epigraphs meant to offer. I tend to discover the epigraphs at some point in the work in progress. I don't think a book has to have an epigraph. In fact, maybe it's a little fussy for a book to have an epigraph—*War and Peace* doesn't have one, and so on—a book should be its own. On the other hand, I've enjoyed other people's epigraphs, and if I find a quote that seems to me to hit it, as a sort of mystical offering given to me, I use it. *The Poorhouse Fair* uses the rather specially worded quote from Luke. [*If they do this when the wood is green, what will happen when the wood is dry?*—Luke 23:31, E. V. Rieu trans.] I meant, if they do this when the wood is green—that is, now—what will happen when the wood is dry— that is, in the future? And there's a good deal of wood imagery, carpentry imagery, in the book, and a sense of dryness—of the old people being dried up. I guess that's a fairly straightforward epigraph, really. . . .

Campbell: Since those words were spoken by Jesus as he was going to the crucifixion, I wondered if there was any indication here that maybe Conner was some sort of Christ-figure or false Christ.

Updike: Certainly the book is a very consciously Christian one. I was twenty-five and very intellectually concerned. I wouldn't have been reading this modern translation of the New Testament if I weren't. I didn't know, in fact, until you said so, that the words were spoken by Jesus on the way to being crucified. I saw Conner as some kind of pseudo-martyr—a martyr of a new religion, really a materialist or social-humanist martyr, not so much as a Christ-figure. Throughout, I was consciously dealing with a period analagous to the early Christian period, that is, a time when the established religion was crumbling and something new was trying to be born and meeting resistance. The book was written by a young man who saw the time he was living in—the Eisenhower years—as a dry period, certainly a dry period for the established church.

And the next epigraph [for *Rabbit, Run*] was from Pascal, as I remember it. [*The motions of Grace, the hardness of heart; external circumstances.*—Pascal, *Pensée* 507] I took the quote as I found it, and it's just, of course, a jotting.

Obviously Pascal meant to elaborate it if he ever wrote the full work that the *Pensees* were meant to be. I think what struck me was that those three things describe, in a way, our lives. The external circumstances are everywhere, in this case the pregnancy and family responsibilities and financial necessities. The motions of grace represent that within us which seeks the good, our non-material, non-external side. And the hardness of heart? Clearly Rabbit shows hardness of heart, and there's a way in which hardness of heart and the motions of grace are intertwined. I was struck as a child, and continue to be struck, by the hardness of heart that Jesus shows now and then in the New Testament, advising people to leave their families, driving the money-lenders out of the temple in quite a fierce way. And I think there seems to be an extent to which hardness of heart is tied in with being alive at all. But, in a way, the epigraph in its darting, fragmentary, zigzaggy form fits the book, which also has a kind of zigzaggy shape, settles on no fixed point. . .

Campbell: You said when you found the other one in Luke you were reading the Bible. Does this indicate that you were also reading Pascal? Do you find yourself in harmony with his basically Jansenist position?

Updike: I first read Pascal in my twenties and was attracted to his particular line of Christian thought, which I take roughly to be the Augustine-Pascal-Kierkegaard-whatever line. This is the one that seems to me to address my plight more than the Thomist—although I did read some St. Tom, too! Yes, I think I clearly am attracted to Pascal, but I confess I never have read him through; I just sort of dart around in it. I happened upon this, and this particular quote seems very apropos.

Campbell: In *The Centaur* the epigraph is from Barth, a rather typical quotation. [*Heaven is the creation inconceivable to man, earth the creation conceivable to him. He himself is the creature on the boundary between heaven and earth.*—Karl Barth]

Updike: Again, I think I came upon the quote while working on the book and was unable to resist it because it did say so tersely and definitely that we're all on a boundary and all are centaurs. It made the book typographically a little unclean since I already in a sense had a long epigraph, the actual Greek story. But, unlike the others, it was tucked in with the title page, and I think it looks quite well there. The book's texture is sort of lumpy, anyway, so it could take one more little bubble on it.

Campbell: The epigraph of *Of the Farm* is Sartrean. *[Conse-quently, when, in all honesty, I've recognized that man is a being in whom existence precedes essence, that he is a free be-ing who, in various circumstances, can want only his freedom, I have at the same time recognized that I can want only the freedom of others.—*Sartre] Is it possible that the epigraphs might sometimes be ironic? It seems to me that freedom is exactly what Joey and his mother and Peggy, all three, don't want—either for themselves or for each other.

Updike: As you know, a critic is entitled to his own reading, and in a way a book is mysterious to the writer. My con-scious intention was to say that if you love someone you want them to have what they want. In a way the mother and Joey forgive each other and there's some kind of blessing bestowed at the end. The book may not really work that way; sometimes the pattern you think you've created doesn't con-nect. It's true that none of the four people are utterly free.

Campbell: It seems to me that Joey does not want to be total-ly free of his mother; she does not want to be free of him, nor does she want him to be free of her. They each want a kind of community.

Updike: You're right, and the book is, in a way, about com-munity—there's more social interaction in a way. . .

Campbell: In *Couples* the first epigraph is from Tillich. [*There is a tendency in the average citizen, even if he has a high standing in his profession, to consider the decisions relating to the life of the society to which he belongs as a mat-ter of fate on which he has no influence—like the Roman subjects all over the world in the period of the Roman em-pire, a mood favorable for the resurgence of religion but un-*

favorable for the preservation of a living democracy.—Paul Tillich, *The Future of Religions*]   The parallel decay of our own time and the Roman empire seems obvious, but I wonder if there may not also be an ironic putdown of Tillich. This was a mood, he says, favorable to the resurgence of religion. But what kind of religion is favored for resurgence in *Couples?* It doesn't seem to be primitive Christianity. . . .

Updike: No, again it's as in *The Poorhouse Fair.* It's the idea of an unchristian religion emerging, a religion of human interplay including sexual interplay. To some extent, in the years since I've written *Couples,* that has happened. There are more formalized ways now of getting together, of touching—T-groups, and so on—and all this is foreshadowed in the book. The generation after mine seems to be attempting to find religious values in each other rather than in looking toward any supernatural or transcendental entity. These epigraphs were meant to be in themselves interesting—I thought Tillich's remark was quite interesting. It's linked with a little Blok quatrain—Alexander Blok. [*We love the flesh: its taste, its tones,/Its charnel odor, breathed through Death's jaws. . . ./ Are we to blame if your fragile bones/ Should crack beneath our heavy, gentle paws?*—Alexander Blok, "The Scythians"]   This, I think, is the first set of epigraphs that appears on a dedication page. It was to my then wife Mary, whose father was a Unitarian minister and a great Tillichite. We had just come back from Russia, and quoting a Russian poet was meant to be a sort of personal touch. I guess, though, the main thing was the sense of sex as something brutal, crushing, barbaric even. It's sort of hardness of heart again, isn't it?

Campbell: In *Rabbit Redux* there are four epigraphs, one at the beginning of each section. The first is from a Russian cosmonaut, the next one from an American astronaut. Then the next one's Russian, and the last one's American. Does this suggest that the problems dealt with, which in one sense seem intimate and domestic and personal and noncosmic, are, in fact, the same sorts of issues that affect international relations and world affairs?

Updike: Sure, there's some attempt in these epigraphs to remind the reader that these domestic events are occurring simultaneously with this unparalleled venture into space and that it wasn't just Americans that did it. I think the first quote, which I've forgotten, was the crucial one—the one that I'd intended to use alone.

Campbell: "It took me quite a while to find you, but now I've got you."

Updike: Yes. But as I went through the literature of what the first cosmonauts and astronauts said, I found a couple of others that seemed too good to leave out, and then I especially love Armstrong saying that it's kind of different out here but pretty. This seemed to be a much more natural remark than the first words he had prepared—much less stilted.

Rabbit's adventures in this book are a kind of launching free of the very terrestrial world of Pop and Mom and Janice to a kind of no man's land. In some way I felt the little ranch house to be a space capsule spinning in a kind of way, and the reunion with Janice—even their bodily jockeyings were meant to be a kind of jockeying in space, like these linkups. I guess that's obvious, although not everybody seemed to know it—to notice it. So in some way the whole thing, the whole fantasy of the book—and the book is a touch fantastic—is related to the true fantasy of our space invasion.

The men, of course, are very much just men, aren't they? Even though they're way out there. The things they said were so mundane; I kind of like that—like that quality. The Russians as much as the Americans, actually, were very informal. Of course, they're all pilots, and I suppose that being a pilot in some ways trains you to tame the unusual.

Campbell: In *A Month of Sundays* the first epigraph is from the Forty-fifth Psalm—"my tongue is the pen of a ready writer." The second is from Tillich: "The principle of soul, universally and individually, is the principle of ambiguity."

How important, if important at all, is the balance of the Forty-fifth Psalm? Are you conscious of the rest of that psalm?

Updike: I doubt if I am, although I'm sure I read the whole psalm through when I picked the quote. What is the psalm about?

Campbell: Well, it's a marriage celebration. The poet opens with the affirmation that his tongue is like the pen of a ready writer or scribe, and then he goes on to sing the glories of his king and his new bride, and there's at least some fairly logical evidence that maybe this psalm was composed for the marriage of Ahab and Jezebel.

Updike: Really?

Campbell: Another possibility would be Solomon and Pharaoh's daughter, or it could have been post-exilic. Certainly it was left in the Psalms because it was allegorized to be the Messiah and Israel, and of course later Jesus and the Church. It is also very fitting—the totality of the psalm to what happens in the book.

Updike: It's not bad, not bad, but I'm not sure if I can claim much credit for it. I was aware of the psalm being one of praise and celebration—indeed, almost all the psalms are—and to that extent I liked it.

These two quotes appear on the same page as the dedication to Judith Jones, who is my editor at Knopf. The first is a little joke on me: I've often been accused of being much too ready a writer, and Marshfield is himself, of course, in the book a very ready writer. I think the book is somewhat ambiguous, even more than the others, and maybe to some extent Tillich's remark made sense of the ambiguity; I think I came upon it later and couldn't resist appending it in the hope that it would somehow be helpful. I like the idea of the principle of soul being ambiguity; it's a very neo-platonic, I suppose, notion.

Campbell: You've said several times that as you begin a novel you frequently have some certain shape in mind. *The Poorhouse Fair* is variously a gladiola or fireworks that shoot up and spread out, *Rabbit, Run* is zigzags or Z's, *The Centaur* is a sandwich, *Of the Farm* an X. How about *Couples?*

Updike: I think I'm maybe running out of shapes! I've forgotten in what interview I produced all those images. It is true that with every book I do begin with some image. Herbert Reed coined or used the word "haptic," trying to differentiate the pleasure that sculpture gives us from the pleasure that painting does—some sense of its *seizability,* or some sense of its mass. I have to have that even before I begin a book. But now you've asked about *Couples*—what was the shape of *Couples?* The shape is the turn that occurs between the first and last paragraphs, even the first and last sentences, where the Hanemas become a different pair of people. In other words, a couple changes—one couple replaces another. Other than that I'm not sure that I can offer a shape.

When I think back over the shape of the book, what I remember is the second chapter, "Applesmiths and Other Games," in which I was trying to show the ground—the kind of social terrain—that these events were occurring in. Although it seemed to some to be a long and unnecessary flashback, to me it was necessary. It was important also that this is a coupling that occurs within the social network and does not harm it. It may harm the people in it, but the couples—the group—remain intact. Then in Piet and Foxy I meant to show that one couple does in fact break out. And they are socially unacceptable. Piet is snubbed at the end in a way he never was in his previous phase. It's no accident that the book is in five chapters, as seems to be a distinctive thing for me. I saw each one as steps, in a way. The turn, the revolution, that turns Piet and Angela into Piet and Foxy was the shape.

Campbell: Did you have specific shape in mind for *Rabbit Redux?*

Updike: I doubt it. I think I've somewhere committed myself to writing four books about this man. *Rabbit Redux* paired up, deliberately, but also happily, with *Rabbit, Run* so nicely that in a way they look at each other—they seem to me to make almost a set. I do think he's learned something. I think that he shows—especially in the second book—the American quality of openness; he is, in a sense, unprejudiced. He is willing to entertain these outlanders in his house. I'd like then to write a sequel showing that he did learn something.

Campbell: One of the recurrent criticisms of your work is that you avoid violence.

Updike: I am aware of this complaint and I detect in myself a wish not to have *false* violence. It's terribly easy when you're sitting at a typewriter, of course, to kill and maim and produce explosions. I think that Mailer's an example of a good writer who nevertheless has much too easy access to violence, so that the violence becomes hysterical, impersonal. I've led a rather quiet life—I think most men would prefer to lead quiet lives if they can. I really haven't witnessed much violence. The incident of the house burning down was based on something that actually happened in the particular section of Pennsylvania that I come from, and it impressed me as a piece of authentic social violence. A black and white couple were living in a house and the neighbors burnt the house down—somebody burnt the house down. This piece of violence did fall within my ken, and I tried to use it.

There is a way in which the television set invades the guy's life. That is, these are sort of headline figures who come upon him, and I think it was true of a lot of us in the late sixties that all the things we preferred not to think about became unavoidable. So in a way he is the middle class man whose living room becomes the scene of atrocities and teach-ins and all those things. I wrote the book rather rapidly. I was trying to work on the long Buchanan thing at the time, and I've kind of forgotten the composition of *Rabbit Redux* except that as I was witnessing these events as they unfolded, they seemed real enough to me. I was trying to let out my own anxieties and doubts, puzzlement over the issues that are raised.

Campbell: Let's go on to *A Month of Sundays.* I was struck here with the possibility of a circle, particulary since we start off with a motel in omega shape and of course he stays a month, which is, in a sense, a circle—the circle of the moon. But I'm not satisfied with a circle because I don't think he returns the same as he left, and here I will just have to put in a little Barth, who insists that history is real—there's not a meaningless cycle, but a purposeful movement. So I don't know—I think circle and then I say no it can't be a circle—maybe a spiral.

Updike: I guess I agree with Barth, if I understand you right, in that nothing is ever the same twice, and that the stream—what does Heraclitus say? We never put our foot in the same stream twice. Marshfield goes to the motel; it is a kind of end point. He is pretty thoroughly disgraced and out of it and yet still obstinately alive, kind of the way Beckett characters are. They are reduced to nothing yet keep talking and refuse to be crushed or dismissed. Of course it is true the motel is a self-enclosed bubble and Marshfield does return and possibly to much the same. . . .Well, I doubt it; I don't think he will repeat those exact same adventures. I meant to show a pattern of absence. That is, when one is violently taken out of one's milieu, it slowly fades. I meant the month to show that the surroundings in the end eclipse the memories of what he's left, so that at about chapter twenty Frankie and Alicia and all those other people fade, and he tries to look at the people around him. I'm not sure it worked, but that was the idea, that Ms. Prynne and his fellow guests come forward and occupy his mind and in some sense refresh him. It's sort of a vacation that's being described. He brings to the desert this mass of emotion and memory and humiliation and so on, and it finally runs dry and the sun keeps coming up on a different kind of terrain.

Campbell: What relationship do you see between painting and fiction? Have you consciously attempted to apply any principles or theories of visual art to your writing?

Updike: In some sense I, of course, do see a book as having a tone before you set out and a certain shape and texture. In *Rabbit, Run* the present tense and so on is very different from the kind of very calibrated prose of *The Poorhouse Fair.* I am a sort of frustrated painter, or rather I have painted a bit and was told I have a very good sense of composition. So maybe I see the book as a canvas with things disposed in it. Of course, as you write it turns out that things that you thought would take twenty pages somehow dismiss themselves in one and other things blossom, so it's not quite as spatial as that. I kind of came to writing a little sideways. My initial talents and ambitions were all in the pictorial-graphic way. My mother took a writing course from a man called Thomas H. Uzzell, who operated out of Texas, I think, somewhere. He would analyze various classics in terms of plots so that you saw the plot as a kind of set of stick directions, and I don't scorn this; I think that when all is said and done some impetus, some direction, some tension or conflict, must be set up. In other words, some movement along a kind of linear way happens, and to some extent the books do break down into this kind of direction or diagram. Detail is bearable only if you feel it's strung or bestowed on some kind of general seizable form; otherwise it becomes suffocating and you're lost in it. I really feel I can only add detail when I know where I'm going and feel the reader is with me—I mean when he cares and has a sense of being taken somewhere.

Campbell: Do you keep up pretty generally with what seem to be at least relatively serious attempts to evaluate or interpret your work?

Updike: It's hard to get a book about yourself that you can ignore entirely. Of course one is interested. In general, that kind of scrutiny is a little painful and a touch unreal for some reason, so I don't think I've really read any of the books through. I've looked at all of them and I'm glad that some man or woman has thought enough of me to want to devote the year or more, or whatever it takes, but I've not read them thoroughly because I just don't think that you can steer your own ship by those stars.

Campbell: Have you found any that you looked at that you find most acceptable or congenial; and have you found any that you think are serious misreadings?

Updike: I do think that the Hamiltons, who I think were almost the first into the field, are wonderfully careful readers, and they're always dredging up puns I didn't know I made, and connections that I wasn't conscious of. Also they take me seriously as a sort of theological or at least religious thinker. And it's true there's a kind of germ of philosophical or moral or even supernatural inquiry in my stuff. On the other hand, they tend to enlist me in their own Sunday School a little too quickly and efficiently so that in some cases where I meant to raise a question they take it that I provided an answer. I remember reading Joyce Markle's book feeling that she was more with it than some others. Alfred Kazin has some pages on me in his sort of survey of the contemporary novel that seem to me to be nice and—nice means what? He likes you? I think I mean that he seems to be able to read the books.

Campbell: How would you respond to David Galloway's concept that your protagonists are examples of the absurd man as saint, particularly George Caldwell and Rabbit?

Updike: I do see them as absurd in the sense that they live in a world with no unavoidable values. In other words, they are adrift and they have to make up their own. Rabbit I would not call a saint. I meant him to be a kind of you and me, or a sort of Everyman. George Caldwell I do see as exceptional in his altruism, but in a way I'm questioning him as a saint, also. In some ways he's an unbearable man: embarrassing to his son, annoying to his wife, and there's an antic mischievous something. But yes, he'd be my candidate for sainthood—if I had one.

The question of sainthood is an interesting one. We *are* interested in saints, and I notice that in the novels my heroes are all males and they all seem to be in some quandary. They're all uncomfortable in this world to a degree, which then suggests that there's another world where they'd be more comfortable; but they're a far cry from saints. The God that they speak of and the God that they search for has some of the hardheartedness that is in the Pascal. He's God of the earthquake, of the volcano, as much as of the flowers.

Campbell: Robert Detweiler has a phrase he uses over and over again. He calls your style and approach "secular baroque."

Updike: Secular baroque? I think I *am* a secular man in the end. And the baroque, yes, I suppose. Classicism, I suppose, suggests a certitude of the kind that I don't seem, as a writer, to have—clear meanings, definite presumptions; I seem to write always in the hope of turning up the truth around the corner somehow, of finding a secret truth, hitherto hidden, that just needed greater and more intense groping.

Campbell: Michael Novak suggests that your sensibility is specifically Christian, an alert, open, human, sensual Calvinism, almost wholly Platonic, with a radical dualism that makes myth and symbolism necessary tools. He says it is difficult for the Jewish sensibility or the hard pragmatic secular sensibility of our critical establishment to understand this world-view. Do you see your sensibility as specifically Christian?

Updike: I think so. I think Christianity is the only world-frame that I've been exposed to that I can actually look through.

Campbell: Novak suggests that one has to accept this world-view in order to understand what's going on in your work. He says Calvinism, but from my point of view I see you as much more Lutheran than Calvinist. Does that distinction make any sense to you?

Updike: It makes a lot of sense to me and I agree with you. I was raised as a Lutheran. Now to an extent all Protestant churches would look alike to a Catholic like Novak. I can't claim to have had a Lutheran upbringing in the rigorous way that Ingmar Bergman, maybe, did. In the county I was from, the Lutheran and Reformed churches existed on the same block, but they were distinctly different churches. The Calvinist church just gives off a different vibe. I do think that in some way the personalities and fundamental emphases of the two great founders show through still. Lutheranism is comparatively world-accepting; it's a little closer to Catholicism than Calvinism. I don't feel much affinity with the New England Puritan ethos insofar as it still persists. No, I would call myself a Lutheran by upbringing, and my work contains some of the ambiguities of the Lutheran position, which would have a certain radical otherworldly emphasis and yet an odd retention of a lot of Catholic forms and a rather rich ambivalence toward the world itself. That is, Luther's feelings about the devil and the world are quite interesting to me. He seems to greatly admire, to adore, the devil.

Campbell: I was struck with Marshfield's one great religious experience, which seems to me very Lutheran—certainly you must have had Luther in mind. When Marshfield calls himself a cheerful sinner, I see Luther's "sin boldly" and Luther's "freedom in Christ" much more than what I associate with Calvinism.

Updike: Quite so. And very few of my critics have been by their own conditioning equipped to make the references you just have, to look to some of Luther's memorable sayings which do add up in the books, especially in this one.

Campbell: All right, if there is a valid distinction between Lutheran and Calvinist, what would be some of the distinctions between a Catholic sensibility and a Protestant sensibility?

Updike: Trying to think with you on this, certainly there is a very clear difference. What strikes me when I think about Flannery O'Connor and Graham Greene is how far they are willing to go in presenting a suffering, apparently Godless world. That is, the very scorchingness with which God is *not* there is something that I don't feel in my own work. It amazes me. In other words, there's something kind of Jansenist—I was going to say Calvinist—in both of these writers. I think there may be a Protestant emphasis on the individual conscience and on attempting to locate a consecrated or a graceful inner state of mind that perhaps is not necessary for these Catholic writers. My heroes, at least, are all struggling for some kind of inner certitude, illumination, or something.

Campbell: Are there any contemporary writers that you think do express the Protestant sensibility?

Updike: Living . . . my own generation has been dominated so much by Jewish writers. . . . I'm trying to think. . . . There were sections of *Nat Turner* in which Styron, it seemed to me, was convincingly evangelical. I was moved by some of Nat Turner's earlier meditations on God, but. . . . You do feel something in Faulkner, certainly, that's Protestant. . . No, I can't think of too many, off hand. Most Protestants who come to writing have pretty thoroughly put it behind them, I guess.

Campbell: Would you accept Novak's dictum that you are Platonic and dualistic, or one of them if not both?

Updike: Yes, if I understand the words, I would. I don't *mean* to be dualistic, but there is a way in which I see things as mind or spirit on the one hand and body on the other. It's more a gut way of looking at things than any sort of intellectualized position. I think Novak, by the way, is one of the better people who have written about me. I'm grateful for the seriousness with which he takes me, and he seems to be able to deal with the Christian matter of the early stuff, the early stories, very well.

Campbell: In reading *The Poorhouse Fair,* I couldn't help thinking what Flannery O'Connor might have done with the mock stoning scene. Why do you seem to deliberately avoid the dramatic moments that are typical of her work?

Updike: I guess my experience fits *The Poorhouse Fair* that I wrote. That is, most pebbles don't brain us and most troubles are non-drastic.

Campbell: Novak cites the centrality of myth and symbol in your work. Certainly your concern with myth and symbol is obvious in the first three novels, and quite overt in *The Centaur.* Would you comment on the importance of myth in *The Centaur?*

Updike: I guess the mythological references mean to show that everybody, the existence of any person, any thing, is in some way magical and highly charged, and rather strange—and gaudy. There's a gaudiness about life that means you almost have to produce an extra effect, you have to bring up fiction to the gaudiness of actuality. Something *extra* has to happen. It might be the verbal play, or these myths. From the standpoint of an adolescent boy who hasn't been anywhere else, all of these ordinary or less than ordinary people are very large and significant. That is, you live the rest of your life with the categories that you build up in these early years.

I think what attracted me to the Chiron legend is the notion, rather rare in Greek mythology, of the centaur sacrificing himself for somebody else. It is true that his life had become unbearable to him in a way that the life of Christ or

293

any Christian martyr had not. In other words, it became a convenient thing to do—it's almost a thrifty thing to do, to give up a life that's become sheer pain and at the same time bail somebody else out. I'm no ancient Greek, and I'm not even a student of these stories. I still would not have written the book without the myths. They are important to me and I think give the book its proper tone of eccentricity, or surprisingness—the sense that everybody comes to us in guises. I think I've used myth less since. There was something in *Couples* almost centaurlike in the texture, without the allusions being so specific.

Campbell: Barth doesn't have much use for myth. He says myth deals with the timeless reality, while the Christian creation story cannot be a myth because it affirms the objective reality of life.

Updike: I think I know what he's saying, and I think there is a limitation. He's saying that the concrete historical reality of Jesus is better than any myth. Myth is part of the cyclical, Asiatic religiosity, and has nothing to do with the real thing. Barth is very absolute, very tough on this point, as I guess logically he must be. In a way it's a little like what evangelists in this country talk about, about the concrete experience of Jesus—again it's something definite, you know, like a hiccough or a shoe-lace. I mean it's something very real: it's not other things disguised as—it's not a flavor of other things—it is a *thing.* Lacking, I think, this kind of concrete experience, I'm not so willing to dismiss myth as Barth is. But basically I'm with him, not so much religiously as for a way of viewing reality: you have to take a thing seriously as itself.

Campbell: Could I say, then, that the point of *The Centaur* is not that George Caldwell is Chiron all over again, but that there is a kind of universality or unity, a continuingness about life. . .

Updike: And in fathers—fathers and sons. In a way every father lays down his life—well, not every, but many—for the son. Or the child. Parents, parents and children. The Greek mythology is probably appropriate to this particular "schoolish" novel because really Greek myths are things we learn in school. They're not imbibed, not even in a landscape; they're just something we learn.

Campbell: You have stressed the "yes—but" quality of your work, and ambiguity does seem to be a recurrent emphasis. How would you compare "yes—but" as you see it to the Kierkegaardian "either/or" imperative?

Updike: Both the "yes—but" and the "either/or" imply there are two sides to things, don't they? So to that extent it is Kierkegaardian, and no sooner do you look at one side than you see the other again. . .

Campbell: And this also would fit with Barth's "God says yes and God says no." And perhaps not fit quite so comfortably with Tillich's "both/and."

Updike: Not so comfortably. Even though I recognize Tillich as a kind of wonderful spirit, and he does have these flashes, I find his overall attempt to have it several ways basically unpossible. It occurs to me that Kierkegaard and I might be tedious in the same way, too, in that this constant turning it over and seeing the opposite side and expounding it is what makes him able to write almost endlessly, and enables me to write a fair amount because, yes, there is a lot to be said on both sides. A book like *Rabbit, Run* was a deliberate attempt to present both the escapist, have-it-my-way will to live versus the social restraints, the social voices in the book, the ministers, and other people's too. . .

Campbell: Also Kierkegaardian would be the individualism, and here we're back to something we mentioned a while ago as something maybe basically Protestant. I wonder if there have been some elements of existentialism that you found particularly viable or attractive. One thing, for instance, specifically: I find in Sartre affirmation of man's radical discontinuity with nature and his radical aloneness. Would you share these affirmations or not?

Updike: We are obviously very much in nature and have to be well aware of it. All our various kinds of health depend upon some recognition that we are natural beings. On the other hand, there is a radical jump between one's individual sense of me—I—and any other kind of reality. One experiences the existence of all these exterior forms. I think I'm attracted to that—or was—and still am, really, because I haven't as much altered my philosophical-theological views as let them sit, and fade, I guess, a little bit. And Kierkegaard, what the existentialists picked up was his insistence on the importance of the individual. He almost says that God is there because I so much want him to be there, doesn't he? There's a building upon terror. The first thing you lay down is the fact that you're terrified. I find, from the standpoint of someone trying to present human experience, existential philosophy more useful in a way than the more social views of humanity which somehow don't come over into fiction terribly well, do they? I don't know why that is. Saying that, I wonder if it's true or not. I do think that somebody like Bellow. . . his fiction is much enriched by his innate sense of society. Not only all the talking his characters do, and all the theories, but his very real sense of the family and the city. That is good, and I guess I can't claim that as my own.

Campbell: In Sartre's radical aloneness I don't find the

I-Thou bit that you get out of Buber, and I feel this possibility at least in your work. I even wonder if Ms. Prynne becomes a Thou at the end of *A Month of Sundays.*

Updike: I was just going to say that there is a touch of the I-Thou in that last ending, the saluting and the—sure. ["What is it, this human contact, this blank-browed thing we do for one another? There was a moment. . .when your eyes were all for another, looking up into mine, with an expression without a name, of entry and alarm, and of salutation. I pray my own face, a stranger to me, saluted in turn."—*A Month of Sundays* 228) She is Thou, and also in some way she is meant to be the ideal reader. I mean the I-Thou is also the writer-reader I-Thou. She is his reader.

Campbell: Do you think there's some possibility your work might develop into some sort of saga?

Updike: I don't mind the interconnections when they come upon me. You know it becomes increasingly hard to work with things you've already established. Often it becomes necessary just to give the thing *spring* somehow. Obviously I have written interlinked short stories, and revived characters. I've written a sequel to one of my novels. There's a way in which *Of the Farm* is a sequel to *The Centaur,* and so on. I'd like my *oeuvre* to have some blend, continuous without being a formal shelf's worth the way in which some of the French writers attempted—Balzac and so on. I think just by moving out of Pennsylvania and living in another region, I have created the discontinuity in my own life that, say, Faulkner did not have.

Campbell: Can we bounce some ideas about *Midpoint* around for just a while? You say in Canto V: "Atomically all writers must begin, the truth arises as if by telegraph,/ One dot, two dots, a silence, then a laugh,/ The rules inhere and will not be imposed,/ *Ab alto* as most liberals have supposed." Is this ironic or not? One dot, two dots—silence. There aren't going to be any more dots? Because the rules inhere and therefore our dots aren't ever going to get anywhere? Or the rules inhere and therefore what we think are random dots turn out to be illustrations of something that comes from beyond?

Updike: I think the latter. The image that I must have had in mind, at least that comes to mind now that I hear it, is scientific inquiry into matter. Instead of beginning with some broad suppositions and trying to make them apply to little phenomena, you look at the little phenomena and try to extract the rules that inhere from them. And so in writing, I try to adhere to the testable, the verifiable, the undeniable little thing. Somehow, I hope the pattern in the art will emerge, and I guess I must have some such hope cosmically.

Campbell: Again in Canto V, after all the heroes, and praise of pointillism, calculus and all and so on, you say "all wrong, all wrong." Now I couldn't exactly see what was all wrong.

Updike: Of course, I've been saying all along since the second line of Canto I that there's something wrong. The author of middle age, the man at midpoint, has the sensation, no matter what he's saying, that something is all wrong. Things are not quite right; there's an unease pervading the poem. He sort of doubts and mocks what he's just asserted. Certainly as the writer of dogmatic couplets I felt uneasy. You could say original sin. I mean original sin says it's all wrong, doesn't it?

Campbell: But when you say "nothing has had to be," I think immediately that Pope wouldn't agree with that— "whatever is, is . . ."

Updike: I think one of my independent philosophical obsessions was that there is a certain gratuitousness in existence at all. That is, however riddles are unraveled, the one of why the void itself was breached remains permanently mysterious, and in its own way, permanently hopeful-making.

Campbell: Here also you say that the author gives intelligent hedonistic advice. Frankly, if you hadn't told me this was hedonistic advice, I would never have known it.

Updike: I think there are two kinds of advice, as I remember, given. One is, you might say, ecologically sound. That, I think, is somewhat distrusted by the author of these lines as being true but somehow something's wrong with it. The other is—which I frequently find myself saying—to be grateful, be grateful for existence, that is, "nothing had to be." And that advice, I think, is religious advice.

Campbell: You also say here in your "argument" that he appears to accept reluctantly his own advice. I think he very plainly does not—

Updike: Does not accept his own advice?

Campbell: —accept this advice, and when he says here at the end, "Henceforth, if I can, I must impersonate a serious man," I think the first, third, fourth, and the beginning of the fifth sections all clearly indicate the irony there. What he's really doing is impersonating a clown. That's what he's been doing all along, when in reality he is a very serious man all the way through. So I don't think at all he is accepting this advice. I think he's rejecting all this well-meaning advice.

Updike: And he's going to keep clowning, you think? . . .I can't help it.

Campbell: But at a deadly serious level.

Updike: I'm glad you're looking at *Midpoint,* by the way. Just in the way you talk I realize that *Midpoint* and *Month of Sundays* are in a way among my franker books. Because Marshfield to some extent is speaking for me. Just the sensation—trying to talk about experiences as it, you know, first arrived—dot, dot. Marshfield's passage about fixing the window sash and how it speaks to him and the sense of. . .["I had never taken apart a window before. What an interlocked, multi-deviced yet logical artifact one is! And how exciting, all the screws unscrewed and stop strips removed, to pull forth from decades of darkness the rusted sashweight, such a solid little prisoner, and fit him with a glossy new noose and feel him, safe once again in his vertical closet, tug like life upon the effortlessly ascendant sash!"—*A Month of Sundays* 115]

Campbell: Yes, he finds in the furniture his Ground of Being.

Updike: Right, right. . .

Campbell: Let's go on to *Month of Sundays.*

Updike: You might be interested to know that my original plan was to have chapter thirty-one blank. The trouble is, being the end chapter, it didn't look blank. That is, it just looked like the book had ended. But then I wrote it as you read it. In this blankness some kind of merger of I-Thou. . . . I might say of the sermons that I meant them not only to sort of pick up the events of six days just past and in a way cap them, but also to show a normalization. The first is meant to be the most blasphemous; it's really a sort of assault on the Bible. The second is somewhat. . .well, the second is also pretty defiant. But by the third sermon you wind up with a fairly orthodox message. And as she [Ms. Prynne] says, the fourth is a sermon that really could be preached. So there is some kind of lessening of anger and whatever, and he is, in fact, despite himself, being returned to usefulness.

Campbell: Well, it strikes me that evidence emerges here in an overt way, or in a more overt way, of concerns that you have had all along.

Updike: It's overt, all right, it really is. It may be also a trying to say goodbye to some of these concerns, to move to something else.

Campbell: Let's talk about Barth a little more. Obviously, you do acknowledge your debt to Barth, saying that at one point in your life his theology seemed to be your whole support. Could you say something about what elements of this Barthian position particularly attracted you?

Updike: I think it was the frank supernaturalism and the particularity of his position, so unlike that of Tillich and the entire group of liberal theologians—and you scratch most ministers, at least in the east, and you find a liberal—whose view of these events is not so different from that of an agnostic. But Barth was with resounding definiteness and learning saying what I needed to hear, which was that it really *was* so, that there was something within us that would not die, and that we live by faith alone—more or less; he doesn't just say that, but what he does say joined with my Lutheran heritage and enabled me to go on.

Campbell: This statement that I referred to was made ten years ago and even then it was referring to a time in the past. Does the past-tense nature of that reference suggest that your enthusiasm has cooled for Barth or that you've found other things in addition to Barth, or does it mean anything?

Updike: I certainly have not renounced Barth, nor have I read him much lately. The great period of my reading Barth— I'm trying to fix the time—I think it was about 1960 or 1961, so I would have been in my late twenties. Either I have become as a middle-aged person kind of too numb to care, or, what I would suggest instead, I am able, having assimilated Barth and somehow being permanently reassured, to appreciate Tillich, say. . . . After one has conquered this sort of existential terror with Barth's help, then one is able to open to the world again. *He* certainly was very open to the world. Wonderfully alive and relaxed, as a man.

Campbell: As I read Barth, I find that he heavily stresses three particular things. First of all is the very centrality of Christology. This is the touchstone—belief in Christ. Then the importance of the church, and then the Christian as new creature in Christ, sign of the resurrection. Now as I read your novels particularly, I find Christ-references relatively rare. And in the second place, I find the church, when it gets in there, is usually portrayed in its bland decadence and seems pointless and useless. And then the new-creature, resurrection images seem distinctly absent in the novels until we get to

Marshfield, where it is very clear at the end. Now my question is, simply, have I missed something obvious, or are these in fact parts of Barth's enthusiasm that you are not concerned to try to illustrate?

Updike: No, I'm afraid you're right, and to that extent I'm a very poor Barthian. As I've said before, my religious sensibility operates primarily as a sense of God the Creator, which is fairly real to me, and secondly as a sense of the mystery and irreducibility of one's own identity, mixed in with fear of the identity being an illusion or being squelched. I'm not a good Barthian—I'm not a good Christian, really, when you come right down to it. I don't find that these emphases on Barth's part get in the way, though, somehow. I'm willing to believe that Christ was real, to him. Barth's own images now and then of the church in action are more scathing than anything I've presented. I do remain fascinated by the church. I'm grateful that there are churches there. I find going to church generally comforting and pleasant, and I admire ministers for trying, as it were, to maintain the impossible in the midst of the all too possible.

Campbell: Barth's view of creation, history, and God's participating in it implies the importance of eschatology, yet I see your work undercutting any apocalypticism. Things do not come to some great end.

Updike: It's true I do see the world as something that, as far as my horizon goes, will plug along. Even the holocaustal disasters turn out to be survivable by humanity in general. And in our own lives we survive all of our disasters but the last one. Yes, I do see the world much more in terms of persistence. I feel that it's going to limp along.

Campbell: I see I've got a red herring in my question, anyway, because Barth's eschotology is not apocalyptic. He, too, in *Dogmatics in Outline,* right after the Second World War, mentions that we made it through all this. People are still people, and he even supplies his own answer to my question: in the Eschaton, he says, light falls from above into our lives, the dailyness. . .

Updike: Barth is not always easy to pin down because he has a way of subjectifying these terms that to Paul's generation were clearly historical events. To this extent, he, too, is a liberal theologian. . . . He, too, is a bit of a "yes, but" and a master of having it both ways. I first read him in the collection of sermons and speeches *The Word of God and the Word of Man.* In one of those, after having presented a devastating picture of our society and of the church's condition, he says do not ask me, then, "What shall I do?" Just go on doing what you are doing— but—doing it differently. As far as concrete action, he seemed to think it was all more or less hopeless in the sense, at least, of producing any absolute result. [See "The Christian's Place in Society," in *The Word of God and the Word of Man* (New York: Harper & Brothers, 1957), 272-327.] I don't know. I think obviously one could find in the vast corpus of Barth's pronouncements a number of shades of opinion on this and that.

Campbell: I have but one other comment. Barth at one point says that "Christian art" is well intentioned but ultimately impotent. A real Christian, he says, wants no imagery. Your work, of course, is full of all sorts of marvelous imagery.

Updike: But I've never really offered it as Christian art. My art is Christian only in that my faith urges me to tell the truth, however painful and inconvenient, and holds out the hope that the truth—reality—is good. Good or no, only the truth is useful.

ALBERTSON COLLEGE OF IDAHO
PS3571.P4.Z6.1987
Updike's novels :thorns spell a word /

3 5556 00090445 8

DATE DUE

WITHDRAWN

PRINTED IN U.S.A.